Draining
the
Cumbrian Landscape

Locations of tile-works which were manufacturing in Cumberland and adjacent counties at some point between 1820 and the early 1900s   [Gen Map UK]

Draining
the
Cumbrian Landscape

a revolution in underdraining with tiles

with

A Gazetteer of Sites and Manufacturers

[on a CD]

Edward & Stella B Davis

CUMBERLAND AND WESTMORLAND
ANTIQUARIAN AND ARCHAEOLOGICAL SOCIETY
2013

Cumberland and Westmorland
Antiquarian and Archaeological Society
Hon. General Editor
Professor Colin Richards

Draining the Cumbrian Landscape: a revolution in underdraining with tiles

RESEARCH SERIES No XI

ISBN 978 1 873124 63 5

Printed by

Badger Press Ltd. Bowness on Windermere
2013

Contents

Gazetteer of Sites and Manufacturers [CD inside back cover]

Figure Credits

The source of each figure, where appropriate, is acknowledged preceding the subject in the caption. Where the figure is a photograph, the photographer and copyright holder, are given following the subject.

Cumbria Archive Service (Carlisle) was the source of the *Carlisle Journal* and other local newspapers. It also provided the majority of OS 1st and 2nd edition 1:2500, and a number of the 1:10560 maps.

The offices at Barrow, Kendal and Whitehaven provided similar material for the areas of the county for which they are responsible.

Carlisle Library Local Studies Collection was the source of most of the 1st and 2nd edition 1:10560, as well as some of the 1:2500 OS maps.

Images including book extracts, maps and photographs in all other figures are from private collections including that of the authors.

List of Tables

Abbreviations

AHEW	*Agrarian History of England & Wales* 8 vols., Cambridge University Press
AHR	*Agricultural History Review*
AO	*Annan Observer*
BBS	British Brick Society
CIHS	Cumbria Industrial History Society
CJ	*Carlisle Journal*
CN	*Cumberland News*
CP	*Carlisle Patriot*
CAS	Cumbria Archive Service (Barrow) (Carlisle) (Kendal) (Whitehaven)
CUL	Cumberland
Cumb P	*Cumberland Pacquet*
CW	*Transactions of the Cumberland & Westmorland Antiquarian & Archaeological Society* 1. Old Series, 2. New Series, 3. Third Series
C&WA	*Cumberland & Westmorland Advertiser*
C&WH	*Cumberland & Westmorland Herald*
D&GS	*Dumfries & Galloway Standard*
D&GS&A	*Dumfries & Galloway Standard & Advertiser*
DFS	Dumfriesshire
DT	*Dumfries Times*
HASS	Highland & Agricultural Society of Scotland
IAR	*Industrial Archaeology Review*
JRASE	*Journal of the Royal Agricultural Society of England*
LAN	Lancashire
LAN(F&C)	Lancashire (Furness & Cartmel)
LRO	Lancashire Record Office
M, H & Co	Morris, Harrison & Co's (1861) *Directory*
M & W	Mannix & Whellan (1847) *Directory*
NBL	Northumberland
NMRS	National Monuments Record Scotland
NSA	*New Statistical Account*
ODNB	*Oxford Dictionary of National Biography*
OS	Ordnance Survey
PO	*Penrith Observer*
P & W	Parson & White (1829) *Directory*
RASE	Royal Agricultural Society of England
RCAHMS	Royal Commission Ancient & Historical Monuments Scotland
SCT	Scotland
SUA	*Soulby's Ulverston Advertiser*
THASS	*Transaction of the Highland & Agricultural Society of Scotland*
TYAS	*Transactions of the Yorkshire Agricultural Society*
VCH	Victoria County History
WES	Westmorland

Acknowledgements

Generous assistance has been given by the staff of numerous record offices, libraries and museums in the north of England and southern Scotland. In particular special thanks are extended to the staff of two organisations, Cumbria Archive Service and Cumbria Libraries, who have for over 13 years given unstinting assistance in response to requests.

The bulk of our research has been carried out in what was Carlisle Record Office situated in Carlisle Castle. Here on a weekly basis, newspapers, maps and archives were produced for us. At the offices in Barrow, Kendal and Whitehaven, members of staff were equally attentive to our requests during sporadic forays to peruse documents on other parts of the county.

In respect of libraries, the members of staff of Carlisle Local Studies Collection have over a number of years responded willingly to requests for maps and books, as have their colleagues in Penrith, Kendal, Barrow and Whitehaven on a less frequent basis.

Further afield, thanks are extended to the staff of record offices, libraries, and museums who have responded to our queries regarding tile-making. All those institutions which have been consulted are mentioned at the beginning of the bibliography. Special acknowledgement is given to the Lancashire Record Office in Preston, the Northumberland Archive Service, the Staffordshire Record Office and the William Salt Library in Stafford.

We are grateful to the assistance given by the librarians of Durham University Library's special collections, the University of Cumbria libraries at Newton Rigg and Ambleside, the special collections of the Library of the University of Newcastle and the Mitchell Library in Glasgow.

Three museums have allowed us to inspect their collections of tiles for which we are indebted - Tullie House Museum, Dumfries Museum and the Museum of Scottish Country Life

Many individuals, too numerous to list; have assisted us throughout our 13 years of research. Special thanks must be given to Ian Caruana who generously provided his notes on tile-making when we first began our project, and to Dennis Perriam who has supplied us with literally hundreds of references. We would also like to thank the Publications Committee of the CWAAS for publishing this work.

Mention must also be made of individuals who have assisted with information or help on specific topics: Ted Relph with regard to Crosby Ravensworth; Mike Jackson and Barbara Smith for tiles and references relating to Bewcastle; Graham Brookes, Geoff Brambles and other members of Cumbria Industrial History Society; the Holker estate for permission to visit Reake Wood; Peter Wilkinson and Rachel Etheridge for references and research assistance; Andrew Humphries for use of his thesis; and finally Peter Robinson for bricks and information relating to railways.

Others have contributed tiles to our personal collection, for which we are very grateful.

Where help by an individual relates to a specific tilery, acknowledgement has been made in the appropriate place in the *Gazetteer of Sites and Manufacturers*.

Apologies are made for any omissions, which are not deliberate but result from our failing memories over the long period of the research.

Foreword

Some aspects of the improvement of agriculture and the transformation of the landscape of Cumbria in the nineteenth century are well known. The parliamentary enclosure of upland wastes and lowland mosses and the rise of the lime-burning industry have attracted recent research. Yet surprisingly little is known about the development of under draining in Cumbria during the nineteenth century, about the associated industry of tile making and about their role in facilitating agricultural development., This seems particularly anomalous because the region has some of the highest rainfall totals in England and the importance of under draining in other parts of England is well known. Underground drainage systems are, by definition, hidden from view and unobtrusive, leaving only subtle traces in the landscape. This may be one reason why they have not attracted more attention from researchers. Today it is often only when the drainage systems become broken and clogged that their existence is realised.

Only occasionally does the extent of under drainage become apparent. In a dry summer in the early 1980s when walking across the Shap fells after a moorland fire had burnt off the topsoil and surface peat I observed regular lines of tile-pipes exposed at the surface. It seemed amazing that any proprietor had considered this land sufficiently promising to be worth the expense of underdraining. It was a salutary example of how mid nineteenth-century attitudes to agriculture, land management and productivity differed from those of modern times.

This book provides a window on a vanished industry; it is based on thirteen years of intensive research, combining archive sources and fieldwork. The authors take care to set their regional findings within a broader national context. The sources used include not just the obvious ones such as early Ordnance Survey maps and census enumerators' books but a wide range of manuscript material relating to the building and management of tile factories. In the process they have identified an important element in the Cumbrian landscape, in its day clearly a significant source of employment. Yet it was a surprisingly short-lived phenomenon, beginning in the 1820s, peaking with 'high farming' in the 1850s and 60s, then declining after 1870 with the onset of agricultural depression. The illustrations of different kinds of tiles and the kilns used for making them, maps of tile-works and photographs of surviving structures add to the understanding of the processes involved in tile manufacture. The effects of the drainage work live on in the landscape long after the industry has declined. A detailed and comprehensive gazetteer of sites is provided on a CD Rom accompanying the book. I suspect that this, together with the many illustrations will encourage many people, myself included, to reach for their wellingtons and set out to explore some of these tile-making sites ourselves.

Ian Whyte
August 2013

1

Introduction

The manufacture and use of clay agricultural drainage tiles was introduced into the historic county of Cumberland between 1819 and 1821. From then until the late nineteenth century production was largely what has been described as a 'home manufacture', confined to small rural sites referred to as 'brick & tile works', 'tile works', 'tileries', 'tile yards' or 'tile kilns', and these are the titles used in this book. However, it should be noted that such sites are now designated 'clay drainage pipe works' with the other descriptions reserved for sites producing roof, floor or decorative tiles.[1]

The term 'tile', originally referring to a flat sheet of clay moulded into a horse-shoe shape, continued to be used throughout the nineteenth and twentieth centuries to describe the objects in Figure 1.1.

Figure 1.1 tile, tile & collar, tile-pipe, pipe [photograph S B Davis]

Even when tiles became tile-pipes or pipe-tiles and then pipes they were widely referred to as tiles, and still are to this day by many farmers.

Our interest in the history of tiles was prompted by a combination of three factors: a small derelict building, information derived from 1st edition OS maps and an article published in 1829. This resulted in thirteen years of research into the introduction of tiles into Cumberland, the location of sites of tile-works, the study of manufacturing, migration of individuals and families working in the industry, and finally, this publication.

When first moving to Cumbria in 1993, a regular route through minor roads in the north-eastern corner of the county took us past a field on the edge of the village of Kirkcambeck, which contained a small brick built structure, with a chimney at one end, and a tree growing on its roof, Figure 1.2.

Figure 1.2 Newcastle kiln near Kirkcambeck [photograph S B Davis]

The origin and purpose of this building, which we subsequently discovered was a Newcastle kiln, became apparent on studying the 1st edition OS map, which showed that it stood on what had been the site of a brick & tile works. As maps covering adjacent parishes also displayed several other sites, it became obvious that north Cumberland in the 1860s was home to a number of centres of this industry.

While studying for the Certificate in Local History of Lancaster University, a title on a reading list provided the reason for this concentration. This was an article, published in *Prize Essays and Transactions of the Highland Society of Scotland* in 1829, written by John Yule the land agent on the Netherby estate, and describing the introduction of tile-making there, the method of manufacture and the buildings required.[2]

Research initially concentrated only on the tile-works in the immediate vicinity of the area in which we had come to live. Within a short period it became obvious that very little work had been carried out into the history of tile-making in the historic counties of Cumberland and Westmorland, and consequently there were few modern publications.
At the same time reading of national agricultural histories to obtain background information highlighted the importance of tile-draining in the nineteenth-century. This created an opportunity for a 'retirement project', which soon expanded beyond the initial geographical constraints.

John Yule's article suggested that making clay drainage tiles for agricultural purposes began in Cumberland on the Netherby estate, and nothing during subsequent enquiries has brought to light any facts to the contrary. This created the obvious starting point for research, prefixed only by exploration of the draining practices prior to, and during, the opening years. The mid-nineteenth century was a period of immense agricultural improvement, and 'Draining was the great improvement of the age'.[3] A national debate was taking place on the system of underdraining known as 'Thorough Draining' with a growing consensus that 'the best materials for draining are tiles'.[4] This placed tile-making at the forefront of agriculture from the 1840s until the late 1860s. A decline followed, brought on by several factors, with the result that by the end of the century tile-making was being carried on by a small number of what were essentially brick-works. Numerically by the 1920s these had reduced even further, giving a closing date for a period to be studied of around one hundred years.

Due to the limited information available on any one site, research extended beyond the area of northern Cumberland. This prompted a decision to try and produce a gazetteer of all traceable tile manufacturers in the historic counties of Cumberland and Westmorland, and to include Furness and Cartmel, formerly part of Lancashire. Subsequently, due to the close links between some tileries in the south-western part of Northumberland, as well as a number of Dumfriesshire works, selected sites from these areas have been included. Although the gazetteer is geographically restricted, the first part of the book attempts to place the progress and evolution of tile-making in our region in the context of developments in both England and Scotland.

Having established the parameters in terms of chronology and geography, initial research set out to establish a list of sites and manufacturers. The first task was to scrutinise all 1st edition OS 6"maps for the relevant counties to give a definitive list of works at the time of the surveys.

Trade directories from 1829 to the early 1900s were similarly treated, with the material from both sources being combined. The information was recorded in the manner explained in the *Gazetteer of Sites and Manufacturers*-essentially using historic parishes and townships, which facilitated comparisons between sources.

The list was then used to follow individuals, initially through nineteenth-century census returns, which as well as providing information on the separate occupations of workers in the industry, gave the place of birth of tile-makers' children. Information in the enumerators' schedules, in a number of instances, revealed the existence of a tile-kiln which had not been recorded on OS maps or in directories.

Details of the place of birth of tile-workers' children established a starting point for research in parish baptism registers, which along with other information provided the father's occupation and helped to fill gaps in the history of a works, between census dates. This gave a picture of what we have called 'tile-making families', Appendix 4, who had a number of members involved in the industry at different places.

The 2nd edition OS 6" maps were examined in the same way as the 1st editions and expanded the list of works. Then, to obtain greater detail, the 25" scale of both 1st and 2nd editions were perused for areas containing sites of tile-works.

DRAINING THE CUMBRIAN LANDSCAPE

Every edition of the *Carlisle Journal* for 70 years beginning in 1819 was examined for advertisements relating to tile-making; this produced substantial quantities of information. For the 1890s to the early 1900s a more selective approach was taken, concentrating on the small number of works still in existence. Many references have been provided by other researchers who are recorded in the acknowledgements.

As the existence of a particular tile-works was established, it became possible to search other archives, using the names of places and individuals. Much material has been located, including accounts of drainage projects, wills of individuals involved in tile-making, and a small number of records relating to individual tile-works. The most fruitful sources have been estate records, including a few relating specifically to estate tileries, which are all recorded in the bibliography.

Where possible, sites have been visited and photographed, although, sadly, with one or two exceptions, very little remains to be seen on the ground. This is partly the result of the practice, when a works closed, of auctioning not only the equipment but the materials of the buildings. Another factor, particularly in the early years, was the condition in some agreements that the site had to be re-instated.

The primary focus of the research has been manufacturers of agricultural drainage-tiles, many of whom also produced bricks, just as many brick-works, often only for a limited period, made tiles. As this was a time when many builders possessed their own brick-field, it has resulted in a number of references to nineteenth-century brick-makers, who may have made tiles but for which there is no verification. Details of many of these are included in the *Gazetteer of Sites and Manufacturers*, but this does not set out to be a complete list of brick-works. In particular a number of the later colliery, and fire-brick works in the west of Cumberland have not been recorded. Also not listed are the names of individual employees, brick-makers and brick-works labourers, especially for areas such as Kingmoor, Stanwix, Whitehaven, Millom, and Barrow, where substantial numbers worked.

For many works it has been possible to establish the years of opening and closing, although not always both. In other cases the dates of the first- and last- located references have been used to define the period of operation.

In the *Gazetteer* all located sources and references for each entry have been recorded to provide a foundation for future researchers. It seemed advisable to concentrate on organising and publishing what we have achieved to date, leaving others to continue and seek out the many documents which must exist in a variety of archives.

Notes

---

[1] Watts (2002) 39, RCHME (2000) *Thesaurus Class List-Industrial* www.gov.uk/thesaurus/mon-types/
[2] Yule (1829)
[3] Chambers & Mingay (1966) 175
[4] Pusey (1842) 173

2

Surface, hollow and deep drains

Agriculture was in a depressed state in Cumberland in the early years of the nineteenth century, when in 1815 at the Carlisle fair, 'cattle could not be disposed of at any price' and grain was sold at prices that could not possibly repay the cultivator. In 1890 it was stated that in the last century 'in no county in England was agriculture at a lower ebb than in Cumberland' and that 'draining was hardly heard of'.[1] Almost as pessimistic was an account of 1853, which recorded that 'little draining of any kind was practised in the county till near the end of the last century; it was too expensive for the tenant farmer to take in hand, and the gentleman landowner of that period seldom paid much attention to this improvement of his estate'.[2] Lancashire was similarly behind other parts of the country; in the first decade of the nineteenth century draining was 'executed in a most slovenly and imperfect manner; the drains were cut only in the wettest spots'. This was despite the fact that it was a county in which, from the quantities of rain which fell and the nature of the soil, draining was 'of necessity, the first requisite step to improve our lands'.[3] It was generally agreed that draining was a 'practise of the first importance' for bringing land into a 'state necessary for further improvement' but throughout the northern counties, apart from the cost, for tenants the lack of incentive to drain could be chiefly attributed to the short terms of leases, making it uneconomic to invest.[4] Other publications were more positive, describing draining in 1805 as 'one of those improvements which has been introduced of late years into the northern counties'. Cumberland was one of the places where it had been adopted, with great advantages being gained by both hollow and surface drains. In Westmorland the importance of having the land lie dry was well known and the practice of draining was 'daily gaining ground'. The middle and northern parts of Northumberland were the areas of the county where draining was mostly practised, with hollow drains generally being used, while on the sheep farms of the Cheviot hills surface drains were cut.[5]

Surface draining as its name suggests, removes water by using channels on the surface of the land, the number and type being modified to suit the composition of the soil. From time immemorial surface draining had been achieved by utilising the ridge and furrows created in the course of ploughing.[6] Water ran off the ridges and into the furrows on either side, which could be altered to direct the flow. This method could work on sloping land, but on flat and low-lying ground only the ridges stayed dry.[7]

Hollow drains were trenches, usually about two feet deep, filled loosely with stones, boughs, bracken, brushwood or straw before either a sod or soil was returned, creating a hollow channel through which water would flow.[8] In Cumberland and Northumberland hollow drains were generally used, the filling, where available, being stone. The system in Cumberland involved setting stones against the side of the drain, these being wedged apart with another block and then filled with small stones. In Westmorland the drains were similarly walled on the sides and then covered with large stones, which were below the depth of a plough.[9] Drains in Lancashire in 1815 were described as being 'two feet in depth and 22 inches in width; they were walled on the sides, and flagged in the bottom where the land was soft, being covered on the top with flat stones' so creating a square passage.[10]

An alternative where stone was unavailable, or considered too expensive, were sod drains which could be formed in a simple manner. In Cumberland in the mosses and level meadows, where the sward was strong enough for the purpose, sods were widely used. They were also the most common form of drain on newly-made moss land in Westmorland, where the system was to cut a two-foot deep trench with a shoulder on either side on which the sods were placed. The same method was employed in Lancashire where they were considered the least expensive form of draining. The major weakness of this type of drain, even when well and deeply formed, was that it could not support heavy cattle and horses.[11]

A variation employed in parts of Westmorland and also in Lancashire was to cut a trench, partially filling it with thorns and brushwood, before placing a green sod in the trench and topping it with soil. This provided a cheap form of draining suitable for peat or moss land.

These two methods, surface draining by means of open ditches or by using ridge and furrow, and hollow draining utilising fillings of various materials, dependent on local availability and cost, were common to all parts of the country.

There was also a third method, a deep draining system, widely used in the midlands and southern counties from its 'invention' in the 1760s. This was what became known as the 'Elkington' system, a form of deep draining based on the location and tapping of springs, and then forming one or two outlets to carry off water from this source.

Joseph Elkington began his drainage experiments in 1764 on land he had inherited. Having dug a trench four to five feet deep along the edge of a bog adjacent to a spring, without the desired effect, he then drove an iron bar into the bottom of the trench, which caused water to gush out. This iron bar, which was replaced by an auger, became his trade mark when searching for the source of water. Although only suited to land where the water damage resulted from springs, the use of Elkington's system spread and he was widely employed to drain estates.

In 1795 he was awarded a parliamentary grant, and the Board of Agriculture sent Mr John Johnstone, a land surveyor, to visit, in company with Elkington, the principal drainage projects that he was executing, and to report on them. This resulted in the publication in 1797 of a book, *An Account of the Mode of Draining Land according to the System Practised by Mr Joseph Elkington* which appeared in a second edition in 1801.

Although feted by many, Elkington's system did not gain universal approval; one account relating to estates in Bedford and Derby described not successes, but 'the want of them'. Similarly in Scotland, it was stated that the system in many instances had not been attended by anything like complete success, even when most carefully carried out.[12]

Despite these doubts his methods were widely used, as illustrated by this advertisement of 1824, Figure 2.1. The Robert Lucock referred to had, prior to 1824, been a land drainer for 16 years, becoming as will be seen one of the most important tile manufacturers in Cumberland.[13]

JOSEPH ROBINSON,

EDEN BANKS, Parish of WETHERAL,

(Successor to RoBT. Lucock, late of LAVERSDALE,)

RESPECTFULLY informs his Friends, and the Public in general, that he has commenced LAND DRAINING in all its Various Branches; and from his scientifical and practical knowledge (having practised for a number of years upon *Elkington's* Approved System), and a determination to do the work entrusted to him in the most effectual manner, he hopes to merit a share of their patronage and support.

Eden Banks, Sept. 29, 1824.

Figure 2.1 CAS (Carlisle) *Carlisle Journal* 16th October 1824

Nationally agricultural improvements were encouraged through local agricultural societies. In Cumberland one of the main exponents of these was John Christian Curwen, Figure 2.2.

Figure 2.2 John Christian Curwen [Lonsdale (1867) frontis]

As well as embarking on an improvement programme on his own estates, he inaugurated in 1805 the Workington Agricultural Society, and in their report of 1806, he declared that 'the basis of all improvement, without which nothing is permanent or effectual' was draining. From 1806 regular premiums of £5.5.0 were awarded by the society for draining, usually at least two being offered, one for a proprietor and one to a farmer. For 1815 the premium was for the greatest number of roods of drains 'sod or open drains not to be entitled to the premium, if the land will admit of stone draining'. The society held annual meetings at which the awards were made, Figure 2.3. In 1821 the premium went to a farmer who drained 1700 roods for which he received £5.5.0 and a silver cup.[14]

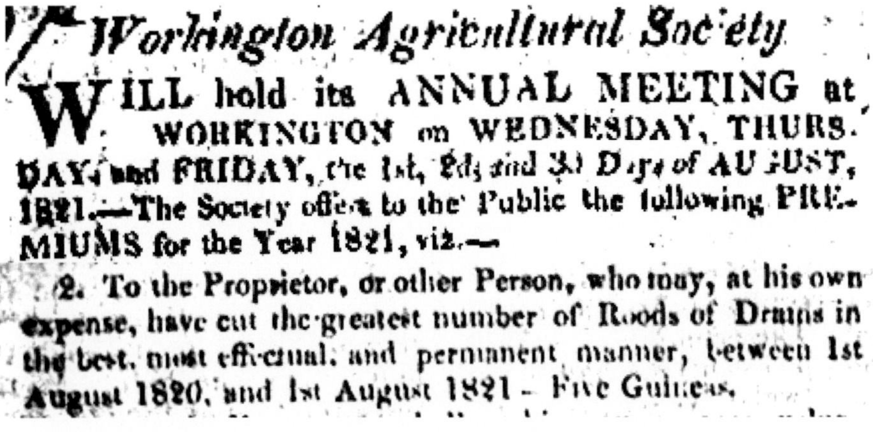
Workington Agricultural Society.

WILL hold its ANNUAL MEETING at WORKINGTON on WEDNESDAY, THURSDAY, and FRIDAY, the 1st, 2d, and 3d Days of AUGUST, 1821.—The Society offers to the Public the following PREMIUMS for the Year 1821, viz.—

2. To the Proprietor, or other Person, who may, at his own expense, have cut the greatest number of Roods of Drains in the best, most effectual, and permanent manner, between 1st August 1820, and 1st August 1821 - Five Guineas.

Figure 2.3 CAS (Carlisle) *Carlisle Journal* 2nd June 1821

All these methods of draining were unsatisfactory in some respects. Surface draining which had limited effect only on certain types of terrain also produced with ridge and furrow a surface unsuitable for the machinery which was beginning to be introduced.[15] The materials used as filling in hollow drains determined their efficiency; stone not always available was heavy and expensive to transport. Sods, brushwood and other 'soft' substances were liable to collapse under the weight of animals. Therefore with the beginnings of the promotion of draining as an essential improvement, particularly on large estates, together with other factors which are detailed in the next chapter, the elements were in place for the widespread introduction of a new conduit for excess water - the clay drainage tile.

Notes

[1] *CJ* 23/9/1815-3/3, Ferguson (1890) 286
[2] Dickinson (1853) 80
[3] Holt (1795) 108, Binns (1851) 16
[4] Dickson (1815) 476, Wedge (1794) quoted in Marshall (1813) 18/19
[5] Bailey & Culley (1805) reprint (1972) 128, 238, 322
[6] Stephens (1846) 5, Mingay (1977) 48
[7] Brown (1993) 11, Mingay (1977) 48
[8] Dickinson (1853) 81, Brown (1993) 11, Mingay (1977) 48
[9] Bailey & Culley (1805) 128, 238, 322, Dickinson (1850) 33, Dickinson (1853) 81
[10] Dickson (1815) 477, 479
[11] Dickinson (1850) 33,Garnett (1912) 58, Dickson (1815) 476, 479, Lovat (1831) 74
[12] Hozier (1870) 7, Harpur (1911) 3, Livesley (1960) 4, Johnstone (1801) v, vi, vii, Farey (1813) 364/5, Dudgeon (1840) 85
[13] *CJ* 21/8/1824-1/1, 16/10/1824-1/1
[14] Ferguson (1890) 287, Hughes (1965) 226 fn citing Report (1806) 27, Beckett (2004) Curwen, John Christian *ODNB*, Jollie (1811) 55-61, Curwen (1809) 207-210, *The Report of the Workington Agricultural Society for the Years 1813 & 1814* page 6 [Carlisle Library, Jackson Library M83] *CJ* 8/6/1819-3/5, 2/6/1821-3/1, 11/8/1821-3/4
[15] Fenton (1976) 23

3

The arrival of tiles in Cumberland c.1819-c.1829

The customary use of stone, turf or wood as the materials for filling hollow land drains had not excluded the experimental use of clay products. Underdraining with tiles did not suddenly materialise in the early years of the nineteenth century. Writers on agriculture over centuries had alluded to the employment of tiles or pipes for drainage systems. Among Roman authors, Pliny suggested utilizing tiles in the bottom of drainage ditches. Pipe drains were used in a French monastery garden in the seventeenth century, and it was claimed that horseshoe tiles were manufactured in Suffolk in the middle of the eighteenth century.[1]

It is a natural progression therefore to find that bricks and tiles were being made in various parts of England from the late eighteenth century specifically for use in agricultural drainage.

The following description, 'an inch thick and a foot long, nearly the shape of a ridge tile, but not being more than 5 inches wide at the bottom and 6 inches semi-diameter' of what the author called 'a brick-arch', was in effect a horseshoe tile made for draining purposes in Shropshire in 1794.[2]

The use of bricks to create the channel of a land drain was reported in a number of counties, including Cheshire in 1794 and Lancashire in 1795. In the latter county it was remarked that brick-drains were experimented with in a number of areas; this suggested that bricks were used, due to the fact that tiles were not considered to be strong enough.[3]

In a section on materials with which hollow drains were filled, a publication of 1801 described how in 'Essex and other counties, pipes of clay, about eighteen inches long, with an opening of three or four inches diameter, are burnt'.[4]

Relating in 1843 how he had commenced underdraining in the Weald of Kent in 1788, John Read recounted that the kiln in which he had made tiles was now used for making pipe-tiles. In this account he does not state when he first made tiles, but elsewhere in 1845, it was recorded that he had 'made and used draining tiles for thirty-five years'.[5]

On one estate in Yorkshire, despite little drainage taking place prior to 1840, some tile drainage was pursued, 'as between 1810-1819 a small sum was shown as tenant expenditure on tiles'.[6]

Tile-draining was reported in 1811 as being practised in several places throughout Derbyshire, using 'stout curved tiles, like Ridge Tiles and hollow or Pipe Bricks'. A list was also given of a number of brick-kilns where tiles were being manufactured for draining purposes.[7]

A description of draining in Worcestershire in 1813 related how on one farm 'tiles, twelve inches long, three and one half inches deep and the same wide were used to good effect'. On another estate 'hollow drains were made in almost every field' with tiles used to form the channel; 'they were of a semi-elliptical form, four inches wide, three inches deep, one foot in length, and one inch in thickness'.[8]

Following the wet summer of 1816, on the Stow Hall estate in Norfolk 'tenants were clamorous for tiles' and wagons came to the kiln-yard as soon as the first tiles were ready.[9]

There are numerous accounts of tiles in other counties: 'pipes and tiles were in use at Histon, Cambridgeshire, 1818-24', and in Lancashire 'drainage tiles were made in about 1820 but were not extensively used until 1840'. Similarly 'on the clay lands of Lincolnshire some under-draining was commenced in the early 1820s using horse-shoe tiles and soles'.[10]

This incomplete summary of the use of tiles in underdraining across England gives a picture of widespread but localised unconnected trials. A publication of 1852 describes how 'almost forty years ago', small pipes for land-drainage were used concurrently by parties who had no knowledge of each other's operations.[11] This endorses the statement that for the spread of underdraining 'there is no clear picture of the timing, rate and spatial pattern of its adoption in the nineteenth century'.[12]

A common complaint when describing the use of bricks and tiles for drainage was the additional cost, imposed in the form of tax under a 1784 act granting duties upon bricks and tiles. Under the terms of the act the 'excise officer was required to take an account of all bricks and tiles, while they were drying, and before they were removed to the kiln or clamp, for burning, and charge the duty'.[13] The previously mentioned 1794 account of Shropshire recounted how 'the excise officer thought them [the brick arch] taxable, and charged 2s 6d per 1000'. This curtailed the use of them for 'nothing can be more irksome than a tax upon material to be used in essential improvement upon land'.[14]

Similar complaints were made in Lancashire in 1815, where it was stated that bricks for draining -both common bricks and specially manufactured ones,-were experimented with but because of the tax were considered overly expensive.[15]

From 1794 a number of acts were passed with the purpose of exempting tiles for land draining from tax. The majority of the acts specified the shapes and sizes in which the tiles could be made to avoid taxation. In 1826 an amending act was passed, stipulating that tiles for drainage would be free of tax provided they were stamped with the word 'Drain', examples of which are in the Tullie House Museum collection in Carlisle.[16]

The 1820s was the decade when although 'drain tiles were very scarce' there was greater availability and underdraining was introduced into many parts of the country.[17]

One such part was the county of Cumberland; here there are no located records of experiments with tiles or draining-bricks before 1819, although as was described earlier, encouragement was given to farmers to undertake draining.

Fortunately, there are two contemporary published accounts by one of the participants in the introduction of clay drainage tile manufacture into the county, which took place on the Netherby estate between 1819 and 1821.[18] It is one of these, published in 1830, that the *Oxford English Dictionary* cites for the term 'tile burner'.

The individual to whom credit must be given for introducing tiles into Cumberland was Sir James R G Graham, Bart, Figure 3.1, working with John Yule his agent and the author of the aforementioned publications. This claim is substantiated by William Dickinson, an authority on tile manufacturing, writing in 1853 who stated that the Netherby establishment was 'the first attempt of the kind in the county'.[19]

Figure 3.1 Sir James R G Graham Bart [Lonsdale (1868) frontispiece]

Netherby, seat of the barony of Liddel, is situated in the north-east corner of Cumberland near Longtown, and is bounded on the north for sixteen miles by Scotland, Figure 3.2.

Figure 3.2 Detail from 1815 map included in Lysons, D & S, (1816) *Magna Britannia*

Approximately 26,000 acres in size in 1819, the estate was divided into small holdings of from 40 to 100 acres in extent; it was farmed by 300 tenants at low rentals and with considerable amounts in arrears.[20]

The management of the estate was entrusted to Sir James by his father, also Sir James, in 1819. Subsequently in 1824 on the death of his father he succeeded to the baronetcy. The estate he took over was in what later agents described as, a ruinous condition, overseen by an agent, Ellis, with very little control and an almost complete lack of accounts.[21] One of the first tasks for Sir James was to replace Ellis with a young efficient agent, John Yule, who was to help 'make Netherby a great agricultural estate, a model of good farming'.[22]

Many improvements were found to be absolutely necessary before farms could be let on advantageous terms and before an improved mode of husbandry could be introduced. Rainfall was excessively heavy in Cumberland making farming largely unprofitable, unless a good drainage system was installed. On the estate 'there was the greatest possible need of drainage, for by far the greatest portion of the country was surcharged by spring and surface water'.[23] It was a matter of grave consideration as to how extensive drainage could be effected, due to 'the general want of stone' and of quarries 'where material might have been procured at a moderate rate'.[24]

Sir James first encountered the use of tiles in draining when visiting Staffordshire in 1819. His uncle William Inge resided at Thorpe Hall and on his estate of around 1000 acres, with conditions similar to those at Netherby, great improvements had been made by draining with tiles.[25] No time was lost; 'having communicated with his agent', they engaged 'a proper person from the neighbourhood of Tamworth' recommended by Mr Inge. This man was Thomas Guy Patrick and he was brought to Netherby for the purpose of examining the estate to discover 'if proper clay could be found for moulding tiles'. A bed of suitable clay was located, and a contract, to last three seasons, was entered into with Patrick for the manufacture of draining tiles to be used on the estate.[26]

During his time at Netherby, Patrick was provided with labour from the estate - young men who learned 'the art of preparing and burning tiles'[27]

The whole process was in active operation in the season of 1821, with a 'proper tile-kiln' and shed having been erected. The tilery was at Sandysike, near Parcelstown, where 'Draining Tiles of various sizes' together with bricks, both 'manufactured by a Contractor from Staffordshire', were offered for sale in June 1821, Figure 3.3.[28]

Figure 3.3 CAS (Carlisle) *Carlisle Journal* 16th June 1821

At this time the second tile-works in Cumberland had been established. An advertisement noted that 'the Price of Draining Tiles will be the same as charged by the Messrs Patrick at Grove'. This was at Linstock where Thomas Guy Patrick was recorded as a tile-maker. Later accounts stated that he had started on his own, having quarrelled with John Yule, which may be correct, as the original three seasons contract would not have expired by this date.[29]

Having inaugurated tile-making Sir James and his agent continued with improvements- amalgamating farms to create units of between 100 and 500 acres, and granting leases of 19 years. To encourage draining, a farming society was formed on the estate and prizes were awarded to farmers who used the largest number of tiles. The quantities of tiles used eventually necessitated the establishment of a second Netherby tile-kiln.[30]

Although Sir James Graham was incontrovertibly the first to introduce tile-making into Cumberland, others were not far behind. A publication of 1868 credited two individuals in addition to Sir James and Thomas Guy Patrick with being among the initial participants in the 1820s. One of these was Quintin Blackburn of whom unfortunately not a single reference connecting him to tile-making has been located. He resided at Knorren Lodge, in the proximity of which two tile-works operated, although neither commenced sufficiently early to be among the pioneers, and no link has been found. As he was buried on the 4th January 1826, any involvement must have been of a short duration.[31]

The second man was Emanuel Demain born in Skipton and resident there until at least 1811. He had arrived in Cumberland by September 1815 when his son was baptised at Hayton near Brampton. At that date and in 1818 he was described as a 'labourer'.

In 1843 Emanuel claimed to have been a tile manufacturer for 21 years, placing his commencement of tile-making in 1822. This is substantiated by a statement in October 1846 to the effect that a John Little had been in the employ of Emanuel Demain as drainer and tile-burner for 32 years. This suggests that before the introduction of tile-making Emanuel had been in business as a drainer.[32] His first recorded involvement with tiles is on the Earl of Carlisle's estate at Naworth, seat of the barony of Gilsland.

The estates of Naworth and Netherby were the two major landowners in the north of Cumberland, with Naworth land extending into Northumberland, as Netherby estate did into Scotland.

Tiles were first mentioned on the Naworth estate in an account of the number of 'Tyles (*sic*) made in 1827 and 1828'; the number of bricks manufactured is also shown. On the verso of this document, under a date of 1829, appears the comment 'E Demain for making bricks &c', suggesting this was payment for the previous two-years production.[33]

If Emanuel Demain really did commence tile-making in 1822 as he claimed, it would seem that Naworth followed very closely behind Netherby in the manufacture of tiles.

An advertisement of 1823, Figure 3.4 proclaimed the setting up of the next tile-kiln in the county and the second commercial enterprise, although as will be seen an estate requiring tiles for their own use instigated the project.

TILE DRAINING.

WANTED, an experienced MAKER of DRAINING TILES,—to whom every Encouragement and Assistance will be given. He may have the occupation of Ten Acres of Ground adjoining the new Glasgow Road, in which there is an inexhaustible Bed of excellent Clay, well calculated for making Tiles; and a suitable Cottage will either be erected on the Ground, or one at a convenient distance, furnished for him. Bricks and other Materials will also be furnished for erecting a Tile Kiln.

The Land is of excellent Quality for keeping one or more Milch Cows, and is in a most central and desirable Situation for Sale of Tiles in the surrounding Country, and into the Borders of Scotland.

For further Particulars apply to Mr. MOUNSEY, at Castletown, Rockliff. (Not to be repeated).

Figure 3.4 CAS (Carlisle) *Carlisle Journal* 27th December 1823

The experienced tile-maker who eventually took the works at Petersyke was Thomas Guy Patrick, the Staffordshire man already operating at Linstock. He entered into an agreement on the 16th February 1825, by which time the kiln and sheds had been erected. The term was seven years and the rent was £25 per annum, or if required, 10,000 three - inch tiles and 2,000 four- inch tiles in lieu. It would seem that the works had already been operational as notes on the verso of the agreement list equipment and repairs required, including 'Bricks for Kiln Bottom those left by Tyers being good for nothing'. This was probably the William Tyers who was still a tile-maker at Petersyke in 1831, presumably then employed by Patrick.[34]

According to an article headed 'Tile Draining' in the *Carlisle Journal* of the 31st January 1824, there were four tile-works established, with another about to commence near Wigton.[35] If this statement is correct, and there is reason to doubt it as two other comments within it are inaccurate, it does raise the question as to which was the fourth. The first was Netherby at Sandysike, the second was Thomas Guy Patrick at Grove, and the third was at Petersyke. It is likely that the fourth could have been a Naworth estate tilery, operated by Emanuel Demain. While it is not possible to confirm or disprove this, what is correct is that the next works was near Wigton.

Robert Lucock had been employed, with his brother Joseph, at Netherby to supervise draining of land under the estate's own management. In this position he was involved with tile-making from its inception in Cumberland. As will be seen he put this experience to good use. In 1830 he was described as 'an enterprising man and the first person who introduced the draining tiles into this country', that is, into the western division of Cumberland.[36]

In February 1824 Robert advertised to be let the making and burning of bricks at Langrigg in the parish of Bromfield, with the clay already dug. This was followed in August with the announcement, Figure 3.5, that manufacturing of tiles, prepared upon the Staffordshire principle, had begun.[37]

DRAINING TILES.

ROBERT LUCOCK, late of LAVERSDALE, LAND-DRAINER, takes this opportunity of return-
ing his grateful Thanks for the very liberal Patronage confer-
red upon him in the above line for the last 16 years ; and
begs to inform his Friends, and the Public in general, that he
has commenced the MANUFACTURE of DRAINING
TILES, at LANGRIGG, in the Parish of Bromfield. He/
intends to prepare them upon the Staffordshire principle, and,
from the arrangements he has made, and a determination to
deliver nothing but the very best article, and on the most reasonable terms, he hopes to give Satisfaction to the Public, and
to merit a share of their Patronage and Support.

N. B.—20,000 Tiles are now ready, and the same Number will be prepared every Nine Days.

R. L. will CONTRACT for DRAINING BOGS, &c.
as usual.

Langrigg, August 9, 1824.

Figure 3.5 CAS (Carlisle) *Carlisle Journal* 21st August 1824

William Dickinson, himself an owner of tile-works, wrote in 1850: 'In 1824 Mr Robert Lucock established the first tile Work erected in the Division [West Cumberland], at Langrigg and in spite of a host of doubts and objections, succeeded in prevailing on his neighbours to try tiles by way of experiment, and in very soon convincing them, on trial, that three inch tiles at 42s per thousand (the price then) were better and cheaper than stones'.[38]

By 1828 the Netherby estate included among its letting of annual contracts, the manufacturing of bricks and tiles, Figure 3.6. It must have been taken by one of the men trained by Thomas Guy Patrick, as John Yule wrote in 1829: 'at this moment, the whole draining tiles required (upward of two hundred and six thousand yearly) are supplied by a native of the estate of Netherby'.[39]

TILE AND BRICK BURNING.

Also to be LET, at the same time and place, the
PREPARATION of the CLAY, and MANUFAC-
TURING of BRICKS, and DRAINING TILES, for
the Estate of Netherby,—at PARCELSTOWN, near
Longtown, for the ensuing Year, 1829.
(One Concern.)

Figure 3.6 CAS (Carlisle) *Carlisle Journal* 1st November 1828

In the same decade that tile-making was being introduced into Cumberland, it was also taking place to the north and east of the county. Across the border 'the first tile works in Scotland was on the Duke of Portland's estate at Cessnock in Ayrshire in 1826', although other accounts place the introduction respectively in 1820 and in 1824. [40]

The earlier date may be correct, as John Johnston, described as the 'father of tile drainage in America', later recounted his experience on the way to Glasgow at the beginning of his journey from Dumfriesshire to America in 1821. In a field he had seen what was described to him as 'the burning of crockery to be put in the ground'. On investigating, he discovered it was the making of tiles. [41]

Whatever the date there was a close relationship, which will be illustrated over the ensuing decades, between tile-making in Dumfriesshire and in Cumberland and Westmorland. This began with an advertisement placed in the *Carlisle Journal* in October 1829 requiring contractors to make a large quantity of tiles and bricks on the Springkell estate near Ecclefechan north-west of Carlisle. [42]

In Northumberland there were at least three rural tile-works in 1825 - at Alnwick, Tweedmouth and Wooler, and a possible fourth, at Ford by 1828. [43]

A directory of 1829 carried the following statement regarding agriculture in Cumberland: 'The system of tile draining is now very prevalent here; and during the last five years about 800,000 tiles have been made annually for this purpose, by three manufacturers near Carlisle, Bowness and Langrigg'. The number of tiles produced may be accurate, but there were more tile works than this suggests, as within the directory several other brick and tile manufacturers were listed. [44]

With the works detailed above, together with the manufacturers in the directory, there were potentially nine tile-making establishments in Cumberland, Table 1.1, sufficient at the end of its first decade to describe them as an industry.

Table 3.1 Tile-works & manufacturers in Cumberland 1821-29

Date	Parish	Manufacturer - Works
1821	Arthuret	Netherby estate - Sandysike
1821	Stanwix	Thomas Guy Patrick - Linstock
1823	Rockliff	William Tyers - Petersyke
1824	Bromfield	Robert Lucock - Langrigg
1827	Brampton	Emanuel Demain – Naworth estate
1829	Bowness	Joshua Ward
1829	Cockermouth	Robert Smithson
1829	"	William Mackreath – St. Helen's Street
1829	"	Thomas Mackreath - Kirkgate

Sources: *Gazetteer of Sites and Manufacturers*

The locations of the sites are shown in Figure 3.7, illustrating the cluster around the first works at Sandysike. Langrigg, as has been described, was opened by Robert Lucock who had been employed at Netherby. As yet there is no indication as to how or why three manufacturers commenced in Cockermouth. Only two are captioned on the map, as the exact position of the third is not known.

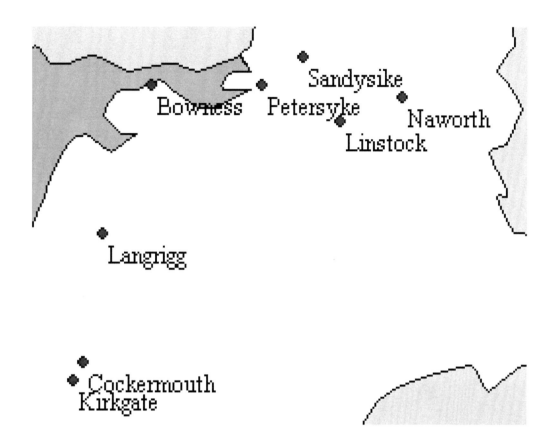

Figure 3.7 Tile-works in Cumberland 1821-29 [Gen Map UK]

The proliferation of early tile-works did not immediately bring about the demise of other forms of draining, as shown by a premium of 10 guineas, to be awarded at the Carlisle cattle show in 1829 for 'the greatest extent of effective and judiciously executed close draining, either with stone or tile'.[45]

John Yule's account of the introduction of tile-making was published in the first volume of the New (2nd) Series of the *Prize Essay & Transactions of the Highland Society of Scotland*, which became the *Highland & Agricultural Society of Scotland*.
It was dated 31st March 1829, Glingerbank, Longtown, at that time his residence as steward to the Netherby estate.
This was followed in 1830 by 'Netherby in Cumberland' in the series 'Farm Reports or Accounts of the Management of Select Farms', which included an Appendix 'An Account of Underdraining by means of Tiles'. In 1840 the work was published in book form as part of *Husbandry* Volume the Third in the Library of Useful Knowledge.

These two publications provide much of the information on which our knowledge of the operating process of an early tile-works is based, as will be shown in the next chapter.

Notes

[1] Klippart (1862) 13-15, Weaver (1964) 2-5

[2] Johnstone (1801) 124, Marshall (1818) Vol.2 180, both citing Bishton (1794)

[3] Marshall (1818) Vol.2 18-19 citing Wedge (1794), Holt (1795) 108

[4] Johnstone (1801) 124

[5] Read (1843) 273-4, Wiggins (1847) 11

[6] Phillips (1972) 199

[7] Farey (1811) Vol.1 453-4

[8] Pitt (1813) 192, 194-5

[9] Wiggins (1847) 34

[10] Turner et al (2001) citing Cambridge RO R62/36, R58/9/4/3, Beesley (1849) 38, Clarke (1851) 352

[11] Gisborne (1852) 29

[12] Phillips (1989) 14

[13] Dowell (1888) 379

[14] Johnstone (1801) 124, Marshall (1818) Vol.2 180, both citing Bishton (1794)

[15] Dickson (1815) 481

[16] Appendix 2

[17] Stephens (1846) 103, Phillips (1989) 14

[18] Yule (1829) 388-400, Yule (1830) 62-68

[19] Dickinson (1853) 82

[20] Yule (1829) 388, Spring (1955) 73, Dickinson (1853) 17

[21] Ward (1967) 55-7, Parker (1907) 61

[22] Spring (1955) 74, *CJ* 18/5/1822-2/4

[23] Erickson (1950) 171, Yule (1829) 388-9

[24] Yule (1829) 388-9

[25] Yule (1829) 389, Salt Library Misc.238 Inge Family 34, White (1834) 401, Parson & Bradshaw (1818)

[26] Yule (1829) 389-90, Yule (1830) 62, Lonsdale (1868) 37

[27] Yule (1829) 390

[28] Yule (1829), *CJ* 16/6/1821-1/5

[29] Parson & White (1829) 445, Lonsdale (1868) 37-8

[30] Dickinson (1853) 17-18, *CJ* 4/9/1824-3/1, Lonsdale (1868) 39

[31] Lonsdale (1868) 38, Willis, T W (1912) *Register of the Parish of Lanercost*, 244, *CJ* 7/1/1826-3/5

[32] CAS (C) PR102/3 Hayton Baptism Register 3/9/1815, 16/2/1818, *CJ* 12/8/1843-1/2, 10/10/1846-3/6

[33] Durham University Library Archives & Special Collections, Howard of Naworth Papers C612/74

[34] *CJ* 27/12/1823-2/5, CAS (C) DMH5/2/2 16th Feb 1825, PR7/6 Rockliff Baptism Register 20/11/1831

[35] *CJ* 31/1/1824-3/2

[36] Lonsdale (1868) 39 footnote, CAS (Whitehaven) D Lec119 Note re-proposal 1830

[37] *CJ* 28/2/1824-1/3, 21/8/1824-1/1

[38] Dickinson (1850) 33

[39] *CJ* 1/11/1828-2/2, Yule (1929) 390

[40] Fenton (1976) 20, *NSA* (1845) Vol.5 Ayrshire, Dundonald (1841) 681, Kilmarnock (1839) 546-7, Highland & Agricultural Society (1878) 61

[41] Weaver (1964) 12

[42] *CJ* 30/10/1829-2/3

[43] Mackenzie (1825) Vol.1, 323, 394, 442, Davison (1986) 6-8, Parson & White (1828) Vol.2, 507

[44] Parson & White (1829) 59,192-3,312,363,445

[45] *CJ* 25/4/1829-2/6

4

Early tile-works

The term 'early' is used to define the period from c.1819 to the mid1840s, prior to the wider introduction of machinery into tile-making.

As was stated at the end of the previous chapter, two publications by John Yule provide a contemporary record of the manufacturing processes of the prototype works. In addition there are a number of slightly later accounts, which, together with newspaper advertisements and manuscript sources, mainly agreements with tile-makers, provide material for the reconstruction of a typical Cumberland tile-works.

Although there were variations in layout, the main elements were common to most rural tile-works. The first prerequisite was a bed of clay from which the raw material was extracted, overwintered in the open and then processed, either by hand or using a grinding or pug-mill. These were initially horse-powered and required either a gin-ring or house. The tempered clay then went to a covered area, adjacent to the largest building, the drying shed, for moulding. This would be in close proximity to the kiln, which was always the most substantial structure on the site. Many works also had additional land on which there was a cottage for the tile-burner. As the industry progressed during the next two decades, and machinery was added, additional buildings were required.

One of the main causes of waterlogged soils necessitating draining is also the material used to produce the article which provides the antidote to the problem. 'Clay' is a popular term for a variety of substances of 'very varied origin and great dissimilarity in their compositions'. Boulder clay or till, occurs over the greater part of northern and central England and a considerable portion of Scotland. Ubiquitous on both sides of the Pennines, it is by far the most extensive of the drift deposits of lowland Cumberland, and is the raw material for most of the brick sand tiles, made in the county.[1] Both 'have been made in the past from boulder clay at Longlands Head' also 'at Millrigg'. The deposit which overlies the Stanwix shales was also utilised with several brick-fields at Kingstown. Another bed, the site of Cumberland's first tile-works, was at Sandysike, and close by 'an old brick-pit was worked 250 yards west of Young's Close' The list could be extended to other parts of the county, but a comparison of these place-names with those of tile-works is sufficient to confirm the origin of the clay used in brick and tile-making.[2]

Due to the numerous types of clay and the variations in purity and tenacity, alternative methods of management were required in various localities; this makes it impossible to have a general rule applicable to all.[3]

The two properties of clay relevant to the production of tiles and bricks are 'that when mixed with a certain proportion of water it makes a plastic material that can be moulded, and that when baked under certain conditions of temperature and time it becomes hard and durable'. The most obvious feature of a piece of moist clay is its 'plasticity' or ability to alter shape under slight pressure. Clays are often spoken of as being 'fat', that is possessing great binding power, or 'lean', deficient in this characteristic, tending to be friable and difficult to mould. Fat clays shrink considerably on being baked, causing cracks on cooling, and rendering them of little value for brick and tile-making. Such clay can be rendered lean by the admixture of sand or 'grog' that is powdered burnt clay or ground-up brick debris.[4] In the opinion of Robert Beart of Godmanchester, one of the pioneers of the tile-machine, 'the clay best adapted for tiles is that which contains a small proportion of sand or marl, or sand may be mixed with the clay when raised in winter'. Clay mixed this way did not contract so much in drying, and the tiles when burnt were sounder.[5]

In nineteenth-century advertisements, numerous superlatives were employed in extolling the attributes of beds of clay suitable for brick and tile-making. No clay was less than 'excellent' and beds were usually 'inexhaustible'; 'there is an inexhaustible bed of excellent clay' was the description of the clay at Petersyke. At Toppin Castle there was an 'inexhaustible bed of fine clay from which the strongest tiles and bricks are made'. Similar expressions of quality were made in the 1830s and 1840s about clay at Wreay, Hesket-in-the-Forest, Calthwaite and Botcherby, to name but a few.

It was common practice before offering a 'bed of clay to be let' for landowners to test the quality of the product. On a farm in the parish of Ruthwell in Dumfriesshire where there was 'a bed of excellent clay' it had been 'tried and found to make Tiles of a very superior quality'.[6] Such trials often proved, as happened at Woodhouselees, Dumfriesshire in the early 1840s, that clay 'of a very coarse quality, being mixed with some portion of sand, and with a good many small sand-stones', the sort of material that most tile-makers would not have used, made tiles that were 'strong and useful' though not fine looking.[7]

According to John Yule 'the clay most suitable for draining-tiles, is of the same description and quality commonly utilised for the coarser kinds of pottery purposes such as the making of house-tiles'. The clay at Netherby lay close to the surface in a bed about five feet thick; 'it is what workmen call *keen* clay, and is quite free of small stones'.[8] The supply of clay for the ensuing season was dug in the months of November, December and January in order 'that it may receive the benefit of the atmosphere through the winter'. Contractors at Woodhouselees were bound to turn over the clay required for the following season 'early in the winter, when it is cut out in thin slices and the stones so far as is practicable carefully picked out'. A little water was occasionally thrown over the clay during the course of the winter; this was particularly beneficial when the weather was frosty.[9]

This practice was universal, with accounts from other parts of the country giving the same advice: 'all clay intended for working next season must be dug in the winter, and the earlier the better, so as to expose it as much as possible to frost and snow'. In addition, if the consistency of the clay required it, around the middle of February the heap of clay was covered with sand. Whether or not it was sanded 'it is turned over twice and watered' before early April when moulding commenced.[10]

Stones, as already mentioned, occurred in clays of most geological ages but particularly in boulder clays. These stones had to be removed from the clay used for tile-making, and the standard method was that given in the instructions to contractors at Woodhouselees, described previously; that was 'to dig in small spits, and cast out the stones as much as possible'.[11] Limestone could form a part of the stony material in clay, and if the grains were large enough, on burning in the kiln they would be converted to lime, so that on exposure to weather the lime absorbed moisture, swelled and caused the tile to disintegrate. There was one allusion in Cumberland to this problem, when tiles advertised in 1840 were described as 'perfectly free from any admixture of Lime'.[12]

The time taken for the digging or 'casting' of clay depended on the quantity required for the coming season; in 1843 Thomas Edmondson was paid two shillings per day for 27 days, and his son the same rate for 26 ½ days casting clay at *Westward Park Tilery*.
Once the top soil had been removed, and the depth of the clay ascertained, a drain had to be cut through the clay-pit to take off the surplus water, which accumulated as the clay was extracted. Thomas Edmondson at the same tilery was in 1842 paid for four days work which included 'cutting drain through clay pit'.[13]
This photograph, Figure 4.1, of old clay-pits on the site of *Burrells Tilery* near Appleby , which was operational in the late 1840s and early 1850s, was taken in 2007 following a period of heavy rain. It illustrates the necessity of draining clay-pits and shows why the OS surveyors in 1897 described the area as 'Tilekiln Ponds'.

Figure 4.1 Old clay-pits at Burrells. [Photograph S B Davis January 2007]

Clay was a valuable commodity, and the Netherby agreement with tile-makers stipulated that the clay was to be 'fairly and properly wrought out to the bottom and no waste was to be allowed'.[14]
Numerous depressions in the landscape can be identified as old clay-pits, due to their proximity to the site of a tile-works and to their appearance on early OS maps. These are usually in areas of rough grazing or surrounded by trees in a small patch of woodland, often named 'Tile Kiln Wood' or 'Plantation'. Many, however, are no longer recognisable for what they were, as from the beginning some landowners required the contractor, after excavating to acquire the clay, to replace the soil and in doing so 'make a regular uniform surface'.[15]

The transporting of clay, initially from the clay-pit to where it was to be overwintered, and during the season to the moulding shed, required a quantity of planks and barrows. The planks were used to create temporary tracks on which the barrows could be wheeled, giving them from the early days their name 'wheeling planks' and, in 1825, 'foreign planks for wheeling out clay'- presumably to describe the fact that they were hardwood. Barrows were also mentioned in inventories of tools to be kept, and left in good condition by the contractor, although this did not always happen, as at Petersyke, again in 1825, where there was one barrow 'to be made good, only one good one being left'. An alternative system was for the contractor to 'find all labour, barrows and tools'.[16]

John Yule recorded that the tile-making season began in the spring as soon as the danger of frost was past, when 'the process of tempering commences, which is done with the greatest care, either by a simple grinding machine, driven by a pony, or by manual labour'. A grinding-mill was also in use at Petersyke in 1825, where the contractor, as with the barrows mentioned above, had to keep and leave in good condition. Among the list of equipment there was also a 'clay knife for grinding'.[17] The date of the general introduction of the pug-mill into brick-making, and therefore into tile-making, is subject to debate. The consensus is that its use did not become common until the mid-nineteenth century.[18] The two references to grinding-mills date from the early 1820s and in our region it was not until the 1840s that pug-mills were mentioned by name; even then the terms 'grinding-mill', 'clay-mill' and 'pug-mill' were often used synonymously.[19] The pug-mill used in tile-making, usually horse-powered Figure 4.2, was similar to other gins in that the animal fastened between the shafts, walked in a circle.

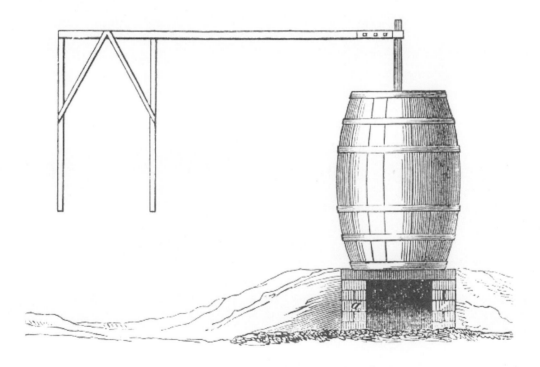

Figure 4.2 Horse-powered pug mill - Dobson (1850)

An account of 1843 described the clay being 'wheeled in barrows along planks to the Pug Mill which is driven by a horse, and is of the ordinary simple construction'. The clay was placed in the barrel of the machine and as the animal trudged around, the central upright from which knives projected, rotated, slicing the clay and pressing it out through the opening at the bottom.[20] The material for the framework of such a machine was detailed in accounts for *Westward Park Tilery* in 1841; this included 30 feet of oak for posts and frame for the gin, and 14 ½ feet of larch for the principal beam. In the same year a pug-mill was offered for sale by the *Beaumont Tile Yard* with no price given, although in that year nationally the cost was £12.12.00. *Hackthorpe Tilery* in 1846 purchased a pug-mill for £10.17.00 from a company in Whitehaven.[21]

Having gone through the mill, the clay was then transported, again by barrow to either a separate moulding shed or to the area of the drying shed used for moulding. As s was happening at *Hackthorpe Tilery* in July of 1848, tiles could be moulded and dried in the open in settled fine weather.[22]

The process of making tiles by hand was very similar across the country, as was the equipment, Figure 4.3, with only slight regional variations in design and terminology.

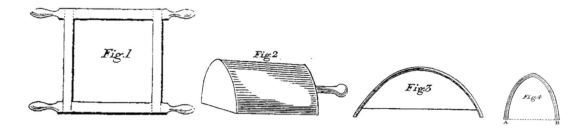

Figure 4.3 Tile mould, tile horse, tile cutter, horseshoe tile [Yule (1829)]

A moulding table was required by each tile-moulder, who would be attended by at least one 'stout' boy, known as a 'tile runner', who would bring the tempered clay in lumps. If the consistency of the clay required it, a quantity of sharp sand would be to hand, as well as a container of water. The mould, Fig.1 was filled with clay to obtain the superficial shape which was then placed on the tile horse, Fig.2, also known as a 'bender'. The clay-cutter, Fig. 3, a strong hoop bent and joined with wire, would be used to remove excess clay. If necessary, the boy having dipped his hands in the water would smooth the tile, before carrying it still on the horse to the drying shed and placing them both on a shelf. This horse was withdrawn when the next combination was placed beside the first, thus providing support for the first tile and preventing it from splaying. This activity required three sets of moulds and tile horses for each tile-moulding team, as illustrated by accounts of 1825 at *Petersyke Tile Works* and 1841 at *Westward Park Tilery*. An expert tile-moulder, of whom four were commonly employed at Netherby, could mould in a day around 1000 three-inch tiles or smaller quantities of larger diameter tiles. Greater quantities of bricks could be produced, varying from 2500 to 3000 per day.[23]

An account of work in a tilery, in Lancashire in the early 1850s indicated how exhausting the job of a tile-runner must have been. 'This carrying–off was no child's play, but one long continued getting up steps and getting down again after placing each wet tile in its place; and this at twelve to fourteen years of age, when repeated hundreds and thousands of times, made rest at eventide sweet and refreshing'.[24] The wages in the 1820s for a 'good moulder' were from 3s to 3s.4d per day, and his boy received 10d or 1s; these rates continued into the 1840s.[25]

The drying shed into which the tiles were placed at Netherby was '135 feet long, and 20 feet wide, open all around for four feet high, supported on strong wooden posts, and covered with thatch'. There the tiles were 'carefully and neatly arranged in layers, crossing each other, and divided by thin pieces of wood, in an open shed'. John Yule stated that the structure and arrangement might be considerably improved were it necessary to rebuild the shed.[26] The improvement which rapidly appeared was shelving, as was illustrated in the first advertisement for a drying shed, or as it was termed 'shade', for *Langrigg Tile Works* in 1828, which had 'fixed shelves to contain 15,000 tiles'.[27] In the records of *Westward Park Tilery*, specifications for a drying shed, which had been sent to Thomas Dixon of Calthwaite in 1830, gave details of the requirements for shelving. This document was probably the blueprint for the shed at Westward Park, erected in 1841 by Jacob Hewetson, using for the shelving timber supplied by E Brockbank of Carlisle's sawmill. Several expressions of interest and estimates were received before the contract was awarded, and references included with these showed that by this date there were a number of builders familiar with the construction of drying sheds. Joseph Fisher stated he had a 'good deal of experience of such work for Jos Mitchell' who was the proprietor of *Parkgate Tilery*, while John Simpson, a carpenter, was described by Robert James of *Sebergham Tilery* as having 'great experience of such buildings'.[28]

Nationally construction was very similar with posts supporting the roof covered with slate, which also became the standard material in Cumberland, where Welsh slate was the norm. The amount of shelf space required by a tilery was determined by the capacity of the kiln. Robert Beart of Huntingdonshire in an article of 1841 described how he had four drying sheds each with shelves capable of holding 6000 tiles. At Annan in 1846 the *Howgill Tile Works* had sheds which could house 23,000 tiles, while the Duke of Northumberland's tilery at Alnwick had 'Drying Sheds calculated to hold 38,000 tiles'.[29]

There were writers advocating producing tiles by the cheapest method, using temporary sheds for drying, constructed with hurdles and thatched, with the tiles stacked on floors. The transient nature of such activities makes it impossible to judge how widespread their use was.[30]

The purpose of a drying shed was, as its name implies to dry the tiles to a point where they could be stacked in a kiln. Contemporary accounts stressed that 'no tiles, if possible should be taken from the drying sheds to the kiln without being thoroughly dry, all dampness being very injurious'. Therefore 'good drying sheds, and plenty of them, are of great service, and a preventative against having damp tiles'. The time required for tiles to stand on the shelves, before being removed into the kiln, depended entirely on the state of the weather. The problem was of course that although the arrangement of a shed was to allow tiles to be dried by a through draught, this allowed the ingress of rain. The solution eventually was a more sophisticated system of wooden louvres; initially however, in some parts of the country such as Norfolk, the openings were 'regulated by moveable reed slats'.[31] In the northern region canvas screens or curtains were used, as recorded in the accounts of *Holker Tilery* in 1843, when £4.19.00 was expended on 'canvas used for screens'. In the 1850s at Newton in Makerfield, the previously mentioned tilery in Lancashire, 'to protect the outer ends of the tiles in wet and windy weather, screens of sailcloth were used, which had to be unfurled or furled as rain or fine demanded'.[32] The screens can be seen in the views of no. 1 drying shed in Figure 4.4.

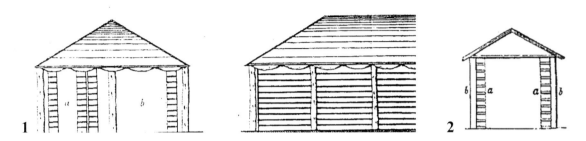

Figure 4.4 Drying sheds - No.1 Bell (1843) No. 2 Beart (1841)

This was erected at Woodhouselees in Dumfriesshire in 1841, where the contractors who operated the tilery were from Cumberland. Their advice had been taken regarding the design of the kiln and drying sheds, and John Yule witnessed the signing of the contract, so it was probably his experience that was utilised in setting up the tilery. The shed was 105 feet long and 17 feet in width, with four lines of shelving having 11 shelves in each line. Materials used included 2290 feet of boarding for shelves, 10,000 Welsh slates for the roof, and linen for curtains. The Shed no. 2 illustrated in Figure 4.4 was the one described by Robert Beart; it contained only single rows of shelves down each side leaving sufficient space for tiles to be stacked on the floor between the lines of shelves.[33] Large estates were at the forefront of innovation; on the Lowther estate at Hackthorpe in 1847, the new drying shed was constructed on stone pillars and heated by flues. In November of that year James Mawson who was overseeing the building work reported to Lord Lonsdale that they were drying tiles by heat and also lighting the shed by lamps to extend the working day.[34]

The best position for the drying shed was considered to be with 'one end close to the pug-mill and the clay heap, only leaving just room for the horse to work the mill, and the other end near the kiln'.[35]

On the Netherby estate the original kiln was 21 ½ feet long by 15 feet wide and 11 feet high, with five furnaces on each side. The walls, constructed of brick, diminished in thickness from two feet nine inches at the bottom to 18 inches at the peak; the structure was 'open at both ends and the top'. Writing in 1829 John Yule considered that as with the drying shed, the construction and arrangement of the kiln 'might be considerably improved'.

Probably the second tile-kiln to be built in the county was at Rockliff (Rockliffe), where in December 1823 an 'experienced maker of Draining Tiles' was required, for whom 'bricks and other materials would be provided for erecting a kiln'. When this kiln was taken over by Thomas Guy Patrick in February 1825 it was not in a good state. 3000 bricks were required for the kiln bottom, 560 fire-bricks for the ten 'Eyes' that is fire-holes, and cracks in the walls required repair.[36]

Kilns are classified by two functions: in relation to the direction of the draught, they may be horizontal-draught, updraught or downdraught, and in relation to the method of operation they may be intermittent or continuous. Intermittent kilns are filled, fired, cooled and emptied and the type used in most rural tile-works in northern England was an updraught version known as a Scotch kiln. This consisted of 'an open topped rectangular structure lined with firebrick, 20-50 feet long, 11-12 feet wide, and 11-13 feet high'. It had a wicket at each end and a series of fire-holes along each side; the walls were thicker at the base, and the fire could burn within the thickness of the walls with a series of flues formed in the base of the stacks of bricks and tiles to distribute the heat.[37] The Netherby and Rockliff kilns match this description, as did the kiln at Woodhouselees, which was built of stone with a brick lining and five 'eyes' on each side. These were covered by a temporary shelter to protect the burner from the weather, and the fire-places from unequal currents of air.[38]

On the Holker estate in Cartmel, there are the remains of a Scotch kiln known as Reake Wood tile kiln or Frith kiln from its location. This has been investigated by Cumbria Industrial History Society who have published their findings[39]

Although used countrywide there were differences; the kilns in use in Lincolnshire were described as being closely related to the common Scotch kiln, with a similar basic design, but with some features of a type rarely found outside the county. A kiln in use at Lower Park Farm in Cheshire in 1841 included 'fire tunnels' in a roofed over area, an open top and one side open for loading.[40] With the increase in the number of tile-works there were, as with drying sheds, builders who became experienced in their construction. One, who tendered to build the kiln at Westward Park in 1841, stated that he had 'a good deal of practise in building tile-kilns for the last 12 years'. Tile-kilns were sufficiently numerous by the late 1840s for a fire-brick works to advertise 'Long Bricks suitable for Tile-Kilns'. In Northumberland a horizontal-draught kiln, known as a Newcastle kiln, was widely used in the manufacture of bricks and tiles.[41]

Coal was the usual fuel used to fire kilns, although 'offal' wood was also used; in 1841 the kiln at Woodhouselees was drawn 20 times using 154 tons of coal during the season. In 1835 an agreement to rent land from Naworth estates for the purpose of making bricks and tiles stipulated that all coals used in burning must be purchased from the Earl of Carlisle's collieries. Carriage charges for coal could be expensive; coals for *Holker Tilery* were delivered by boat to Reake End, a short distance from the kiln, but the freight charges were 4 shillings per ton on a load of 49 tons. In 1842 206 tons were required for *Westward Park Tilery* at a cost of £63 with an additional £25 for carriage.[42]

Frequent firings during the season resulted in constant repairs being required, which was one of the reasons for the manufacture of bricks as well as tiles. Bricks were used for lining the kiln and for the kiln bottom. Both required regular attention as illustrated by these comments from Thomas Edmondson, a tile-burner in 1843: 'we should make a few more bricks very soon as the kiln will want lining she is all to pieces'. With regard to the kiln bottom he stated that it, 'will be better and cheaper and take no more coals by laying her bottom every time with new made bricks instead of fire-bricks'.[43]

Dry tiles were placed in the kiln on end, horseshoe tiles were interlocked into one another, and great care was required to keep them perpendicular and firmly set. The size of the kiln obviously determined the number of tiles being burned. In 1841 the kiln at Woodhouselees averaged 15,807 per firing, with the total number in the season being

316,149. When the kiln was filled the entrances were bricked up before firing commenced. The expertise of the tile-burner was the key factor in obtaining well-burned tiles, as no instruments existed to show how long the tiles needed to stay in the kiln. This skill was only acquired by practice and resulted in the early years of complaints about quality, as when in 1829 in Cheshire it was stated that tiles were so badly burned that in a delivery of 1000 one third were broken.[44] Advertisements extolled the quality of tiles, as in 1835, when they were described as 'well burnt', in 1836 as 'sound, hard true shaped' and in 1849 as 'very smooth on their surface, well shaped, and of most excellent metal'.[45] Once the fires were lighted in the kiln, they were kept burning continuously from between three to seven days, the time depending on the nature of the clay, the quality of the coals, the draught, and the state of the atmosphere. At Hackthorpe in 1847 the kiln was 'filled, burned and unloaded once every fortnight'.[46]

The 'contractor', and at this time the term was used synonymously with 'tile-maker' and 'tile-burner', was required to tender at so much per 1000 tiles 'counted out of the kiln' or 'ready for the market'. In addition to this payment a cottage and garden were usually provided rent free. These terms were usual when tiles were required for an estate; alternatively, land containing clay was let, as in 1835 at Kirkcambeck where one and one half acres was leased for 12 years at six pounds per year rent. If the works was erected by the landowner, as it was at Petersyke in 1835, the rent was higher- in that case £17.10.00 per annum for three years.[47]

The incentive for an estate owner to set up a tilery was to obtain tiles at a much reduced price, which had to be balanced against the construction costs. Nationally it was estimated that that the costs of erecting a kiln and drying shed, together with equipment, was in excess of £300. The cost in the northern region was considerably less; the tilery at Woodhouselees in 1841 cost £139. In addition to cheaper tiles, or a rental return, owners could also, where they possessed the mineral rights, receive clay royalties. Robert Lucock in 1835 paid for land at Curthwaite a yearly rent of £10; in addition for every superficial yard of clay in excess of 800 excavated, he paid an additional three pence.[48]

The basic layout and structure of tileries remained the same during the nineteenth century as their numbers increased. As will be seen four types of works developed: firstly the tilery erected solely to provide tiles for an estate; secondly a similar establishment which also sold tiles commercially. The third category was the purely commercial tilery, set up to exploit the growing demand for tiles, and finally, some brick works which also seized the opportunity, either on a permanent basis or for limited periods, to manufacture tiles.

Notes

[1] Searle (1912) 2, 65, Arthurton & Wadge (1981), Taylor (1971) 93

[2] Dixon et al. (1926) 91, Trotter & Hollingworth (1932) 180

[3] Hodges (1844) 553, Etheredge (1845) 463

[4] Raistrick (1943) 217, Searle (1912) 29

[5] Beart (1841) 100

[6] CJ 27/12/1823-2/5, 5/9/1840-2/4, 1/8/1840-1/2, 16/11/1839-2/4, 5/1/1839-2/2, 2/11/1844-1/1, 7/6/1845-2/6, 2/12/1837-1/3

[7] Bell (1843) 746

[8] Yule (1929) 391

[9] Yule (18290 391, DUL Archives & Special Collections, Howard of Naworth Papers C612/2 Agreement for making tiles & bricks at Netherby 19th August 1836, Bell (1843) 746
[10] Hodges (1844) 553, Wiggins (1840) 351
[11] Searle (1912) 7, Hodges (1844) 553
[12] Searle (1912) 10-11, 127, *CJ* 22/8/1840-2/3
[13] CAS (Whitehaven) D Lec119 Thos Edmondson 1843, July 24th 1842, Bell (1843) 746
[14] DUL Archives & Special Collections, Howard of Naworth Papers C612/2 Agreement 19th August 1836
[15] CAS (Carlisle) DMH 5/2/2 Agreement for lease of Tile Kiln 1825
[16] Bell (1843) 744, CAS (Carlisle) DMH 5/2/2 Agreement 16th February 1825, *CJ* 23/1/1836-2/4, CAS (Whitehaven) D Lec 119 Work at Tile Kiln 1841
[17] Yule (1829) 391, CAS (Carlisle) DMH5/2/2 Agreement 16th February 1825
[18] BBS *Information* 89 November 2002 Pug-Mills
[19] Bell (1843) 745, Dobson (1850) 53
[20] Bell (1843) 746, Hodges (1844) 553-4
[21] CAS (Whitehaven) D Lec 119 Work at Tile Kiln 1841, *CJ* 24/4/1841-1/4, Beart (1841) 95, CAS (Carlisle) D Lons L15/1/1/29
[22] Bell (1843) 746, CAS (Carlisle) D Lons L1/2/178 13th July 1848 Mawson to Lonsdale
[23] CAS (Whitehaven) D Lec 119 Work at Tile Kiln 1841, CAS (Carlisle) DMH 5/2/2 16th February 1825, Wiggins (1840) 352, Yule (1829) 391-2, Yule (1830) 63, Bell (1843) 744, 747
[24] Lane (1916) 160 Peter Mayor Campbell worked as a boy at Newton-in-Makerfield
[25] Yule (1829) 392, Bell (1843) 749
[26] Yule (1829) 393
[27] *CJ* 5/4/1828-1/4
[28] CAS (Whitehaven) D Lec 119 Letter addressed to Thomas Dixon 1830, Work at Tile Kiln 1841, Letter 15th May 1841, Letter 16th May 1841
[29] Wiggins (1840) 352, Beart (1841) 94-5, *CJ* 4/7/1846-1/3, *CJ* 13/6/1846-3/1
[30] Hodges (1844) 554
[31] Bell (1843) 747, Boyle (1851) 99, Wiggins (1840) 352
[32] LRO (Preston) DDCa 13/299 15th February 1843, Lane (1916) 159
[33] Bell (1843) 738-9, 744-5, 747, Beart (1841) 97
[34] CAS (Carlisle) D Lons L15/1/3/4 Letter 15th November 1847
[35] Hodge (1844) 554
[36] Yule (1829) 393, *CJ* 27/12/1823-2/5, CAS (Carlisle) DMH 5/2/2 Agreement 16th February 1825
[37] Hammond (1977) 171
[38] Bell (1843) 744-5, Boyle (1851) 96
[39] Keates (1998) 29-43, www.cumbria-industries.org.uk/reake, Brambles, G 'Tile Kiln at Frith – An Update', CIHS
[40] Redmore, K 'Some Brick Kilns and Brick Makers of East Lincolnshire' BBS *Information* 108, September 2008, 12-24, Poynton Collieries: Subsidiary Industries, www.brocross.com/poynton
[41] CAS (Whitehaven) D Lec 119 Letter 1841, *CJ* 13/2/1847-2/3, 28/4/1848-2/1, Day & Charlton (1981) 289
[42] CAS (C) D/Lons L15 Box 1232 Offal wood, D U Library Archive & Special Collections, Howard of Naworth C612/250 Agreement with H Little 1835, LRO (Preston) DDCa 13/299 22nd April 1843, CAS (Whitehaven) D Lec 119
[43] CAS (Whitehaven) D Lec 119 Thos Edmondson 1843
[44] Boyle (1851) 99, Bell (1843) 739, 748, Day & Charlton (1981) 290, Palin (1844-5) 79
[45] *CJ* 28/2/1835-3/4, 23/1/1836-2/4, 21/9/1849-2/3
[46] Boyle (1851) 101, CAS (Carlisle) D Lons L1/2/178 Letter 7th December 1847 Mawson to Lonsdale
[47] CJ 23/1/1836-2/4, CAS (Whitehaven) D Lec 119 Westward Park, Yule (1829) 393, *CJ* 20/12/1835-1/1, D U Library Archive & Special Collections, Howard of Naworth C612/250 CAS (Carlisle) DMH 5/2/2 Agreement 21st February 1835
[48] Yule (1829) 394, Beart (1841) 95, Wiggins (1840) 352, Bell (1843) 745, CAS (Whitehaven) D Lec 119 Clay at Curthwaite 10th November 1830

5

The hand-moulding era c.1830 – c.1844

Horseshoe tiles manufactured in the nine tile-works operating in Cumberland by 1829 were all moulded by hand in the manner described in the previous chapter. During the next one-and-a-half decades, characterized here as the 'hand-moulding era', production continued in much the same manner. This is not to suggest that after 1844 all tiles were machine made; on the contrary, moulding tiles by hand continued into the 1860s, often at tileries where machines were also being employed. The use of machines in Cumberland commenced in 1845, heralded by the appearance of the first advertisement offering for sale 'superior machine made tiles'. This was only two years after the RASE meeting at Derby, where, for the first time two machines for making tiles and bricks were exhibited.[1] Individuals who had been involved with tile-making on the Netherby and Naworth estates were foremost among the entrepreneurs responsible for the next phase of expansion. The first of these, Thomas Guy Patrick the Staffordshire tile-maker who had been brought to Netherby to set up the first tilery, opened the second works in the county at Linstock in 1821. In 1825 while continuing this enterprise, he took a seven-year lease on *Petersyke Tile Works*, which had opened two years earlier. His active involvement in tile-making seems to have ended by 1833 when he leased *Linstock Tile Works* to James and Adam Creighton, who advertised that they were making tiles 'where the same business was lately carried on by Thomas Guy Patrick'. Their venture did not last long; in 1835 the 'Tile Works at Linstock, lately in the occupation of James and Adam Creighton' was again to be let, with applications to be made to the owner Thomas Guy Patrick. When his lease on *Petersyke Tile Works* expired, Patrick did not renew. Instead in 1835 it was let for a period of three years to John Beaty and Thomas Phillips. They also did not continue, as in 1839 a Robert Kirkup signed a seven-year lease. This constant change of manufacturers suggests that operating a tile-works in the infancy of the industry was not as rewarding as it may have first appeared. The fact that one year after relinquishing the lease on Linstock the Creightons were advertising for all those indebted to them for tiles to pay immediately, illustrates one of the problems experienced.

Thomas Guy Patrick died in December 1840 aged 52, having in the 21 years he was in Cumberland provided the expertise to establish tile-making, opened the first commercial tilery and left a legacy which was to benefit the agriculture of the county in perpetuity.[2]

Robert Lucock was born in Irthington c.1774 and commenced working as a land drainer in about 1808. He was employed with his brother Joseph at Netherby to supervise draining on the estate during the period when tile-making was being introduced. It was here the brothers acquired their tile-making expertise which Robert utilised to establish several works which resulted in him being described in 1830 as 'an enterprising man and the first person who introduced the draining tiles into this country'-referring to the western division of the county. His subsequent operations resulted in him being acknowledged as 'the greatest tile-burner in Cumberland'.

Having opened his first tilery at Langrigg in 1824, his next venture was at Broughton Moor in 1830 followed by West Curthwaite in 1831. All three works were advertised in 1833 in the *Carlisle Patriot* and *Carlisle Journal*, Figure 5.1.[3]

DRAINING TILES.
ROBERT LUCOCK

RETURNS his most sincere and grateful Thanks to those Gentlemen, Agriculturists, and Farmers who have favoured him with their Support since he commenced the above Business, and will be happy to serve those who may want DRAINING TILES, at his different Works—at LANGRIGG, in the parish of Bromfield; WEST CURTHWAITE, in the parish of Westward; & BROUGHTON-MOOR, in the parish of Bridekirk. And, as he is anxious to serve all his Customers alike, and not being able to *lead* Tiles for all, he will do so for none,—but will supply them with the very best article at the following reduced Prices, viz. :—

Three Inch Tiles... ...£1 10s. per 1000.
Four Inch   do....... 2 0s.   do.
Six Inch   do....... 3 0s.   do.
Langrigg, Jan. 23th, 1833.
(Not to be repeated.)

Figure 5.1 CAS (Carlisle) *Carlisle Journal* 2nd February 1833

The expansion continued with an announcement in 1836 that he had 'commenced making tiles at Fitz in the Parish of Plumbland'. This brought the number of his tileries to four, at which in 1837 it was estimated that he manufactured 2,400,000 tiles. His enterprises flourished, and in an advertisement of 1844 he thanked the public for their support during the 'twenty years he has been in the Tile Business', and stated that his various tileries were in active operation.[4] Robert's brother Joseph worked initially in the first tilery at Langrigg as a tile-moulder, moving to West Curthwaite as manager when it opened, and he remained there until his death in 1871.[5] As both Robert's and Joseph's sons were involved in the businesses, there was a Lucock dynasty (see Appendix 4) who played a major role in tile manufacture in Cumberland for almost 50 years.

Emanuel Demain's early involvement with tile-making for the Naworth estate has already been described. In 1836 he advertised that he had removed his tile works from Middle Farm, which was on the Naworth estate, to Becks in the parish of Hayton. The new works was on a parcel of land he had leased in 1832 for a period of nine years. At the end of the period he did not renew the lease, as in 1840 the land and tile works were advertised 'to be let'. Becks had become Troutbeck, with the works described as adjoining the farm of Toppin Castle, which was the name used for the business that was to be operated by various manufacturers until the early 1900s.

Emanuel's next venture, in a different township of the same parish only a short distance away, was the *Allen Grove Tile Works*; he offered tiles from there in 1843. He remained there until his death in 1871, being succeeded by his son James who in turn was followed by one of Emanuel's grandsons (see Appendix 4).[6]

The next phase of expansion was generated by a number of individuals, with tileries gradually beginning to extend further from the north-eastern corner of Cumberland and reaching the borders of Westmorland in 1836 with the establishment of *Culgaith Tile Works*.[7]

An advertisement of 1831, Figure 5.2, was a preliminary to the opening of *Lambfield Tile Works* and *Sebergham Tilery* under the joint ownership of Robert James and Henry Denton.

WANTED IMMEDIATELY.

AN active PERSON, who thoroughly Understands the Practice of TEMPERING the CLAY, and MOULDING and BURNING BROWN POTS and DRAINING TILES, in the Parishes of Castlesowerby and Sebergham.

For Particulars apply to Mr. Mr. ROBERT JAMES, Chalkside, near Rosley; or Mr. H. DENTON, Sebergham ;—If by Letter, post-paid.

Figure 5.2 CAS (Carlisle) *Carlisle Journal* 8th January 1831

This included one of the few links between pottery and draining tiles in the early years of the industry - perhaps surprising considering that the same type of clay was used for both coarse pottery and tiles. The fact that the same clay was also used for brick-making was probably one of the reasons for the involvement of builders in tile-making. Thomas Atkin, a builder and brick-maker, advertised draining tiles from *Stanwix Tilery* in 1836, which were manufactured from the clay he also used for brick-making.[8]

In 1833 an article in the *Cumberland Pacquet* stated that there were 18 tile manufactories in Cumberland, chiefly in the neighbourhood of Carlisle, producing in 1832 a total of 4,000,000 tiles, which was sufficient to drain approximately 2,000 acres.[9]

During the 1830s there were opportunities for those wishing to exploit the potential of tiles with offers of beds of clay and encouragement to tile-makers, Figure 5.3.

TO TILE AND BRICK MAKERS.

EXCELLENT CLAY for the above purposes may be had on application to Mr. DIXON, of Calthwaite, who will give every Encouragement to skilful and industrious Workmen.

The increasing demand for Tile in the Neighbourhood will secure constant and unlimited Orders for Draining.

Calthwaite, 1st January, 1839.

Figure 5.3 CAS (Carlisle) *Carlisle Journal* 5th January 1839

This and the subsequent advertisement, Figure 5.4, illustrated the cooperation of the landowner and the tile-maker which resulted in the setting up of *Calthwaite Tile Works*.

BRICK AND TILE WORKS NEAR
CALTHWAITE.
TO MASONS AND CARPENTERS.

JOSEPH PEARSON, having rented from Thomas Dixon, Esq., of Calthwaite, a piece of land, in which there is excellent Clay for the above purposes, is desirous of receiving Proposals for the immediate Erection of a Kiln, Sheds, &c., &c., the undertakers to find Wood, Stone, Fire and Common Bricks, Iron, and all necessary materials.

Specifications may be seen, and Estimates are requested to be left with the said T. Dixon, Esq., Sealed up, and the Contractors will be declared at Calthwaite, on MONDAY, the 11th day of MARCH.

Figure 5.4 CAS (Carlisle) *Carlisle Journal* 2nd March 1839

As has been described in a previous chapter, construction of a new tilery provided employment to a growing number of masons and carpenters, who became skilled in the erection of the required structures. The coal and haulage industries also benefited, as demonstrated by the letting of 'the finding and leading of coals' to *Curthwaite Tilery* in 1842, with around 12 tons required weekly during the season.[10]

As the number of tileries increased a system of manufacture by contract became established. Netherby estate used this method in 1830 when they needed a contractor 'for preparing the clay and manufacturing such Draining Tiles' as were required for the use of the estate. This contract was to be for either one, two or three years. Others were often for a specified number of tiles with a price per thousand, as in 1835 at Stapleton, when 'proposals stating the terms the burner will charge per thousand' were requested. Works were also being erected, to be let for a given term, with the tenant operating a commercial tilery.[11]

A tile works on or close to a farm was considered an asset by 1840, when offers to let contained comments such as 'there is excellent clay and a Tile Works upon the premises' and 'There are Tile Works adjoining the farm'. Works were also erected solely to drain a farm, as with Leaps Rigg in Walton parish, for which an advertisement 'to let' stated that a 'Tile kiln is erecting upon the premises'.[12]

This proliferation of tile works created new occupations, the names and descriptions of which appeared in an increasing number of advertisements. The initial shortage of skilled workers was marked by the stress placed on the requirement for 'a person who perfectly understands the making and burning', which appeared twice in 1831.[13] The two main skills were moulding and burning; often an individual proficient in both was required, as in Figure 5.5. The term which became most common was eventually 'tile-maker'.

WANTED IMMEDIATELY,
A PERSON to undertake the MOULDING
and BURNING of several Thousands of
DRAIN TILES.—For further Particulars apply
to Mr. GRAY, Coffee-House, Carlisle.

Figure 5.5 CAS (Carlisle) *Carlisle Journal* 11th February 1832

As a separate occupation 'moulder' figured during the 1830s, used with a requirement for someone who 'understands the Business' at *Middlefoot Tile Works*, Figure 5.6.

TO TILE MAKERS.
WANTED, at MIDDLEFOOT TILE
WORKS, in the Parish of Stapleton,
TWO or THREE good MOULDERS, who un-
derstand the Business in general.

Figure 5.6 CAS (Carlisle) *Carlisle Journal* 25th February 1837

An analysis of advertisements in the *Carlisle Journal* for the years between 1830 and 1840 produced the following results for tile-making occupations. There were five separate requirements for moulders, with a total of 12 needed, while a further seven stipulated moulding and burning. There were also five burners, three makers, one manufacturer and one manager of a tilery sought. During the ten-year period 22 advertisements were placed by tileries seeking 29 workers. These figures obviously reflect only the businesses which needed to advertise for labour.[14]

The 1841 census for Cumberland produced a total of 125 workers with 'tile' in their occupation. Only one individual, Robert Lucock, was described as a 'tile manufacturer', the majority occupation being 'tile-maker', with a total of 104 having this description. This ranged from individuals who were either the proprietor or contractor, to adolescents. In addition there were five tile-burners, three tile-moulders, two tile-runners and ten tile-labourers. 'Tile-runner', as described previously, was the term given to the young person who brought the clay to the moulding table and carried the tiles to the drying shed – an occupation for which in 1841 at *Westward Park Tilery* payment was 5 shillings per week-about half of the wage of an adult labourer.[15] Among the total of 19 young people aged 15 and under, consisting of two aged 13, five aged 14 and 12 aged 15, two were described as 'tile-runners', ten as 'tile-makers' and seven as 'tile-labourers'.

What is apparent from these results as well as from other sources, such as the father's occupation in baptism registers, is that 'moulder', 'burner' and 'maker' were interchangeable, and as hand-moulding was replaced by machines, 'tile-maker' became the predominant description.

These individuals were employed in the 'no fewer than thirty-six' tileries which were in full operation by the late 1830s.[16] It is often difficult to ascertain the exact date of the commencement and closure of a tilery, but it is possible that the 36 enumerated in Table 5.1 may be the ones referred to.

.**Table 5.1** Cumberland tile-works operating in the late 1830s

	Date	Parish	Tile Works or Manufacturer
1	1821	Arthuret	*Sandysike Brick & Tile Works*
2	1821	Stanwix	*Linstock Tile Works*
3	1823	Rockliff (e)	*Petersyke Tile Works*
4	1824	Bromfield	*Langrigg Tilery*
5	1827	Brampton	*Middle Farm Tile Works*
6	1829	Bowness	Joshua Ward
7	1829	Cockermouth	*Kirkgate Brick & Tile Works*
8	1829	Cockermouth	William Mackreath
9	1829	Cockermouth	Robert Smithson
10	1830	Bridekirk	*Broughton Moor Brick & Tile Works*
11	1831	Burgh by Sands	John Glaister
12	1831	Castle Sowerby	*Lambfield Tile Works*
13	1831	Kirklinton	*Young's Close Tile Works*
14	1831	Sebergham	*Sebergham Tilery*
15	1831	Westward	*Curthwaite Brick & Tile Works*
16	1833	Beaumont	*Beaumont Brick & Tile Works*
17	1833	Hayton	*Toppin Castle Brick & Tile Works*
18	1834	Bowness	*Millrigg Tile Works*
19	1834	Irthington	*Laversdale Lane End Tile Works*
20	1834	Kingmoor	Richard Wright
21	1834	Stanwix	*Eden Place Tile Works*
22	1834	Wigton	*Parkgate Tilery*
23	1835	Arthuret	*Netherby Tile & Brick Works*
24	1835	Carlisle	*Wragmire Tile Works*
25	1835	Lanercost	*Kirkcambeck Tile Works*
26	1835	Maryport	Nicholson & Pearson
27	1835	Stapleton	*Crossings Tile Works*
28	1836	Kirkland	*Culgaith Brick & Tile Works*
29	1836	Plumbland	Robert Lucock
30	1836	Workington	*Winscales Tile Works*
31	1836	Dean	*High & Low Edge Tile Works*
32	1837	Camerton	*Seaton Tile Works*
33	1837	Stapleton	*Middlefoot Brick & Tile Works*
34	1837	Wreay	*Potter Pits Tile Works*
35	1838	Scaleby	*Longpark Tile Works*
36	1839	Stanwix	*Houghton Tile Works*

Sources: *Gazetteer of Sites and Manufacturers*

As can be seen from the list of parishes the locations of most of the works were as described in 1833. However as illustrated in Figure 5.7 the geographical spread of the tileries in the table, together with the other 1839 openings, was gradually moving southwards.

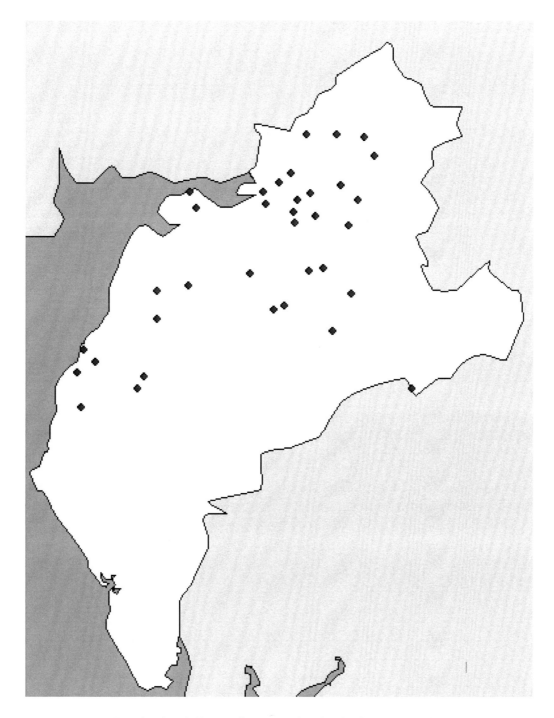

Figure 5.7 Cumberland tile works operating in the late 1830s [Gen Map UK]

The presence of tileries became more apparent through advertisements for their products in newspapers, including the *Carlisle Journal*, in which there was one in 1831, one in 1833 and two in 1834.[17] The second one in 1834 was an offer from the Netherby estate of tiles in excess of their own requirements, Figure 5.8.

DRAINING TILES
ON SALE AT SANDYSIKE TILE KILN,
NEAR LONGTOWN, CUMBERLAND.

A Larger quantity of TILES having been made than are required this Season upon the Estate of Netherby, the overplus, consisting of very excellent Three and Four Inch TILES, will be SOLD in quantities to suit Purchasers.

Figure 5.8 CAS (Carlisle) *Carlisle Journal* 6th September 1834

The year 1835 produced three announcements of tiles for sale, as did 1836; this was followed by a decline, with only one advertisement in both 1839 and 1840, suggesting perhaps that in those years demand within the immediate vicinity of most tileries precluded the need to advertise.[18] The early 1840s generated an increase in notices of the availability of tiles, with two in 1841, two in 1842 and six in 1843.[19] In the northern part of the county this increase, combined with a fall in the price of tiles, implies that it was the year when supply caught up with demand. The first advertisement of the year offered tiles at a reduced price of 28 shillings per 1000, followed by three other tileries offering their tiles at 26 shillings per 1000. Both prices were a reduction on what had become the standard price of 30 shillings per 1000 -itself a fall from the 42 shillings per 1000 of the early 1820s.[20]

Until 1843 there was no indication of tile-making in Westmorland but then in December of that year an advertisement, placed by a Mr J Crosby of Kirkby Thore, required an experienced tile burner to contract for moulding and burning tiles. In February of the following year Wm Thwaites of Appleby wanted a tile burner 'this season'. Unfortunately in both cases the place of manufacture was not specified.[21]

In Cartmel tile-making began in the early 1840s with the erection of a tilery at Reake Wood on the Holker estate. Shortly afterwards the Earl of Burlington added two other tileries to his estates - at Sowerby Hall and Roose in Furness- and offered all three to let in 1846, Figure 5.9.[22]

TILE YARDS IN NORTH LANCASHIRE.
TO be LET, with immediate possession, TWO TILE YARDS, situate in LOW FURNESS, and one in CARTMEL, belonging to the Earl of BURLINGTON.

Figure 5.9 CAS (Carlisle) *Carlisle Journal* 9th May 1846

Generally in Lancashire, although drainage tiles had been made earlier, including some on a Fylde estate in 1833, they were not extensively used until the 1840s. The 'earliest built tile-kiln' was 'erected in 1840-41' and by 1849 there were 31 tile-kilns in operation. 20 were on estates and 11 belonged to private individuals who were manufacturing for sale to the public.[23]

As has been related earlier, a number of tileries were erected in Northumberland in the 1820s, and as the system of thorough-draining spread, more were opened. These included one at Bothal built in 1830 which provided tiles for draining the Duke of Portland's estate and a second constructed in 1834 to keep up with demand.[24]

When the Earl of Carlisle erected a tilery at Hepscott on his Northumberland estate in 1838, he turned to Cumberland to obtain tile-makers, Figure 5.10.[25]

TO TILE MAKERS.
TO be LET, the CASTING, PREPARING the CLAY MAKING, &c., of from TWO to THREE HUNDRED THOUSAND DRAIN-ING TILES, at HEPSCOTT, near Morpeth, Northumberland.

Figure 5.10 CAS (Carlisle) *Carlisle Journal* 22nd December 1838

Similar advertisements were placed in the *Carlisle Journal* in January 1839 and December 1840 when *Espley Tile Works* near Morpeth was seeking a contractor. This suggests that Cumberland was recognized as an area where tile-making expertise was available.[26]

Among the 125 tile-makers recorded in the 1841 census, there were 18 whose place of birth was Scotland, a country which experienced considerable growth of tileries during the 1830s. The *NSA* recorded tile works in many parishes, particularly in Ayrshire where tile-making was first introduced into the country. The Duke of Portland established two manufactories on his estates, one at Galston and one near Kilmarnock. Tileries were also opened in 1833 at Coylton, in 1838 at Dreghorn, and in 1839 at Riccarton, Stewarton and Beith.[27]

Closer to Cumberland there was activity in Dumfriesshire, where in 1836 the *NSA* recorded that at Canonbie the Duke of Buccleuch had erected at his own expense 'kilns for making draining tiles'. This enterprise known as the *Tarrasfoot Tile Works* advertised in the *Carlisle Journal* in 1840 for '12 experienced Drain Tile Moulders'. Also at Canonbie in 1841 a tile-works was erected to drain the estate of Woodhouselees. As previously mentioned, this was designed and operated by Cumberland tile-makers.[28]

Two works opened near Annan: *Whinnyrigg Tile Works* advertised tiles in the *Dumfries Times* in 1842, and *Howgill Tile Works* required a contractor to make tiles in 1843. This position was advertised in the *Carlisle Journal* as was a similar notice for Springkell estate at Kirkpatrick Fleming in 1841.[29]

In view of previously-cited tile prices it is interesting that *Woodhouse Tile Works* also at Kirkpatrick Fleming, was advertising three-inch drain tiles at 28s per 1000 in 1842.[30]

Scotland also played a part in the introduction of tile-making into the USA, when John Johnston who had emigrated from Dumfriesshire in the 1820s, imported horseshoe tiles from Scotland to use as patterns when hand-moulding of tiles began in Waterloo, NY in 1838.[31]

The growth of tile-making in this period of hand-moulding was only a precursor of the expansion which was to occur, both locally and nationally, from the mid to late 1840s. This was fuelled by several factors including the acceptance of systems of underdraining, which were expounded in articles in the *JRASE* and other publications, followed by legislation to allow loans for draining, and the introduction of tile-making-machines which could produce the large quantities of tiles required.[32]

Before continuing with the history of tile-making from 1845, the next three chapters will explore these topics.

Notes

[1] *CJ* 15/2/1845-1/2, Parkes (1843) 460

[2] CAS (Carlisle) DMH/5/2/2 February 16th 1825, *CJ* 28/9/1833-2/5, *CJ* 26/12/1835-1/1, CAS (Carlisle) DMH/5/2/2 February 21st 1835, December 14th 1839, *CJ* 10/12/1836-2/5, 10/12/1836-2/5, CAS (Carlisle) PR117/13 Stanwix Burial Register 6th August 1837,

[3] *CJ* 13/2/1830-1/2, *CJ* 12/2/1831-2/6, *CP* 2/2/1833-1/2, *CJ* 2/2/1833-1/1

[4] *CJ* 18/6/1836-2/7, 'Agriculture of Cumberland' *The Farmer Magazine* (1838) 335, *CJ* 30/3/1844-1/5

[5] CAS (Carlisle) PR140/5 Bromfield Baptism Register, *CJ* 11/8/1871-3/7

[6] *CJ* 26/11/1836-2/5, CAS (Carlisle) D/Ric/154, *CJ* 5/9/1840-2/4, *CJ* 12/8/1843-1/2

[7] *CJ* 23/1/1836-2/4

[8] *CJ* 2/4/1836-3/1

[9] *Cumberland Pacquet* 5/2/1833-3/4

[10] *CJ* 2/4/1842-2/2

[11] *CJ* 24/7/1830-2/1, *CJ* 10/1/1835-1/4, *CJ* 21/8/1841-2/6

[12] *CJ* 1/8/1840-1/2, *CJ* 22/8/1840-2/2, *CJ* 15/8/1840-1/2

[13] *CJ* 1/1/1831-1/2

[14] *CJ* 1/1/1831-1/2, 8/1/1831-2/2, 11/2/1832-1/1, 20/12/1834-2/5, 28/2/1835-3/4, 27/6/1835-2/5, 4/7/1835-2/5, 31/10/1835-1/2, 23/1/1836-2/4, 5/3/1836-3/3, 6/8/1836-2/1, 24/9/1836-2/2, 25/2/1837-1/4, 25/3/1837-2/5, 6/5/1837-1/1, 20/5/1837-2/4, 30/12/1837-2/7, 5/1/1839-2/2, 9/3/1839-1/1, 18/5/1839-3/3, 8/2/1840-2/6

[15] CAS (Whitehaven) D Lec 119

[16] 'Agriculture of Cumberland' *The Farmers Magazine* (1838) 335

[17] *CJ* 12/11/1831-1/1, *CJ* 2/2/1833-1/1, *CJ* 11/1/1834-1/4, *CJ* 6/9/1834-2/3

[18] *CJ* 31/1/1835-2/6, 1/8/1835-1/1, 14/11/1835-1/1, 5/3/1836-3/3, 2/4/1836-3/1, 18/6/1836-2/7, 24/8/1839-2/3, 22/8/1849-2/3

[19] *CJ* 27/2/1841-1/7, 13/3/1841-2/7, 26/3/1842-1/3, 17/12/1842-2/6, 14/1/1843-2/3, 11/2/1843-3/1, 4/3/1843-2/6, 8/4/1843-1/2, 5/8/1843-2/6, 12/8/1843-1/2

[20] Yule (1829) 394, Dickinson (1853) 83, *CJ* 2/2/1833-1/1

[21] *CJ* 9/12/1843-2/5, *CJ* 17/2/1844-1/2

[22] LRO (Preston) DDCa 13/299 1842/3, *CJ* 9/5/1846-1/2, Binns (1851) 105

[23] Beesley (1849) 38-9, Fletcher (1962) 110, 112

[24] Phillips (1989) 161

[25] *CJ* 22/12/1838-2/6, Phillips (1989) 162, NSMR 03-11726

[26] *CJ* 5/1/1839-2/2, *CJ* 9/3/1839-1/1, *CJ* 26/12/1840-2/7

[27] *CJ* 8/5/1830-3/4, *NSA* Volume 5 Ayrshire, Galston (1837) 184, Kilmarnock (1839) 546/7, Beith (1839) 590, Coylton (1841) 569, Riccarton (1839) 613, Stewarton (1840) 737

[28] *NSA* Volume 4 Dumfriesshire, Canonbie (1836) 498, *CJ* 1/2/1840-2/8, Bell (1843) 738

[29] *DT* 25/7/1842-1/A, *CJ* 2/12/1843-1/2, *CJ* 9/1/1841-1/4

[30] *DT* 31/8/1842-1/A

[31] Weaver (1964) 58-60, Klippart (1862) 29

[32] Wade-Martins (2004) 37, Orwin & Whetham (1964) 2nd ed. (1971) 100, Chambers & Mingay (1966) 175

6

Thorough draining and the use of tiles

Having described the circumstances surrounding the introduction of tiles into Cumberland and examined the methods of manufacture and the type of works in which it was taking place, it seems appropriate to consider how, and in particular why, the tiles were being used in increasing quantities.

Low prices for farm produce during the first half of the nineteenth century brought a realisation that 'only efficient farming could be made to pay', which meant 'economising the cost and increasing the amount of production' and to achieve this, improvements had to take place.[1]

Wet land was slow to warm up in the spring, and could not carry implements without suffering damage until it had dried out, delaying both cultivation of the soil and the growth of the crop. This created agreement among agricultural writers that, 'as a means of improvement draining is the most important, the most permanent, and that which ought to precede every other'. This sentiment was reiterated throughout the 1840s and 1850s and underpinned the massive expansion of underdraining with tiles, using the system which became generally known as 'thorough draining'.[2]

The term 'drain', which is 'an artificial conduit or channel for carrying off water', covered a number of practices in land drainage, generally divided into either surface or hollow drains. The term 'underdrain', 'to drain by means of underground trenches', is derived from an agricultural work of 1805, which spoke of 'under-draining' and another of 1832 which used the terms 'underdrained' and 'underdrainers'.[3] Prior to the universal use of 'thorough draining' other terms were widely used, particularly in Scotland, a result, as will be seen, of the work of one man, James Smith. These descriptions included 'frequent drains' as in 'the frequent drain system', 'parallel drains', both self-explanatory as was 'furrow drains', drains which were placed in the water furrows of ridges.[4]

In addition to removing water from the land, underdraining had other beneficial effects including stimulating the establishment of spade-making works to provide the variety of implements used in digging the trenches. It also removed the necessity for ridge and furrow contouring, which had been an obstacle to the use of machines. Tile drainage and ridge levelling went together, producing well-drained level fields which facilitated the use of new horse-drawn equipment.[5]

All of which suggests that comments such as 'thorough draining is to the land as foundations are to a house' did not overstate the case. This belief was also held by James Smith, the first of the two men who were responsible for the principles and practices which, with some refinement, became the accepted standards of thorough draining with tiles.[6]

James Smith born in Glasgow in 1789 was brought up by his uncle Archibald Buchanan, an engineer who was a managing partner of the Deanston cotton mill. While attending school and university in Glasgow, James Smith spent vacations in Ayrshire with his uncle who was involved with another cotton works at Catrine. Here James learned industrial processes and engineering in the textile mill, before serving an apprenticeship with Richard Arkwright. Following this, he was appointed manager of Deanston cotton mill where during the next 35 years, he extended the works and designed and patented machinery. Farming was also an interest of James's uncle which he transmitted to his nephew who in 1823 leased Deanston Farm. It was there that he developed not only agricultural machinery, including a subsoil plough, but also experimented with different types of drains and drain fillings. These resulted in his 'frequent drain system' an account of which was published in 1833. The method was initially widely used in Scotland where it was also known as 'Deanstonization'.[7] This original paper presented some difficulties for a wider audience as it was aimed at Scottish agriculturalists and recounted the history and introduction of thorough draining into Scotland and using local measures. The practice was brought to the attention of English farmers with the publication of a letter from Sir James Graham to the editor of the *Journal of the Royal Agricultural Society of England*, and published in its first issue in 1840. In this he described the 'Deanston Frequent Drain System' and the use of the sub-soil plough invented by James Smith, which penetrated the sub-soil, breaking and pulverising it without bringing it to the surface. Sir James further outlined his experiments with the system at Netherby and described the successful results.[8]

The seventh edition of James Smith's pamphlet was published in 1844, Figure 6.1, in a version aimed at both a Scottish and English readership.

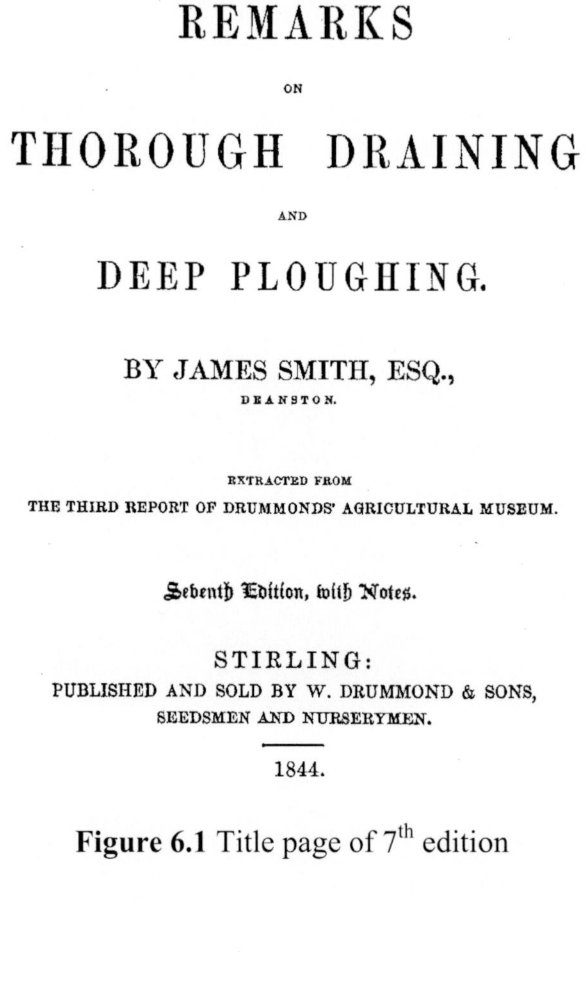

REMARKS

ON

THOROUGH DRAINING

AND

DEEP PLOUGHING.

BY JAMES SMITH, ESQ.,
DEANSTON.

EXTRACTED FROM
THE THIRD REPORT OF DRUMMONDS' AGRICULTURAL MUSEUM.

Seventh Edition, with Notes.

STIRLING:
PUBLISHED AND SOLD BY W. DRUMMOND & SONS,
SEEDSMEN AND NURSERYMEN.

1844.

Figure 6.1 Title page of 7th edition

In this he set out his belief that 'The portion of land wetted by water springing from below, bears but a very small proportion to that which is in a wet state, from the retention of the water which falls upon the surface, in the state of rain'

To remove this water he advocated digging a main drain, at least three-feet deep and if possible up to four-feet, ideally flagged in the bottom. Into this were discharged the ordinary or parallel drains, running at regular distances throughout the field. These 'parallel frequent drains' were 10-15 feet apart in strong soil, 18-24 feet in lighter soil and up to 40 feet apart in very open soil. The depth of these drains was 24 inches when using tiles and 30 inches when broken stone was used.[9]

This method of having drains throughout the field is in direct contrast to Elkington's system of finding springs, and draining from them, as previously described.

The flagged main drain and Smith's preferred method of setting tiles using a stone infill is shown in Figure 6.2.

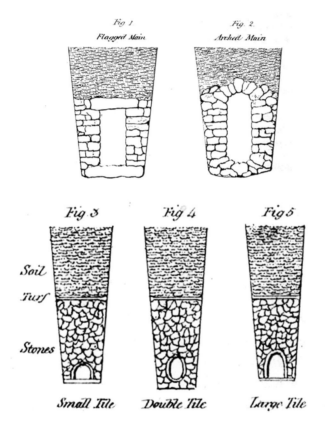

Figure 6.2 Types of tile-drains from Smith (1844)

At the same time as James Smith was setting out his principles of drainage, a second individual was developing his own theories on the subject. He was Josiah Parkes, born at Warwick in 1795, and like James Smith, in his early years worked in the machinery department of a mill, although a wool-spinning mill rather than cotton. After the failure of the mill he continued in engineering, becoming in 1837 a member of the Institution of Civil Engineers. He worked on the draining of Chat Moss in Lancashire before being appointed in 1843 as the first consulting engineer to the Royal Agricultural Society of

England. This position placed him at the centre of the debate on the most appropriate system of draining. His experiences in Lancashire, and his examination of draining methods in other areas of the country, persuaded him of the effectiveness of deep draining, as opposed to the drainage then being carried on at 'a depth too shallow'.[10]

The principle he expounded was that 'that a less depth of drain than four feet in any soil' would not be accompanied by beneficial results. He appealed to agriculturalists to abandon the incomplete system of shallow drains and promoted his own practice of drains 'executed at depths of from 4 to 6 feet deep, according to the soil' at 'distances varying from 20 to 66 feet'. As a conduit, Josiah Parkes advocated the small bore pipe with collar, in particular the one-inch diameter pipe, which he considered was sufficient to remove excess water. He stated that the expenditure using his system could be around £3 per acre, although he pointed out that the cost of main drains and other work was not included in this figure.[11]

Josiah Parkes was employed by many estates to supervise their draining programmes, in particular when the work was being financed with money borrowed under drainage legislation. One such was the Lowther estate where he appeared to have been involved with all aspects of the work including the estate tilery at Hackthorpe. In 1852 he negotiated the agreement with the tile-burner and set the selling prices of tiles. Then in 1854 he ordered on behalf of the Earl of Lonsdale a tile-making-machine from John Whitehead & Co in Preston. The quantities and sizes of pipes manufactured reflect the influence of Josiah Parkes; the stock accounts for 1853 and 1854 show that the largest quantities were of the one-inch diameter with collars.[12]

The drainage carried out on estate lands in both Cumberland and Westmorland, using the tiles manufactured at the tilery at Hackthorpe was financed by money borrowed under the Private Money Drainage Acts.[13]

During the 1840s the system of underdraining known as 'Thorough Draining' was based on the principles of Josiah Parkes, building on the methods of James Smith. The characteristic views of James Smith were [1] frequent drains [2] shallow depth [3] parallel drains [4] infill stones and tiles. Set against these were the opinions of Josiah Parkes which were [1] less frequent drains [2] deep drains [3] parallel drains [4] preferred conduit pipes of one-inch bore. There were obviously other factors in each system, and while both agreed on the need for parallel drains, it was their disagreement over depth and distance which was to be the subject of argument and dispute over the ensuing years.[14]

Discussions on draining became a regular feature of agricultural meetings including one in Newcastle in 1846 and another in Carlisle in the same year, at which both protagonists attended to present and defend their own views on draining, Figure 6.3.

Figure 6.3 CAS (Carlisle) *Carlisle Journal* 18th July 1846

Following the lecture by Josiah Parkes, a reply was given by James Smith, Figure 6.4.

Mr. Smith, of Deanston, was then called for, and spoke for some time in defence of his own system of draining and in opposition to that of Mr. Parkes, which he said had not the recommendation of matured experience.

Figure 6.4 CAS (Carlisle) *Carlisle Journal* 18th July 1846

The lecture was extensively reported locally, including the chairman's comments after both speakers and the discussions. In his remarks he stated that 'the nature and situation of the soil must ever guide farmers in the plan adopted'.[15]

Agreement was needed, according to a writer on agriculture in Northumberland in 1847, on 'how this improvement, draining, is best carried into effect'. He described how, on the Duke of Northumberland's estates, drains were 'cut 3 feet deep and 20 feet apart', while on some other estates it was the practice to 'cut drains 5 feet and 30 feet apart'. His conclusion was that as long as such opposing plans were followed by persons of great experience, it was impossible for him to give an opinion and he looked forward to a 'speedy resolution of the dispute'.[16]

Writing in 1853 on Cumberland, William Dickinson stated that 'about 1835 the mania for shallow draining began to exhibit itself', and the 'depth was gradually lessened to 20 inches and even 18 and 16', then, 'after it had been practiced for a few years, the discovery began to be made that an immense expenditure had been incurred, and a good deal of harm done'. The conclusion was reached that 'the deep drain must be the most effectual remedy for the defects of the shallow system'. Then 'the 5 feet drain, as first recommended by Mr Parkes, was adopted by a few and forced upon others', but it was soon found that its 'universal application could not be a general remedy'[17]

Gradually what prevailed was the opinion expressed by the chairman of the Carlisle meeting. Among others Henry Stephens, author of *A Manual of Practical Draining* and *The Book of the Farm*, commented that both parties were right, when the subsoil was suited to their view, but both were wrong, in trying to apply their particular view to every condition, since 'subsoils of various qualities require drains of various depths and at various distances'. The consensus on average depth eventually settled around three to four feet, which was the situation in Lancashire in 1851 where 'the best and most effectual drains are set three and four feet deep, according to the nature of the subsoil and other circumstances'. Many shallow systems were replaced, as at Brayton where thousands of roods of old drains were taken up. Even on the Netherby estate it was said in 1852 that shallow drains were being lifted and relaid.[18]

Information about draining, which had been the enthusiasm of only a small number of pioneering improvers, was from the 1840s available through a variety of channels. The principal ones were agricultural societies, ranging from the two national societies, RASE and HASS, through regional and county organisations, down to local farmers' clubs. Increasing numbers of printed sources, periodicals, newspapers and books became available, often provided by landlords and on their behalf by their land agents.[19]

Nationally the *Journal of the Royal Agricultural Society of England* commenced publication in 1840, while its Scottish counterpart, which began in 1784 and had numerous changes of name, was from around 1835 known as *Transactions of the Highland and Agricultural Society of Scotland*. Articles in both of these publications helped to create what was described for Cumberland in 1853 as a 'more reading and reasoning' farming community. According to Sir James Graham, the *JRASE* had by 1855 become the 'Fountain of agricultural knowledge and useful information'. Between 1840 and 1855 over 10% of the articles in each issue related to draining and irrigation. After this date, as principles and practices became established, the number reduced dramatically.[20]

Associations, national and local, as well as some individuals, encouraged dissemination of information by agriculturalists through prizes offered for the best essays. Some of these were published in the national journals; including John Yule's which, as previously noted, has provided much of the information on the introduction of tiles at Netherby. *The Prize Essay of the Newcastle-upon-Tyne Farmers Club on Draining Strong Clays* by Peter Laws, a farmer of East Heddon was published in 1850. Three major prizes were presented in the early 1850s for publications on the agriculture of Cumberland. All went to William Dickinson who at North Mosses, Arlecdon, farmed his own, and two neighbouring properties, totalling around 600 acres. He was also a land surveyor and valuer, whose duties took him 'into nearly every field in West Cumberland and a portion of the Eastern Division and the adjoining counties'. William Dickinson was also a tile-manufacturer with interests in several tileries. Such a background made him eminently qualified as a recipient of the awards, the first of which was the premium offered by the Rev Canon Parkinson the Principal of St Bees' College, which was awarded on October 4th 1850 for his *Essay on the Agriculture of West Cumberland*. In 1852 the prize of £50 given by the Earl of Lonsdale and adjudicated on his behalf by the committee of the Cumberland & Westmorland Agricultural Society was presented to William Dickinson for his *Essay on the Agriculture of East Cumberland*. The third prize was from the RASE for 'On the Farming of Cumberland' published in *JRASE* Volume XIII, and also in book form.[21]

In 1819 there were local agricultural societies at Abbey Holme, Wigton, North Lonsdale, Kendal and the best known Workington. This society under the patronage of J C Curwen was a significant organisation; the annual meeting was attended by agriculturalists from all over the country. Its influence in transforming the agriculture of Cumberland has already been noted. Netherby had its own farming society from c.1820 and many other agricultural societies, large and small, were formed. The East Cumberland Agricultural Society which began c.1831, covered a wide area; others such as the Bolton Fell End Agricultural Society were more parochial. Societies formed included those at Barrow in Furness, Cartmel, Millom & Broughton, Penrith and Windermere; others areas such as Raughton Head and Furness had farmers' clubs. In Westmorland it was considered that the various agricultural societies had a greater and more lasting effect in stimulating the smallest class of farmers in the remotest areas than any other influence.[22]

A number of the clubs acquired collections of literature; William Blamire who was appointed tithe commissioner in 1836 and tithe, copyhold & inclosure commissioner in

1845 was honorary president of Raughton Head Farmer's Club, formed in 1839. He donated to the club 'newspapers, pamphlets, and other publications pertaining to the subject of agriculture'. Another club, the Hexham Farmers' Club in Northumberland, had 200 volumes by the end of its fifteenth year in 1861.[23]

Probably for many farmers the most important function of societies and clubs was the annual show. It was through these that premiums were offered by the organisations and often landlords to encourage good agricultural practice. Sir James Graham was one of the first to offer prizes for draining with tiles, although in 1829 stone could still be used Figure 6.5.

> —(Applause.)—I wish for improvement in agricul-
> ture; and I should be proud indeed, if the two small
> premiums I now beg leave to offer shall in any way
> conduce to that end. Sir James Graham then read
> the conditions of his two premiums—10 guineas for
> the greatest breadth of well managed summer fallow;
> and 10 guineas for the greatest extent of effective and
> judiciously executed close draining, either with stone
> or tiles. To be decided at the next Carlisle Cattle
> Show.

Figure 6.5 CAS (Carlisle) *Carlisle Journal* 25th April 1829

From 1831 through to 1837 the Preston Agricultural Society offered, 'to the person draining the greatest quantity of land with tiles or stone', a silver cup valued three guineas.[24] Again stone was still an acceptable material for use as the infill of the drains.

At the annual meeting of the Royal North Lancashire Agricultural Society in September 1848, a public discussion on the drainage of land took place. This prompted a letter to the *Preston Chronicle* in which the writer agreed with the importance of draining but took exception to the suggested depths, contending that the depth of drains must depend on the nature of the soil. The letter was reprinted in *Soulby's Ulverston Advertiser* at the request of the North Lonsdale Agricultural Society, which also awarded premiums for draining. In 1848 there were five competitors for the award which went to a farmer at High Frith, who drained 1269 roods with tiles.[25]

As an encouragement to undertake all improvements, including drainage, leases of a reasonable duration were important to both landlord and tenant. During the period of the lease, 14 years on the Netherby estate, the tenant benefited from his labour, while at the end of the term the landlord had a more valuable property. Leases as used on the Netherby estate and on most of the Earl of Carlisle's north Cumberland lands, enabled the landlord to have more control over farming practices and allowed the supervision of improvements. With regard to drainage, the division was that the tenant normally carted the tiles and paid an additional five per cent rent; while the landlord carried out and met the cost of tiles, drainers and the supervision of the project. This expense to the landowner was, from 1847 onwards, widely funded by money borrowed under the new drainage legislation, which was the catalyst for a rapid expansion in drainage.[26]

In 1845 a Committee of the House of Lords sat to hear evidence as to the benefits to be derived from enacting legislation to enable possessors of land to borrow capital for draining and other improvements against a charge on their estates. This resulted in the passing over the ensuing years of a number of public and private money drainage acts [see Appendix 3].[27]

One previous attempt to provide funds for drainage, Mr Philip Pusey's Act of 1840, had been very largely unsuccessful. Its terms required loans to be approved by the Court of Chancery, a condition which deterred applicants. Only 11 requests were made, of which possibly four were taken up.[28]

In 1846 the first Public Money Drainage Act, 9 and 10 Vict. c.101, known as 'The Drainage Act', was passed, making available two million pounds for draining. Under this act which was administered by the Inclosure Commissioners, money borrowed by landowners was repaid over 22 years. Large sums were applied for by major northern landowners including the Earls of Carlisle and Lonsdale. Lancashire estates also sought loans, as three of the largest applications were from that county. Prior to the loan being approved, the land was inspected by an assistant commissioner or inspector, usually a leading local land agent. If his initial report was favourable a provisional certificate was issued. During, and on completion of, the work the inspector checked the drainage, and if satisfactory, the funds were released.

Such a scheme was carried out on several farms in Cumwhitton, Ainstable and Kirkoswald, part of the Aglionby estate. The loan of £700 was applied for in March 1853 and a provisional certificate was issued for that sum in September 1854. The inspector was John Barker, a land agent of Greystoke who was involved in tile-making.[29]

Owners of tile-works recognised the advantages to themselves from the acts, as shown in Figure 6.6.

TILE WORKS AND SAW MILL.
TO be LET, for One or more Years, and Entered upon immediately, THE SEBERGHAM TILE WORKS.

The Clay, from its plastic nature and freedom from Stones, is well adapted to the manufacture of Drain Tiles and Pipes by machinery.

A very extensive Sale may be expected from the numerous applications for loans under the Drainage Act. If not Let immediately, Proposals will be received for the Making of Tiles. &c., at per Thousand.

Figure 6.6 CAS (Carlisle) *Carlisle Journal* 15th May 1847

Applications made under 'The Drainage Act' were advertised in the press. The first three which appeared in the *Carlisle Journal* in January 1847 were from clergymen for glebe lands. Loans of over £5000 were applied for by seven individuals and estates, for land in Cumberland and Westmorland, during January, February and March 1847.[30]

Following altering and amending acts in 1847 and 1848, the second 'Drainage Act', 13 and 14 Vict. c. 31 was passed in 1850, again administered by the Inclosure Commissioners. The applications of 23rd January 1852, Figure 6.7 covered eight estates in Cumberland and required a total of £1870 in sums varying from £50 to £700.[31]

THE INCLOSURE COMMISSIONERS for ENG-
LAND and WALES hereby give Notice that
Applications have been made by the under-mentioned Persons for the Advance of the under-mentioned Sums by way of Loan, under the Provisions
of the Act of the 13th and 14th Vict., cap. 31, for
the Drainage of Lands hereinafter specified :—

Figure 6.7 CAS (Carlisle) *Carlisle Journal* 23rd January 1852

Regular advertisements appeared in local newspapers for the companies authorised to advance money under the various public and private money legislation. These included the 'Landowners' West of England and South Wales Land Drainage and Inclosure Company', Figure 6.8.

LANDOWNERS' WEST OF ENGLAND AND
SOUTH WALES LAND DRAINAGE AND
INCLOSURE COMPANY.
ESTABLISHED 1844.
Incorporated by Act of Parliament.
This Company is prepared to Contract with Land-
owners for the Drainage, Inclosure, Irrigation, or
Improvement of Lands in any part of England,
Ireland, or Scotland. Owners of Settled Estates in
England may, through the Company, Drain, Inclose,
or Improve their Lands, and charge the Inheritance
with the permanent value.—Apply to
Mr. THOMAS MAY, Secretary,
9, Bedford Circus, Exeter.

Figure 6.8 CAS (Carlisle) *Carlisle Journal* 15th June 1849

Advertisements for 'The General Land Drainage and Improvement Company' first appeared in the *Carlisle Journal* in 1851, Figure 6.9 and continued to do so into the 1880s.

THE GENERAL LAND DRAINAGE AND IM-
PROVEMENT COMPANY.
HENRY KER SEYMER, Esq., M.P., Chairman.
JOHN VILLIERS SHELLEY, Esq., Deputy-Chairman.
Empowered by Act of Parliament to execute all
works of drainage (including outfalls through adjoining estates), to erect Farm Buildings, and carry
out every kind of permanent improvement upon
estates under settlement ; to provide the money,
or to enable the landowner to employ his own capital and execute the works by his agents under the
superintendence of the Company, and to secure repayment of the outlay by a charge on the property
improved, spread over a number of years. Applications to be addressed to
W. CLIFFORD, Sec.
Offices, 52, Parliament-street, London.

Figure 6.9 CAS (Carlisle) *Carlisle Journal* 29th August 1851

Numerous applications were made to 'The Lands Improvement Company', Figure 6.10 during the 1850s and 1860s including substantial sums such as the £3000 required by Sir Ralph Henry Vane for his Hutton estate. The local inspector for the company was Isaac Harrington, a land agent based in Carlisle.[32]

THE LANDS IMPROVEMENT COMPANY hereby give Notice, that application has been made by WILLIAM BELL, Esquire, of No. 3, ABBEY STREET, CARLISLE, in the County of Cumberland, for the advance of a SUM not exceeding that understated by way of LOAN, under the Provisions of "The Lands Improvement Company's Act, 1853," and of "The Lands Improvement Company's Amendment Act, 1855," to be applied to Improvements on the Lands understated, and to be repaid with interest by way of Rent-charge or Annuity, in the terms of the said Act.

Figure 6.10 CAS (Carlisle) *Carlisle Journal* 7th March 1856

Under 'The Land Loan and Enfranchisement Company' Act, Sir Henry Tufton borrowed £2000, and in 1878 the Earl of Lonsdale applied for £3000, Figure 6.11, both to be repaid over 25 years.[33]

THE LAND LOAN and ENFRANCHISEMENT COMPANY Hereby Give Notice that application has been made by the RIGHT HON. ST. GEORGE HENRY, EARL of LONSDALE, of WHITEHAVEN CASTLE, in the County of Cumberland, for the advance of a sum not exceeding that understated by way of Loan, under the Provisions of "The Land Loan and Enfranchisement Company's Act," to be applied to Improvements on the Lands understated, and to be repaid with Interest by way of Rent-Charge or Annuity, in the Terms of the said Act.

Name of Estate	Parish.	County.	Sum applied for—viz., the maximum amount proposed to be applied to the Improvements.	Term of Years over which it is proposed the Rent-Charge shall be spread.
Part of the Whitehaven Estates.	St. Bees. Moresby. Workington. Arlecdon. Distington. Cleator. Flimby.	Cumberland.	£3,000.	25 years.

Witness my hand this Tenth day of July, in the year of our Lord one thousand eight hundred and seventy-eight. T. PAIN, Managing Director. Land Loan and Enfranchisement Company, 22. Great George Street, Westminster, S.W.

Figure 6.11 CAS (Carlisle) *Carlisle Journal* 12th July 1878

In Cumberland between 1847 and 1899 loan expenditure, solely on draining, under the various public and private money acts totalled £129,688. This compared with borrowings of £38,484 in Westmorland and £127,968 in Lancashire.[34]

A major problem from the 1830s through until the 1850s was the need for drainers who understood the new system. This was particularly difficult in the early years of thorough draining when it could be said that 'theory and practice are yet defective'. In 1833 a Northumberland agent wrote that he had no person in his employment that was conversant with the system.[35]

Many of the problems encountered by landowners undertaking drainage were recounted in a book by Chandos Wren Hoskyns. His drainer responded to a request to open the entire length of a trench before laying the tiles, rather than lay and backfill each tile, with the retort that he had been draining for forty years and ought to know what he was doing. The frontispiece to the book (Figure 6.12) reflects the need for greater understanding of what was required! [36]

' We shall learn of him another and a greater lesson, some day.'

Figure 6.12 Hoskyns, C W (1854) *Talpa or the Chronicle of a Clay Farm*

A description of the practice on the Netherby estate was given in 1830 when 'in all cases the drains were cut as narrow as workmen can conveniently work in them, decreasing as they approach the bottom'. 'The drains being cut to the required depth, with all the top soil laid on one side, and all the subsoil thrown out on the other, a narrow mouthed spade (technically called a spit) corresponding to the breadth of the tile to be used is then introduced, and with this instrument a bed for the course of the tile carefully and neatly excavated, the strictest attention being paid to preserve a fair equality in the bottom, and a regular descent for the water'. It also stressed that frequent use of a spirit level was commonly necessary. When finishing after the tiles were laid, the turf, grass side down was first replaced, followed by surface soil and finally the subsoil, but not clay. It was also stressed that before commencing draining all ditches should be checked, cleared, deepened and scoured.[37]

As the amount of thorough draining increased, a division of labour and responsibilities developed. Large estates such as Lowther and Springkell had a 'Drainage Superintendent', while for schemes under the Public Money Drainage Acts, as mentioned above, an inspector for the Inclosure Commissioners was appointed. One set of estate accounts in 1857 described the cost of supervision as 'setting tiles and superintending £7.13.4'. An account dated 1849 for tiles for the Naworth estate was signed by Thomas Morley, a farmer and draining inspector.[38]

There were also draining contractors such as Joseph Robinson who regularly advertised for drainers, often in large numbers, as in 1855 when he required 'about forty able drainers'. Draining tasks were divided into 'setting and laying' carried out under supervision by the master drainer, cutting and filling, and also carting, An advertisement for a total of 19,300 roods of drains on three properties in different parishes clearly indicated these separate responsibilities, Figure 6.13.

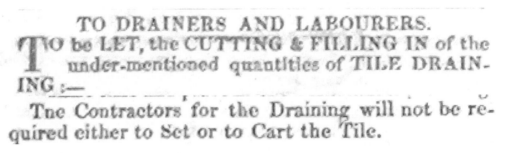

TO DRAINERS AND LABOURERS.
TO be LET, the CUTTING & FILLING IN of the under-mentioned quantities of TILE DRAIN-
ING :—
The Contractors for the Draining will not be re-quired either to Set or to Cart the Tile.

Figure 6.13 CAS (Carlisle) *Carlisle Journal* 15th November 1850

A regular feature of the columns of the *Carlisle Journal* of the 1850s and 1860s was advertisements for both 'Drainers wanted' and 'To be let the cutting and filling of roods of drains'. One contract of 1856 for the cutting of 6000 roods of drains included a cottage and coals supplied gratis.[39]

As tile-works did not normally deliver, when the landlord was meeting the cost of the draining, the carting of tiles was usually the task of the farmer, In other situations draining contracts specified carting, as in 1849 when one stipulated 'the carting of about sixty thousand pipe-tiles'. Similarly in 1860 the draining of land at Knardale in Northumberland required 'the carting of tiles from Slaggyford Station'. Obviously the cost of transporting the tiles would depend on the distance between the nearest tilery and the area to be drained. When land at Thornbarrow, in Hesket-in-the-Forest was being drained in 1844, an amount paid for leading tiles was £23, this for £44 worth of tiles purchased from a tilery about three miles away. The number of tiles would have been in the region of 30,000, consisting of around 100 cartloads. One solution, using a traditional practice, was found in February 1857 when friends and neighbours of a farmer assembled to give him a 'Boon Tile Leading', from the *Culgaith Tile Works* with about 30 carts utilised.[40]

Some advertisements specified that the cutting and filling was for tile-drains, and in one instance, was for the taking up of old drain tiles, Figure 6.14.

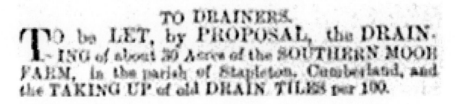

TO DRAINERS.
TO be LET, by PROPOSAL, the DRAIN-ING of about 30 Acres of the SOUTHERN MOOR FARM, in the parish of Stapleton, Cumberland, and the TAKING UP of old DRAIN TILES per 100.

Figure 6.14 CAS (Carlisle) *Carlisle Journal* 24th January 1868

With the emphasis here on the use of tiles, no attempt has been made to analyse the demographics of drainers. Nevertheless there was one example of how Josiah Parkes brought drainers with him when overseeing the draining of the Lowther estate. In 1851 at Hensingham there were in total 12 drainers recorded in the census, of whom seven were from Surrey, two others from outside the county and only three from Cumberland.[41]

The resolving of the dispute over the depth of drains in favour of deeper ones was reflected in the majority of advertisements in the 1850s, which specified drains to be cut 'from three to four feet deep'. Robert Faulder of Kirklinton applied in June 1857 for a loan of £500 under the Public Money Drainage Act. In July he advertised the letting of cutting of about 1000 roods of drains from three- to four- feet deep, confirming that this was the depth being specified by the Inclosure Commissioners. The distances apart of the drains varied between seven and ten yards, occasionally greater, dependent on the nature of the soil.[42]

Several factors affected the price of cutting and filling drains, particularly supply and demand of labour. In 1853 the cost of cutting and filling a rood of seven yards of three feet deep varied between 4 ½ d. to 6 ½ d., and four feet between 7 d. to 9 ½ d. Other circumstances such as the type of ground and the time of year would have an impact. The higher of the two prices applied to the Western division and the lower to the Eastern.[43]

There were few specialised implements for drainers; the spade was the basic tool, supplemented by a long-handled scoop and by a long-handled pipe layer with a spike to insert into a pipe to place it in the trench. At the RASE Show in Carlisle in 1855 sets of draining tools were among the exhibits, Figure 6.15.[44]

ARTICLE No. 44.—Set of *Lyndon's* Patent DRAINING TOOLS.

The Prize of £5 was awarded to *Mapplebeck and Lowe* for these Tools, at the Northampton Meeting of the Royal Agricultural Society. Also, the Prize at Lewes, 1852.

Containing Spade, Two Grafting Tools, Thompson Shovel, One Scoop, One Pipe Layer, One Mattock and Handle, and One Pick and Handle. PRICE, £1 12s. 3d.

Figure 6.15 Cumbria Libraries (Carlisle) *Catalogue of Agricultural Implements* 1855 Drainage Scoop & Drainage Spade [without handles] Personal Collection

Draining was normally carried out during the winter months; most advertisements for draining to be let appeared between September and November and, if earlier, specified 'to drain this winter'. This practice continued into the twentieth century on the Netherby estate where, 'draining was normally carried out during the winter months'.[45]

During the early years of the establishment of 'Thorough Draining' stones continued to be used as a filling. In 1845 William Wallis took over the farm of Duncowfold and during the ensuing months he described in his daily record the draining carried out. From 1st to the 13th April men were employed in digging and deepening drains in various fields, including South Moss Close. On 14th April 'led some stones about 4 cartloads to the drain on South Moss Close which the two men began filling'. The filling continued on the 15th and 17th when a further 12 cartloads of stones were brought, followed by 8 cartloads on 18th, and 15 more on the 22nd. Filling was completed by the 25th when the field was ploughed and then harrowed. While this work was taking place, stone-picking was being carried out elsewhere on the farm, with 'a woman gathering stones' on the 22nd and 24th, and continuing on the 29th when the woman was assisted by a boy.[46]

Tiles were used initially, as stated in 1834 'where stones do not abound', but then gradually became the first choice. This enabled a writer in 1838 to say that 'had it not been for the introduction of tiles' much recent draining in Cumberland would not have taken place. Increasingly, farms to let were advertised with, 'part of the land tile-drained', and others, with promises that 'tenants will be supplied with tiles'. To facilitate this on some farms tile-kilns were erected. One of the first to use tiles in Cumberland was John Rooke of Akehead, Wigton, who as a result of successfully draining with stone had been visited by, and gained the friendship of, both William Blamire and Sir James Graham. John Rooke purchased tiles from Thomas Guy Patrick's tilery at Linstock and transported them from there to Akehead. It was as a result of seeing the carts delivering these tiles that Robert Lucock visited Akehead and obtained John Rooke's assistance in locating a suitable site for making tiles in the area, resulting in the establishment of *Langrigg Tilery*. An article of 7th September 1839 recounted how it was 'twenty years this spring since tile-draining was first introduced into Cumberland'. Since then increasing amounts of land had been tile-drained and more could have been done if there had been sufficient tiles. On the Netherby estate in the 24 years from 1822 until 1846 about 4800 acres on tenants' farms were drained.[47]

The first tilery in Cartmel was set up in 1842 on the Holker estate. Westmorland followed in 1846 when a tilery was established to provide tiles to drain the Lowther estate. This, influenced by Josiah Parkes, produced large quantities of small bore pipes. These were to be a topic of discord, with the opinion of many being that they had no recommendation other than cheapness, and that pipes for drainage should never be less than two inches in diameter. Referring to tiles, John Yule had in 1830 described the three- inch as the most useful for all ordinary purposes. After a short period, mainly on large estates, the use of small bore pipes declined and the most widely used size, of what became known as the pipe-tile, reverted to the three-inch.[48]

The situation in the late 1840s was that nationally as well as locally, despite the fact that some disagreements over depth and distance would continue, the general principles of 'Thorough Draining' were accepted. Information was being disseminated nationwide through the *JRASE* and *THASS* and other journals, as well as at county level through agricultural societies and improving landlords and their agents.

Long-term finance was available through the various drainage acts, and to meet the demand generated by this money the number of tileries, both public and farm or estate, was increasing.

What was now required was for these tileries to increase the quantities of tiles produced and for them to be of a consistently higher standard. The solution to both quantity and quality was the tile-making-machine, which was moving out of the experimental stage to a situation where reliable machines were available nationally.

The next chapter outlines the introduction of machines into tile-making and describes how the products of some manufacturers came to dominate the market.

Notes

[1] Chambers & Mingay (1966) 131, Prothero (1912) 352

[2] Burke (1840) *Husbandry* Vol.3 'Report of Select Farms' 39, Harvey (1956) 4, Laws (1850) 3

[3] *Oxford English Dictionary*, 2nd edition, Dickson (1805) 13, 'Farm Reports' (1832) 25 in Burke (1840)

[4] *NSA* (1845) Vol.5 613, 658, 766, Vol.6 383, 599, Smith (1844) 4, *Encyclopaedia Britannica* (1911) 'Drainage of Land'

[5] Fenton (1976) 23, Fenton (1987) 116

[6] Pusey (1842) 170, Caird (1852) 304 'this necessary improvement, the foundation of all others'

[7] *ODNB* (2004) Cheape, H 'Smith, James of Deanston (1789-1850), Dudgeon (1840) 94-5, *NSA* (1845) Vol.6 Lanarkshire, Carstairs (1839) 558, Vol.9 Fife, Kennaway (1835) 383, Vol.13 Banff, Cullen (1842) 335.

[8] Smith (1844) 3, Graham (1840) 33-37

[9] Smith (1844) 4, 6, 7, 8

[10] *ODNB* (2004) Phillips, A.D.M. 'Parkes, Josiah (1793-1871)', Institute of Civil Engineers, Minutes of Proceedings, (1872) Vol. XXXIII, 231-6 'Josiah Parkes', Parkes (1843) 369-79, Parkes (1846) 251

[11] Parkes (1846) 256, Parkes (1845) 126, 129

[12] Dickinson (1850) 34, CAS (Carlisle) D Lons L15/1/3/4 July 2nd 1852 letter, L15/1/1/27 August 11th 1852 Agreement, L15/1/1/3 July 15th & August 4th 1854 Delivery Note & Invoice, L15/1/1/21 & 22 Stock Account 1853-54

[13] Garnett (1912) 61, *CJ* 7/11/1862-8/1

[14] Phillips (1996) 2, Denton (1883) 2, *CJ* 18/5/1844-2/3 Deanston Farm

[15] *CJ* 18/7/1846-3/1

[16] Colbeck (1847 437

[17] Dickinson (1853) 82-3, *CJ* 15/6/1839-2/4

[18] Stephens (1846) iv, v, Stephens (1852) Vol. II, 617, Binns (1851) 17, Dickinson (1850) 38, Caird (1852) 354, *CJ* 18/7/1851-2/2, 24/1/1868-8/3

[19] Goddard (1991) 166 in Holderness & Turner (1991)

[20] Dickinson (1853) 83, Goddard (1991) 168 in Holderness & Turner (1991)

[21] Fox & Butlin (1979) 52, Yule (1929) 388-400, Laws (1850), Dickinson (1850), Dickinson (1853), *CJ* 6/5/1853-4/2

[22] *AHEW* Vol. 6 376, 377, Fox & Butlin (1979) 49, *CJ* 8/4/1853-6/4, 15/8/1862-8/4, Binns (1851) 106, Garnett (1912) 210, *CJ* 4/9/1824-3/1, 15/8/1862-8/4, 27/11/1863-8/2

[23] Lonsdale (1857) 218-9, 266, 283, Fox & Butlin (1979) 48

[24] *CJ* 25/4/1829-2/6, *Preston Chronicle* 1/10/1831, 6/10/1832, 28/9/1833, 20/9/1834, 26/9/1835, 1/10/1836, 14/10/1837, *CJ* 4/9/1824-3/1

[25] *SUA* 28/9/1848-2/5, 2/11/1848-1/2, 26/10/1848-4/3

[26] Caird (1852) 353, Winchester (2005) 43, Dickinson (1853) 86, Wade Martins (2004) 59

[27] Wiggins (1847) 1

[28] Phillips (1989) 51, Spring (1963) 143-4, Denton (1868) 123-4

[29] Phillips (1989) 51-2, Phillips (1996) 12, Fletcher (1962) 116, *CJ* 11/3/1853-2/3, CAS (Carlisle) DBS 4/3 Aglionby 38 Estate Improvement

[30] *CJ* 15/5/1847-2/4, 16/1/1847-1/5, 23/1/1847-1/5, 13/2/1847-1/4, 27/2/1847-1/4, 13/3/1847-1/7

[31] *CJ* 7/9/1850-1/4, 6/12/1850-1/5, 23/1/1852-2/3

[32] *CJ* 15/6/1849-1/5 [repeated], 29/8/1851-1/6, 29/6/1860-4/3, M H & Co (1861) 19, CAS (C) WPR7/1/5 Letter 20/2/1862

[33] Garnett (1912) 61, *CJ*12/7/1878-1/5

[34] Phillips (1989) 74

[35] Dickinson(1853) 84, Phillips (1989) 161, Harvey (1956) 28

[36] Hoskyns (1854) 16

[37] Yule (1830) 65,67

[38] Census 1851 HO107/2440/206/6 Richard Miller, Superintendent Drainer, *CJ* 19/10/1860-4/1 Robert Tinniswood, Drainage Superintendent, CAS (Carlisle) D ING 23 Draining Expenses 1857, DUL (Special Collections) Naworth Papers C612/208, Census 1861 RG9/3906/62/15 Thomas Morley

[39] *CJ* 10/6/1837-2/4, 26/1/1855-4/1, 16/1/1857-4/1, 2/10/1857-4/1, 29/10/1858-4/1, 21/1/1859-4/1, 4/12/1860-1/1, 18/10/1861-4/1, 15/2/1867-4/1 'Drainers Wanted', *CJ* 19/10/1849-2/2, 15/11/1850-2/1, 5/3/1852-1/2, 12/11/1852-2/4, 27/1/1854-1/4, 20/10/1854-1/6, 26/10/1855-1/4, 12/12/1856-1/5, 19/11/1858-1/2, 21/1/1859-4/1, 4/2/1859-1/3 'Cutting and Filling' *CJ* 7/11/1856-1/4 'A Cottage and coals found gratis'

[40] Webster (1868) 25, *CJ* 2/2/1833-1/1, 19/10/1849-2-2, 12/10/1860-4/2, CAS (Carlisle) D ING 46 February 1844, Bouch & Jones (1961) 230-1, *C&WA* 10/2/1857-4/4 cited in Shepherd (2003) 133

[41] Census 1851 HO107/2437/19/7, 30/29, 41/8, 42/10

[42] *CJ* 20/10/1854-1/6, 30/3/1855-1/4, 8/2/1856-1/2, 26/6/1857-4/1, 10/7/1857-1/3, 7/3/1862-8/4

[43] Dickinson (1853) 83, Dickinson (1859) 36-7

[44] *Carlisle Meeting Catalogue of the Various New and Improved Agricultural Implements and Husbandry Tools exhibited at the Carlisle Meeting of the Royal Agricultural Society of England July 25th, 26th and 27th 185 5 by* Mapplebeck & Lowe, Birmingham [Cumbria Libraries (Carlisle) Jackson Library Box N8 item 8/20]
Drainage Scoop length with handle 55", Scoop blade 14", Spade with handle 39", blade 12", width 5"

[45] *CJ* 14/9/1855-1, 28/9/1855, 19/10/1855-1, 26/10/1855-1/4, 30/11/1855-1/1, 18/7/1851-2/2, Mounsey, H 'Rambling Reminiscences of 55 Years ago on the Netherby Estate –Part Two' *Bewcastle Journal* Vol 7, June 1997, 18

[46] *Collins Memoranda & Daily Register 1845 of William Wallis of Duncowfold* [Cumbria Libraries (Carlisle) Jackson Library B561]

[47] Burke (1834) 458, *The Farmers Magazine* 1838, 'Agriculture of Cumberland' 334, *CJ* 27/1/1844-2/8, 5/9/1840-1/2, 14/12/1939-2/5, Lonsdale (1872) 222-4, *CN* 2/3/1956-10/5&6, Spring (1955) 77, Ward (1976) 61, *CJ* 7/9/1839-3/3

[48] LRO (Preston) DDCa 13/299, CAS (Carlisle) D Lons L15/1/1/29, Fussell (1952) rep. (1981) 28, Johnson (1847) 564, Laws (1850) 17, Yule (1830) 67, Dickinson (1850) 34

7

Introduction of tile-making machines

As with most things new, either practices or equipment, opinions were voiced both for and against tile-machines. The reasons given to justify their introduction also varied, as did the criticism levelled against them.

It has been suggested, based on the remarks by Phillip Pusey in 1843, that the RASE encouraged the use of tile-machines that were labour intensive. What in fact Pusey advocated was for landlords to carry out improvements which would result in the employment of country labourers who were 'standing unwillingly idle'. These proposed activities included the procurement of a tile-machine.[1]

One argument against the tile-machine was that the same money laid out to make the tiles by hand would be more beneficial to the labourers. The introduction of tile-machines did not mean that the number of labouring jobs was reduced. The fact that larger quantities of tiles were produced at a lower cost increased the amount of draining, therefore more labourers were required. This proposition was put forward by the Duke of Bedford's steward, when on acquiring a Beart machine he wrote 'it will no doubt be a means of giving greater scope for the employment of labour, as more than twice the quantity [of tiles] may be used without any increase in the expense'.[2]

A different concern was that 'a tile-machine requires four hands to work it'. This was countered by pointing out that common labourers could make tiles with a machine, which were superior to those produced by the most experienced hand-moulders.[3]

The aim of achieving greater production of better quality tiles at a lower price, which would result in more draining taking place, drove the development of tile-machines. Progress in reaching this goal was remarkably rapid, as improvements were made to the first basic models introduced in the mid 1830s, and new manufacturers entered the market.

The RASE annual show provided a venue for exhibiting tile-making-machines, as well as the opportunity to compare the operation of a number of them through practical trials. One of the earliest was patented by Robert Beart of Godmanchester, Huntingdonshire, whose machine for making tiles and soles attracted considerable attention at the Cambridge show in 1840. He registered the first of his patents in 1833 for a machine for 'making or producing tiles for draining land'; other patents followed for improvements to this, and also in 1834 'apparatus for the manufacture of bricks'. Beart's main interest became the production of perforated bricks, both by his Patent Brick Company Ltd with works in Godmanchester and Bedfordshire, and through licensing the patent to other companies, including, as will be described later, to Thomas Nelson in Carlisle.[4]

In an article in the *JRASE* in 1841 entitled 'On the Economical Manufacture of Draining Tiles and Soles', Robert Beart described the complete process of producing tiles and gave an estimated cost for each operation. The machine used was his own, priced £12.12.00, and its functions were fully illustrated, Figure 7.1.

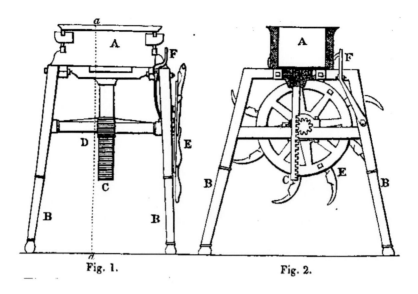

Fig. 1.   Fig. 2.

Figure 7.1 Mr Beart's patent machine for making drain-tiles

An end view is shown in Figure 1 and a side view in Figure 2. The cast-iron box for clay A is fitted with a moveable bottom or piston, attached to a bar C, which is operated by turning the wheel E. When one spoke of the wheel was turned, the piston raised a slab of clay the thickness of a tile, which had to be sliced from the top of the box with a wire bow. The slab was then lifted off by a boy, who laid it upon a tile-horse, similar to that previously illustrated in Figure 4.3, and bent it into shape. One man and two boys worked the machine.[5] The only advantage of this type of machine was the fact that it could produce multiple slabs as opposed to the single slabs of hand-moulders.

The writer of an article published in 1842 suggested that there was 'no doubt that Mr Beart greatly reduced the price of tiles in Huntingdonshire'. However a footnote by a different commentator stated 'Beart's so called "machine" though useful in the preparation, is, in fact, a mere tool, the tile being actually made entirely by hand.'[6]

A second individual who was a major influence on the spread of tile-making machines in the 1830s and 1840s was George Hay, eighth Marquis of Tweeddale, whose interest in agriculture and his knowledge of mechanics resulted in his invention, and in 1836 and 1838 his patenting, of machines for 'making tiles for draining'. As would be expected these machines were widely used in Scotland where in Yester, the parish of his birth, it was recorded as early as 1835 that the Marquis of Tweeddale 'has invented a very ingenious machine for forming the tiles, which will greatly facilitate the operation of tile-draining'. Also in the county of Haddingtonshire, at North Berwick in 1839 there was a foundry manufacturing the Tweeddale machines. Its use had spread to Ayrshire by 1841 where Robert Boyle at his tile-works used 'the Marquis of Tweeddale's patent tile-machine, the only one at present in operation in Ayrshire'. At the HASS meeting at Dumfries in 1845 Mr Boyle exhibited a tile-making-machine which 'took the fancy of every one who saw it work'. Machines were also exhibited by John Ainslie of Middlesex and John Charnock of Wakefield, with all three exhibitors being awarded premiums.[7]

The Tweeddale machine differed from Beart's in that the clay was drawn through two revolving cylinders which compressed it to the thickness of a tile. The flattened clay was then drawn forward by the machine on a web of canvas to pass through a mould which gave it the required shape, Figure 7.2.

Figure 7.2 Tweeddale tile-making-machine

This process gave the tiles a superior quality owing to the greater density given to the clay. A review of 1843 considered that the apparatus was brought down to 'the power of a common labourer not necessarily acquainted with the process of tile-making'. The tiles could be made at the rate of about 15 per minute and were considered by some to be 'superior to all others'.[8]

The patent for the manufacture of Tweeddale tiles was assigned to the Tweeddale Patent Tile and Brick Company, which in 1841 had seven establishments producing tiles across the country, with a further five being erected.[9]

There were, of course, dissenting voices regarding the quality. The Duke of Bedford's steward wrote in 1841 regarding Tweeddale tiles that 'they are below the mark held out to us - as bad as any'.[10]

In addition to those of Beart and Tweeddale there were other similar machines being produced; but it is not possible to state who was the manufacturer of the first tile-making-machine used in Cumberland. What appears to be certain is that the first tiles to be made by machine in the county were produced at *Sebergham Tilery* and offered for sale in February 1845, Figure 7.3

DRAIN TILES.
ON SALE, a large Quantity of superior MACHINE MADE TILES, of different sizes, at moderate Prices, at the SEBERGHAM TILE WORKS.
By WILLIAM WILSON.
February 15th, 1845.

Figure 7.3 CAS (Carlisle) *Carlisle Journal* 15th February 1845

This was followed in 1846 with an advertisement, Figure 7.4, describing the machine-made tiles as very superior to those made by hand.

DRAINING TILES.
ON SALE, at the SEBERGHAM TILERY, a quantity of TILES of various sizes.
The above being made by powerful and efficient Machinery, and well burnt, are recommended as very superior to Tiles moulded by hand.
Sebergham, Dec. 15, 1846.

Figure 7.4 CAS (Carlisle) *Carlisle Journal* 19th December 1846

The only other information regarding the machine appeared when the works was offered 'to let' in April 1847 with the equipment for sale, including a 'Patent Tile Machine'.[11]

A tile-machine was in use in Cartmel at the *Holker Tilery* in 1845, as in March of that year an amount for 'carriage of a tile-machine' appeared in their accounts. In the following year, among the expenditure in the erection of a tile-kiln and sheds at *Hackthorpe Tilery* in 1846, was the sum of £25 for a tile-machine from W. B. Webster.[12]

Nationally the increase in the number of tile-making-machines can be charted from the 'Reports on Exhibition of Implements' at the RASE annual shows. At Derby in 1843 two machines were exhibited; the following year at Southampton seven firms exhibited 13 machines. In 1845 at Shrewsbury 11 manufacturers showed 14.machines, with three, by Clayton, Beart and Scragg, being given trials. The prize was awarded to Thomas Scragg whose machine; Figure 7.5, also came first at Newcastle-upon-Tyne in 1846.

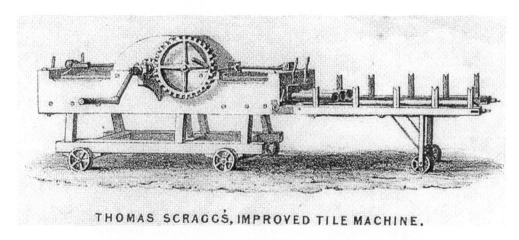

THOMAS SCRAGG'S, IMPROVED TILE MACHINE.

Figure 7.5 Thomas Scragg - trade leaflet (1847)

A number of machines were included in the trials at Northampton in 1847 where the prize was awarded to Henry Clayton while the machine of Thomas Scragg was considered too expensive. The number of machines peaked at 34 in 1848 at the York show, which was five years after Derby where only two had been exhibited. The prize at York went to John

Whitehead of Preston, so beginning the rivalry between the top three names, Clayton, Scragg and Whitehead. The machines of these three were described at Norwich in 1849 as being the most improved, making it difficult to decide, particularly in relation to Scragg's and Whitehead's which was the best. Only two of the three, those of Scragg and Whitehead, exhibited at Carlisle in 1855 when John Whitehead was awarded the prize.[13]

While these developments were taking place nationally, the references to tile-making-machines in our region were becoming more frequent. The second tilery in Cumberland to make tiles by machine may have been *Dearham Tile Works,* which in 1847 specified 'making by hand and machine', although no information was given regarding the type of machine. Apart from estate tileries where details occasionally appeared in the accounts, it is usually from an advertisement that announced the sale or closure of a tilery, which produced facts regarding a tile-machine but not often the name of the manufacturer. A tile-machine was offered for sale at *Chapel Hill Tilery,* Wreay, in February 1850; it was described only as 'of the best construction, nearly new and in good working order'. *Sebergham Tilery* closed in 1854 and in the public auction in February there were '3 iron framed machines for making all kinds of tiles'. In a second sale in October, an 'excellent cylinder tile-machine' was included. A tile-machine to produce round pipes was installed in 1850 at the Netherby tilery. This was capable of producing two and one half thousand per man per day. Unfortunately in all of these examples no manufacturer's name was provided.[14]

Despite the lack of information about which machines were being used, by the early 1850s the requirements of advertisements suggested that more were in operation. Joseph Rome who took over the *Eden Place Tile Works* required a manager in 1851 who 'must understand the making of pipe and other tiles by machinery'. Similarly, in 1855 the *Broughton Moor Tilery* wanted a man 'accustomed to making tiles and pipes with a machine'. The wording in both instances suggested that such machines were by then a normal piece of equipment in tileries in Cumberland.[15]

Although the machines manufactured by Whitehead, as will be shown, became predominant in the north-west, here, as well as generally in the north of England, other manufacturers were represented, even if only as exhibitors at shows.

As observed above, John Ainslie whose machine was patented in 1841 exhibited at the HASS meeting at Dumfries in 1845 where he was awarded a 'Medium Gold Medal'. His machine was marketed by the Ainslie Brick & Tile Machine Company of which James Smith of Deanston was a director. Although a leaflet for this company is included in the archive of *Hackthorpe Tilery*, no evidence has been located of its use there or elsewhere in Cumberland or Westmorland.[16]

The other exhibitor of a tile-making machine at Dumfries in 1845 was John Henry Charnock of Wakefield, who in August of that year also exhibited at the Tyneside Agricultural Society show at Hexham. In the same month an advertisement for the machine appeared in the *Carlisle Patriot.* Charnock's machine was included in the trial of implements at the Yorkshire Agricultural Society's show at Beverley in 1845 where it won a prize. Three men and a boy were required to carry out its operation: one man to feed clay, another to turn the wheel, another to cut off tiles or pipes, and a boy to take them away.[17]

The first machine recorded in use at *Hackthorpe Tilery* was supplied by William Bullock Webster, a draining engineer and inventor. A Webster machine was displayed at the RASE meeting in Newcastle-upon-Tyne in 1845 where he had an advertisement in the show's *Hand-Book*. It would seem that his machine had some problems, as when it was exhibited at York in 1848 it was not in a position to be included in the trials. This was the second occasion that this had happened.[18]

Another early machine which reached the north of England was that patented by Frederick William Etheridge in 1842, which was exhibited in both hand-powered and horse-powered versions at the RASE Southampton show in 1844. The judges preferred the hand-operated machine, which was awarded a silver medal. It would appear that this was the one used at the Duke of Northumberland's tilery in 1846, Figure 7.6.

THE DUKE OF NORTHUMBERLAND'S TILE MANUFACTORY.—The tilework in the vicinity of Belford is in active operation. The buildings have been reconstructed 200 yards westward of their former site, where they have the advantage of freer air. This establishment, we understand, should turn out a million tiles in the season. With Etheredge's patent machine, so beautiful and quiet in its movements, Mr. William Sibbald, foreman under Mr. Hall, tile-maker, Alnwick, is now making 8,000 tiles (equal to 4,000 tiles and 4,000 soles) a-day. The drying shades are calculated to hold 38,000 tiles; and the two kilns, when finished, will contain 20,000 each. Visitors may also see Mr. John Sibbald at this establishment turn out with the hand no less than nine bricks in a minute. This tilework must prove an immense advantage to the Duke's tenants in the district.—*Berwick Warder.*

Figure 7.6 CAS (Carlisle) *Carlisle Journal* 13th June 1846

A number of companies exhibited at the RASE show in Carlisle in 1855 including Fowler & Fry of Bristol who displayed eight articles, among them a 'Drain-pipe Making Machine'. It was probably one of these horse-powered machines which contained a double piston alternating between two boxes, which Robert Wigham, who had a number of tileries in Northumberland, offered for sale in 1861. One of his works *Featherstone Tilery* closed in 1867 when he advertised a 'Fowlers Patent' machine, which must have been an improved model as it was powered by steam.[19]

Among the machines William Williams of Bedford brought to Carlisle were two for making pipes and tiles, one hand-powered, the other capable of being powered either by hand or horse. The first of these had won a prize in 1847 at Northampton, where it was described as simple, strong and cheap. Despite these virtues no record has been found of its use at tileries in the region.[20].

As described above, at RASE shows the machines of three manufacturers, Scragg, Clayton and Whitehead, became acknowledged as the best.

The 1847 machine of Thomas Scragg, Figure 7.5, was recommended by Josiah Parkes when advising the Clifton of Lytham estate on the erection of a tilery. It was probably also on his suggestion that one was in use at *Hackthorpe Tilery* in 1847. Thomas Scragg exhibited at the RASE show in Carlisle in 1855, with two single-action machines on his stand. Despite being 'highly commended', it would appear not to have found favour locally as there are no located references to its use in Cumberland.[21]

Henry Clayton patented his machine for the 'manufacture of tiles, drain pipes or tubes and bricks' in 1844. Unlike those of Scragg and Whitehead which extruded pipes horizontally, this had a perpendicular cylinder giving a vertical delivery. The pipes were pressed out at the bottom to be cut off by a wire, a method which was considered particularly suitable for large diameter pipes. This vertical delivery was commended at RASE shows at York in 1848 and Chelmsford in 1856. A lithograph of Clayton's patent machine was included in Dempsey's *The Machinery of the Nineteenth Century* published in 1852, Figure 7.7, which included best examples of machines at the 'Exhibition of the Works of Industry of all Nations' of 1851.

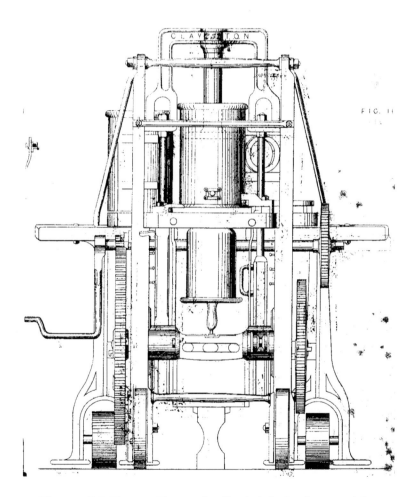

Figure 7.7 Henry Clayton's tile, brick & pipe machine

The machines were in use in Lancashire in 1849, when on a farm tilery near Preston 'two machines were used, a Clayton for large pipes and a Whitehead for smaller bore'. Then in 1851 it was said that on the Earl of Derby's Fylde estate 'two of Clayton's machines are kept constantly at work'. An agricultural implement maker in Preston advertised in the *Carlisle Journal* in 1851 that they were agents for Clayton's tile machine.

Further north in Scotland, at Hawick in 1854, the *Birneyknowe Tile Works* offered for sale a pipe-tile machine by Clayton which was no longer required.

Although Clayton's machines were in use in Lancashire and Scotland, and in 1863 John Whittle in Whitehaven was an agent for Clayton, no references have been found of them being used in Cumberland. In Westmorland, it was only in 1891 that a machine that may have been made by Clayton was described at *Julian Bower Brick & Tile Works.* [22]

John Whitehead entered the business of tile-making-machines rather late, at a time when most practical difficulties had been surmounted by others. In 1839 John Whitehead describing himself as a 'Furnishing Ironmonger and Ironmerchant etc' took over a shop at No.9 Fishergate, Preston. Nine years later his entry in a directory of 1848 listed him as an 'Agricultural Implement Maker of 9, Fishergate'. At the RASE show at York in the same year his tile-making-machine, noted for its strength and good workmanship, had the edge on both those of Scragg and Clayton and was described as undoubtedly the most complete machine yet exhibited. This opinion was repeated in an 1848 publication on agriculture, in which the author stated that 'the two machines which have had the greatest run, are those of Mr Clayton and Mr Scraggs', but there was one 'lately invented by Mr Whitehead of Preston, which seems to surpass them'. Presumably it was these positive comments which resulted in a Whitehead machine being purchased for the *Holker Tilery* in Cartmel in November 1848, the first to be recorded in that part of Lancashire.[23]

Whitehead's machines continued to be awarded prizes at RASE shows as was described in his advertisement of 1855, the year the event was held in Carlisle, Figure 7.8.

THE PRIZE DRAIN PIPE & TILE MACHINES, BRICK MACHINES, PUG MILLS, CLAY ROLLERS, &c.

JOHN WHITEHEAD, PRESTON, LANCASHIRE.

WHITEHEAD'S TILE MACHINES are adapted for the manufacture of DRAIN PIPES of all kinds: TILES of every description; HOLLOW BRICKS, SANATORY TUBES, and Mouldings of all kinds. These Machines are now extensively in use throughout Great Britain and the Continent, and may be seen at work in almost any district. They have had awarded the prize or commendation of the

ROYAL AGRICULTURAL SOCIETY OF ENGLAND

at every Meeting since 1848 at which they have been exhibited, and also the Medal of the

GREAT EXHIBITION OF 1851.

Figure 7.8 CAS (Carlisle) *Carlisle Journal* 13th April 1855

In the previous year a John Whitehead machine was purchased for *Hackthorpe Tilery* - ordered on their behalf by Josiah Parkes whose preferred machine had previously been that of Thomas Scragg. The one selected was the 'No.1 Tile Machine', Figure 7.9 which was exhibited along with other machinery at Carlisle.

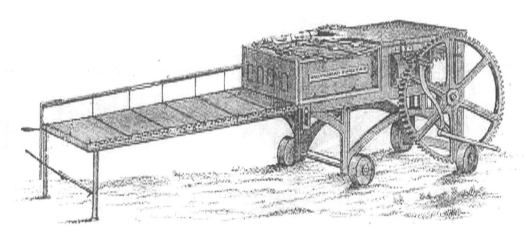

Improved Tile Machine, N.º 1, Whitehead, Maker, Preston.

Figure 7.9 John Whitehead, Preston - trade leaflet 1851

It was a horizontal machine made of iron which had one clay box with a wrought iron-hinged lid, within which worked the piston, Figure 7.10 [b], attached to two racks and moved by two pinions, set in motion using the winch. Dies, Figure 7.10 [a], placed at the front, were of the size of the pipes to be formed. Similar dies, or moulds, were mentioned in auction sales, and examples can now be seen at the Museum of Scottish Country Life.

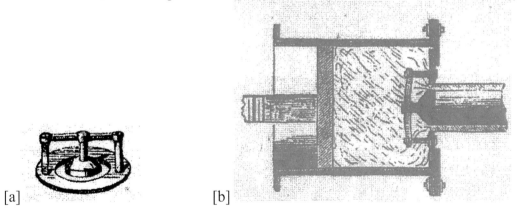

[a]   [b]

Figure 7.10 [a] Tile-mould [b] Clay box with piston

The machine could be worked by one man and two boys; the former filled the clay box, which held sufficient clay to make 48 pipes of two-inch diameter, and turned the winch while the boys cut and carried away the pipes. The price of the machine with the receiving table was £21.

In addition to the 'No.1 Tile Machine' there was a similar, reduced-size version, aimed at the smaller tilery. Also, for larger tileries there was a 'No.2 Double-box Tile Machine', which required two men to operate it, one to fill the boxes and the second to turn the winch.[24]

The tile-making machines of John Whitehead continued to be manufactured into the twentieth-century. Of nationally-manufactured machines, only those of John Whitehead were recorded more than once in Cumberland, Westmorland and Furness & Cartmel. His machines are mentioned 12 times between 1848 and 1891, including one as previously mentioned at *Holker Tilery*, three at *Hackthorpe Tilery* when it closed in 1866, and another at *Julian Bower Brick & Tile Works* in 1891. In Cumberland, there was one at *Eden Place Tilery* in 1859, another used by Robert Hinde at Maryport in 1865 and one at *Calthwaite Tile Works* in 1867. *Bolton Tile Works* in 1870 had one machine, as did *Wragmire Tile Works* in 1878, while at *Sebergham Common Tilery* there were two in 1877.[25]

.

An attempt by some early machine manufacturers to create a system of licensing, by which a purchaser was obliged to pay a royalty per thousand tiles or bricks made, seems not to have lasted for long. One of the exponents of this practice who had to discontinue it was the Ainslie Tile Machine Company, who in a leaflet, unfortunately undated, set out their reasons. These were, according to the directors of the company, representations from applicants for the machines, and the difficulty in collecting the royalty; therefore they stated that their machines would in future be sold at a fixed price.

As already noted Robert Beart's company licensed Thomas Nelson in November 1853, for the exclusive use of two patents in Carlisle, and, 'at or in all of the other towns, villages, parishes and places situate within the district', during the remainder of respective terms granted by letters patent. The patents for improvements to machinery had been granted in 1845 and 1850 for terms of 14 years. Under the terms of the licence Thomas Nelson was to pay to Beart's company, six pence royalty for every 1000 bricks or tiles produced. In 1854 he erected at Murrell Hill, a new manufactory for making tiles and perforated bricks, 'by the patent process invented by Mr Beart'.[26]

Tile-machines manufactured locally were used at a number of tileries; the first was mentioned in 1851, when *Sebergham Tilery* announced that they had purchased one of Thomas Brayton's powerful pipe machines. His name appeared again in 1855 as the maker of a 'double-action horizontal drain pipe and tile machine', Figure 7.11.

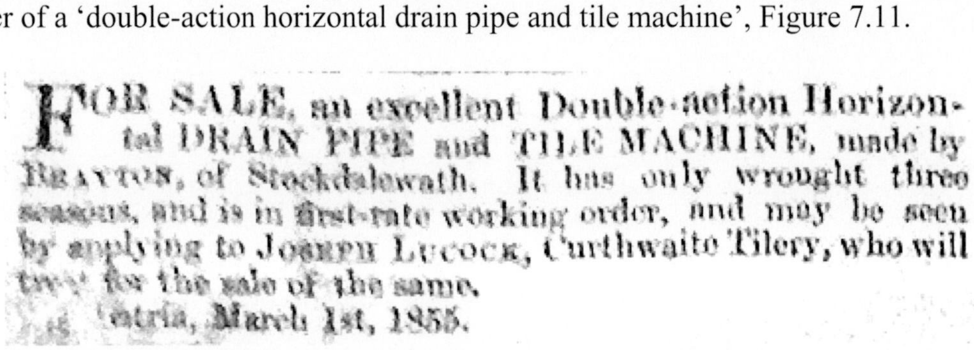
FOR SALE, an excellent Double-action Horizontal DRAIN PIPE and TILE MACHINE, made by BRAYTON, of Stockdalewath. It has only wrought three seasons, and is in first-rate working order, and may be seen by applying to JOSEPH LUCOCK, Curthwaite Tilery, who will [illegible] for the sale of the same.
[illegible] atria, March 1st, 1855.

Figure 7.11 CAS (Carlisle) *Carlisle Journal* 2nd March 1855

The third reference to one of his machines was in 1867 when an auction at *Calthwaite Tile Works* included a tile-machine 'after Brayton's pattern'.[27]

Joseph Lucock of Aspatria, not the Joseph of Figure 7.11 [see Appendix 4], a tile manufacturer, also invented a tile-making machine which was manufactured for him in Carlisle by William Bell, and exhibited at the RASE show in Carlisle in 1855, Figure 7.12.

Stand No. 78.—*Joseph Lucock, of Aspatria, near Carlisle, Cumberland.*

Article No. 1.—*(New Implement.)*—A Drain-Tile and Pipe Machine; invented and improved by the exhibiter; and manufactured by William Bell, of Carlisle. This is a very powerful machine, being constructed entirely of iron; is very portable; and is peculiarly adapted for either a large or small tilery. It consists of two rectangular boxes placed side by side, upon suitable frame-work, with a piston and slide fitted to each, worked by a wheel and crank motion; so that while the tiles or pipes are being forced out of one box the other is filled with clay, and thus no time is lost in the return of the piston or in stopping the machine to refill the boxes. The continuous rotary motion of this machine renders the application of horse, steam, or water power very simple. The die-plate is sufficiently large to admit a pipe 7 in. in diameter inside. To this machine is attached a self-acting cutting apparatus, which cuts the tiles and pipes into lengths of 14 in. Price £45.

Figure 7.12 Cumbria Libraries (Carlisle) RASE Catalogue of Implements July 1855

One of these machines must have been purchased for the *Eden Place Tilery* by Joseph Rome, as it was included in an auction of equipment in 1859 sold by order of his trustees. Other auction sales included named tile-machines; at the closing sale of *Hackthorpe Tilery* in 1866 there were 'three Craig's Pipe-making machines', and in a sale at *Calthwaite Tile Works* in 1867, a 'Young's Tile-machine'. These are the only places where these names appear in relation to tile-making machines.[28]

Another local company which exhibited at the RASE show in 1855 was Porter, Hinde & Porter of Carlisle, which in 1882 became Porter Bros & Co, Figure 7.13.

Please require a Printed Receipt on Payment of this Account.

VICTORIA FOUNDRY, Denton Street, Carlisle, 30th Sept 1896

⊕ PORTER BROTHERS & CO.,
(*Successors to PORTER, HINDE & PORTER,*)
IRON AND BRASS FOUNDERS, ENGINEERS, MILLWRIGHTS AND SMITHS.
Patentees and Manufacturers of Brick Making Machinery.

Figure 7.13 Detail from billhead 1896 [Personal collection]

Their machine had been patented by John Francis Porter in 1853 and was described in the show catalogue as being on the principles developed by Ainslie. A combined pug-mill prepared the clay which was expressed through dies by means of rollers. The purpose of the machine was for forming 'bricks and like articles', which presumably could include pipe-tiles. At the Cumberland & Westmorland Agricultural Society show in 1852, Sir Richard Tufton was awarded a prize for tiles and a tile-machine, presumably manufactured locally, but about which nothing further is known.[29]

The rapid evolution and widespread use of tile-making machines engendered a presumption that they were almost universally replacing manual labour. There seemed little doubt that hand-moulding would soon be entirely superseded by machine. What appeared to happen in the late 1840s, and throughout the 1850s, was that both hand- and machine-moulding coexisted. In 1848 *Dearham Tile Works* required workers capable of making by hand and machine, as did an advertisement of 1857, Figure 7.14, which specified 'two hand-moulders', in addition to one accustomed to making by machine.[30]

TO TILE MAKERS.

WANTED, TWO HAND-MOULDERS, and ONE accustomed to make with a MACHINE.— Apply to Mr. T. STOCKBRIDGE, *Three Crowns Inn*, Ricker-gate, Carlisle.

Figure 7.14 CAS (Carlisle) *Carlisle Journal* 1st May 1857

The earliest tile-machines were operated by hand, with one worker turning a winch - a method, which as previously noted, was preferred to horse-power by judges at the 1844 RASE show. The situation had changed considerably by the RASE show of 1855, where although most of the machines were still available for hand operation, alternative methods of providing the motive power could be used. One of the machines exhibited by William Williams of Bedford could be operated by hand-, horse- or steam-power, as could the tile-machine invented by Joseph Lucock and manufactured by William Bell of Carlisle. The motion to the machine displayed by Fowler & Fry was given by a 'lever working round and round as in the ordinary horse-works'. All of the machines on the stand of John Whitehead were capable of being hand-operated, or by using an apparatus supplied by the manufacturer, easily converted to work by steam-power.[31]

The conversion of a hand-operated Ainslie tile-machine to steam-power by one Scottish tile-manufacturer was not for reasons of efficiency but to save money. Having purchased an improved Ainslie machine in 1848, and agreed piece-work terms with his workers, he found that they became so proficient that 'the quantity made was out of all proportion to the remuneration sufficient for the mere manual labour performed'. He therefore connected the tile-machine to a high-pressure eight-horse-power steam engine, and found that the tile-machine worked much more steadily. There was also an increase in the quantity produced and a very material saving in the cost of making, compared with the hand-operation.[32]

The first mention of steam-power in relation to tile-making in Cumberland was in 1854, when Joseph Lucock of Aspatria offered for sale a five- horse-power steam engine. In the following year in Westmorland, *Wetheriggs Pottery*, also a tilery, advertised a three-horse-power steam engine for sale. When advertising the contract for the making of tiles in 1856, *Brackenhill Tile Works* described the machinery as driven by horse-power, with the proprietor finding and feeding the horses. An account in the *Carlisle Journal* the following year announced the purchase by the Brackenhill estate of a Clayton, Shuttleworth & Co's portable steam engine. This six-horse-power engine, which had aroused much interest at the Great Exhibition of 1851, was to be used for general estate purposes 'such as tile-making', Figure 7.15.[33]

of Clayton, Shuttleworth, and Co.'s improved portable steam engines has been purchased by Mr. James Clarke, of this city, for the estate of W. Pery Standish, Esq., of Brackenhill. It was exhibited in the corn market on Saturday week, and attracted much attention. The engine is of 6-horse power, and will consume between 5 and 6 cwt. of coal per day of ten hours. We believe fixed engines have already been introduced on several farms, but this is the first portable engine which has been brought into this district. It may be applied to general purposes, such as tile making, sawing wood, thrashing, &c. The price is two hundred guineas. We have no doubt that many

Figure 7.15 CAS (Carlisle) *Carlisle Journal* 6th February 1857

These were the first of what became frequent references to the use of steam-power in tile-making. In 1857 the *Rydale Tile Works* in Dumfriesshire announced that 'steam power had been introduced' as did the *Whinnyrigg Tile Works* at Annan. When the plant of the *Whitrigg Tile Works* was offered for sale in 1860, a steam engine was included. Steam engines were also incorporated in tile-works sales at Maryport in 1865, Holme Cultram in 1866 and Featherstone in Northumberland in 1867.[34]

It is believed that one other form of motive power, that of water, was used by only one Cumberland tile- works. In August 1870 when *Culgaith Tile Works* was for sale, the plant included a waterwheel which according to a subsequent advertisement was used to drive the crushing and pug-mill.[35]

Machinery other than a tile-making-machine was in use from the early days, as has been described in Chapter 4. The type of equipment required was determined by the quality and consistency of clay, its plasticity, and the quantity and size of gravel and small stones it contained. In the various records of tile-works, a number of different machines figured, although it is possible that alternative names referred to the same type of machine. Equipment for crushing clay was variously described as a 'Crushing Mill', 'Crushing Rollers', 'Crushing Machine' and a 'Clay Crusher'.[36]

A 'Washing Machine' or 'Clay Washer', used for removing gravel or small stones, was mentioned at four tileries and referred to as either, a 'Washing Machine', 'Washing Mill' or a 'Clay Washer'.[37]

There are several references to a clay-mill or a mill for grinding clay, Figure 7.16. These may have been crushers or pug-mills. The terms were used synonymously, as described in an account of 1850, which referred to 'the pug-mill used in tile-making for pugging, or, as it is termed, grinding the clay'. In 1844 Henry Hutchinson, an authority on draining, wrote 'I would recommend the use of a pair of metal rollers, for the purpose of grinding the clay, and making it more available for the purposes to which it is applied, and it also removes pieces of stone or other things found in the clay, which very often, after the process of burning (if it is not got out) swell, and fly and crack the tiles'.[38]

O N SALE, a MILL for GRINDING CLAY, with a quantity of Shedding for Tile Drying.— Apply to Mr. Jos. Scott, Blackwell Wood.

Figure 7.16 CAS (Carlisle) *Carlisle Journal* 25th April 1851

The pug-mill, an early version of which was described in Chapter 4, contained blades attached to a central shaft, Figure 7.17, with the type and position varying between machines.

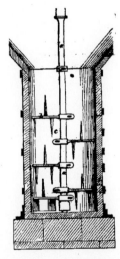

Figure 7.17 Section of a pug-mill – Klippart (1862)

Following an accident at a brick & tile-works in Carlisle in 1856, a detailed description of the operation of a pug-mill was compiled. This described how 'the pug-mill is formed of iron and circular in shape, and in which, works an upright shaft'. The clay was brought up an incline and passed between rollers onto a slide which conducted it into the pug-mill.[39]

When a tile-works was offered for sale, almost every list of plant included a pug-mill. Occasionally additional information was given as in 1873 at Cockermouth, when there was a reference to a 'Large Iron Horizontal Pug-Mill'. When Joseph Lucock advertised a steam-engine for sale in 1854, Figure 7.18, he also included all the equipment necessary to connect it to a pug-mill.

TO TILE MANUFACTURERS, AND OTHERS.
FOR SALE, by PRIVATE TREATY, a 5 Horse
High Pressure STEAM ENGINE. Diameter of
Cylinder 10 inches, Stroke 20 inches, Boiler 12 feet by 3 feet
3 inches.
 Also, all the Framing, Shafting, Gearing, &c., of a PUG
MILL, connected with the above.

Figure 7.18 CAS (Carlisle) *Carlisle Journal* 20th October 1854

Although separate pug-mills continued to be used, including one invented, and manufactured by John Whitehead, a number of tile-machines were produced with the capability to screen out stones and pug the clay.[40]

Making tiles by machine had a number of advantages over moulding by hand. The operation could be carried out by unskilled workers, a point stressed in the advertising of many manufacturers. It was only by machine that pipe-tiles could be mass produced; moulding by hand, although possible was a laborious process.

Of the other two major benefits, the ability to produce large quantities more speedily was stressed, although for small tileries, the number of tiles required in any one cycle was determined by the capacity of the drying sheds and kiln.

Probably the most important factor regarding machine-made tiles was quality; unlike with hand moulding the standard and size were consistent. This enabled a variety of sizes and shapes to be manufactured, all alike, simply by changing the dies on the machine. It is this wide range of shapes and sizes which will be examined next.

Notes

[1] Watt (2002) 49, Pusey (1843) 49

[2] Lincolnshire Archives 3ANC7/23/47 Lincolnshire Estate Letters May-Nov 1845, Watt (2002) 49-50, Bedfordshire Record Office R3/3638 cited in Cox (1979) 37

[3] Stephens (1846) vii, viii

[4] Goddard (1988) 48, Patent 6426 25/5/1833, Patent 6738 23/12/1834, Hounsell, P (2004) 'Beart, Robert (1801-1873) *ODNB*

[5] Beart (1841) 93, 98-9

[6] Pusey (1842) 175, footnote by J. French Burke 174

[7] Keene, H G (1995) 'Hay, George, eighth Marquis of Tweeddale 1787-1876' *DNB*, Keene, H G (2004) 'Hay, George, eighth Marquis of Tweeddale 1787-1876' rev. James Falkner ODNB, *NSA* (1845) Vol.2 Haddingtonshire, Yester (1835) 163, North Berwick (1839) 335, *NSA* (1845) Vol.5 Ayrshire, Coylton (1841) 659, *CJ* 11/10/1845-2/6

[8] Hunt (1841) 148-9, Parkes (1843) 370, *The Builder* (1843) Vol.1 No. XVI May 195, Pusey (1842) 174 footnote J French Burke

[9] Hunt (1841) 149, Parkes (1843) 369

[10] Bedfordshire & Luton Archives R3/44B9 Correspondence of Duke of Bedford's Steward 27/12/1841

[11] *CJ* 15/2/1845-1/2, 21/2/1846-1/3, 10/4/1847-2/1

[12] LRO (Preston) DDCa 13/262 6th March 1845, CAS (Carlisle) D Lons L15/1/1/29

[13] *JRASE* Vol.4 (1843) 460, Vol.5 (1844) 388-391, Vol.6 (1845) 318-320, Vol.7 (1846) 692-3, Vol.8 (1847) 354-7, Vol.9 (1848) 395-8, Vol.10 (1849) 547-9, Vol.16 521

[14] *CJ* 31/12/1847-2/1, 22/2/1850-2/1, 10/2/1854-1/5, 13/10/1854-1/5, Netherby ms Brown to Sir James Graham 1st March 1850 cited Humphries, A. B. *Agrarian Change in East Cumberland 1750-1900*, Thesis, University of Lancaster 1981

[15] *CJ* 18/4/1851-1/8, 4/5/1855-4/1

[16] Patent No.8966 22/5/1841, *CJ* 11/10/1845-3/4, CAS (Carlisle) D Lons L15/1/3/6

[17] *CJ* 11/10/1845-3/4, Davison (1986) 14, *CP* 15/8/1845-1/2, *TYAS* 1845 No.8 'Trial of Implements' 26-7

[18] CAS (Carlisle) D Lons L15/1/1/29, RASE (1846) *Meeting at Newcastle-upon-Tyne, The Hand-Book and Visitors Guide to the Show* Advertisement 9, *JRASE* Vol. 9 (1848) 377-421

[19] Cumbria Libraries (Carlisle) Jackson Collection N4/14 RASE *Catalogue of the various Agricultural Implements Exhibited at the Societies Show at Carlisle* 1835 Stand No.35, *CJ* 15/3/1861-1/5, 27/9/1867-1/6, Northumberland Libraries (Haltwhistle) Leaflet *Featherstone Tile Works* 23rd September 1867

[20] Ibid. N4/14 Stand No.32, *JRASE* Vol.8 (1847) 354

[21] LRO (Preston) DDCL 2232/12 Clifton of Lytham – Letters – Josiah Parkes 29th July 1847, CAS (Carlisle) D Lons L15/1/1/19 Account of Pipes at Tilery 18th September 1847 – 'Made by Scraggs Machine', op. cit. N4/14 Stand No.8, *JRASE* Vol.16 (1855) 521

[22] Klippart (1862) 342, *JRASE* Vol.9 (1848) 377-421, *JRASE* Vol.17 (1856) 571, Glasgow University Library Special Collections Dempsey, G. D. (1852) *The Machinery of the nineteenth century* Part 1 plate Clayton's patent tile, brick & pipe machine, lithograph after C. J. Light, Garnett (1849) 21-2, Binns (1851) 133, *CJ* 12/9/1851-1/2, 26/5/1854-1/6, 6/3/1863-4/1 [repeated], 24/4/1891-1/3

[23] LRO (Preston) DDCL 1186/30 August 20th 1839, Slater (1848) Preston, *JRASE* Vol.9 (1848) 396, Rawstorne (1848) 93-4, LRO (Preston) DDC/a1/118 November 1848 Holker Estate Accounts

[24] *CJ* 13/4/1855-4/4, *JRASE* Vol.16 (1855) 521, op. cit. N4/14 Stand No.65, Klippart (1862) 343, Dobson (1882) 205, *CJ* 5/5/1865-1/6, Museum of Scottish Country Life, Wester Kittochside, Land Gallery, Exhibits 17 & 18

[25] *Gazetteer of Sites and Manufacturer*, *CJ* 6/5/1859-4/6, 7/3/1862-8/5 [repeated], 13/3/1863-8/2 [repeated], 25/3/1864-1/1

[26] CAS (Carlisle) D Lons L15/1/3/6 Ainslie leaflet, *CJ* 14/7/1854-5/1, 17/11/1854-1/3, CAS (Carlisle) DX 1648/1/1, 1648/2/1

[27] *CJ* 18/7/1851-2/3, 2/3/1855-1/5, 22/2/1867-1/6

[28] Op. cit. N 4/14 Stand No. 78, *CJ* 4/3/1859-1/3, *C & W A* 20/11/1866-2/2, *CJ* 22/2/1867-1/6

[29] Op. cit. N 4/14 Stand No.93, Patent 11/10/1853 No.2336, *CN* (2000) Perriam 'Past & Present, *CJ* 27/8/1852-3/2

[30] Dobson (1850) Vol.1 43-4, *CJ* 31/12/1847-2/1, 1/5/1857-4/1

[31] Op. cit. N 4/14 Stand No.32, 35, 65, 78

[32] Allardyce (1851) 70, 72

[33] *CJ* 20/10/1854-2/2, 3/8/1855-1/, 4/1/1856-1/3, 6/.2/1857-5/3

[34] *D&GS* 18/11/1857, *D&DSA* 9/7/1862, *CJ* 13/11/1857-1/6, 21/12/1860-1/6, 5/5/1865-1/6, 23/2/1866-1/5, Northumberland Libraries (Hexham) Handbill 23/9/1867

[35] *CJ* 19/8/1870-1/2, 21/3/1873-8/2

[36] CAS (Carlisle) D Lons L15/1/3/2, *CJ* 21/8/1868-1/4, 21/12/1860-1/6, 30/5/1873-8/3, 5/12/1873-2/3, 14/12/1888-8/2, 10/1/1862-1/1, 25/7/1862-1/5, 3/2/1865-1/4, 1/4/1870-1/5 [repeated 8/4/1870]

[37] *CJ* 14/11/1856-1/6, 2/1/ 1857-1/3, 4/3/1859-1/3, 22/2/1867-1/6, 30/5/1873-8/3, OS 1st edition, 6" Sheet XXXIX, surveyed 1860, Searle (1936) 33

[38] *CJ* 10/4/1847-2/1, 25/4/1851-1/3, 4/3/1859-1/3, 10/1/1862-1/1, 25/7/1862-1/5, 7/2/1873-1/5, Dobson (1850) Part 2, 52, Hutchinson (1844) 201

[39] Klippart !862) 340, CAS (Carlisle) DX1648/2 Lawsuits, *CJ* 11/1/1856-5/3

[40] *CJ* 14/11/1856-1/6, 21/12/1860-1/6, 3/2/1865-1/4, 24/3/1865-1/5, 22/2/1867-1/6, 19/12/1873-8/3, op. cit. N 4/14 Stand No.65 & 93

8

Tiles from horseshoe to pipe

The tile of the hand-moulding period gradually evolved into the pipe-tile or tile-pipe, then finally the pipe, with a major diversion into pipes with collars, and more modest excursions into square, tapered and other shaped pipes. Unlike other objects manufactured from clay, such as bricks, roof-, floor- and wall- tiles which are visible when used, drainage-tiles were buried. The majority remain so, with new drainage systems often being laid alongside the original ones, resulting in only a small random selection of tiles reaching the surface again. It is therefore mainly from documentary evidence-accounts of tiles manufactured, together with advertisements of tiles for sale-that it is possible to give an indication of the variety of sizes and types which were in use.

Legislation [see Appendix 2] may have had some impact on tile-making in terms of dimensions and location of manufacture. In 1784 an act was passed imposing duties on bricks and tiles. Tiles for draining land came under the remit of the act, resulting, due to lobbying by agriculturalists, in a number of amending acts absolving draining tiles from duty, subject to certain conditions. The most visible one, contained in an act of 1826, exempted from duty tiles 'stamped or moulded with the word DRAIN'. Examples of such tiles are in many museum collections, both national and local, including Tullie House Museum, Carlisle. An act of 1850 finally repealed all duties on bricks and tiles.[1]

Consistency in quality and dimensions were the main achievement of 'the introduction of machinery into the manufacture of drain-tiles'. The thorough working of the clay in a pug-mill and the subsequent compression in the tile-machine greatly increased the density, and therefore the strength, of tiles. Improvements in the construction of kilns, and the acquired skill of tile-burners, resulted in tiles which were burned to a uniform texture. These were essential advances since 'if tiles are not properly or sufficiently burnt, of what use is it to put them in the ground', Under-burnt tiles were spongy, absorbed water and ultimately failed, while over-burnt tiles were brittle, apt to break when knocked, and almost always crooked.[2]

Quality was an issue from the early years of the industry, resulting in advertisements by manufacturers extolling the properties of their products. In 1834 and 1844 *Sebergham Tilery* offered 'well burnt tiles', while those from *Culgaith Tilery* in 1836 were 'all sound, hard true shaped'. Tiles from *Rydale Brick & Tile Works* at Troqueer in 1837 were of 'superior texture', and those of *Topping Castle Brick & Tile Works* in 1840 were 'very superior quality'. In the same year tiles from the *New Inn Tile Works* were 'perfectly free from any admixture of lime' - very important, as even a small quantity remaining, and being converted to quick lime by burning, would slake when subject to moisture.[3]

To satisfy the public that the quality of their articles were superior, *Moorfield Brick & Tile Works* of Kilmarnock, who in 1851 were offering tiles delivered to both Carlisle and Penrith stations, gave the following guarantee. All purchasers could 'throw aside any improperly burned or misshapen article' or any other, to which reasonable objection could be found. Emphasis on 'well-burned' continued into the 1860s and 1870s with advertisements still commenting on this aspect.[4]

The first tiles made in Cumberland had diameters of three, four and six inches, and were 12 inches in length; there was also an eight-inch diameter tile 18 inches long. The measurements of diameters related to the internal opening, with the thickness of the tile regulated according to the clay used. Lengths in different parts of the country varied between 12 and 15 inches, and continued to do so as tiles changed to pipes. In 1843 tiles available from *Toppin Castle Brick & Tile Works* were 13 inches long, which was 'the size of the tile most in use' in Cumberland by 1850. Different sizes continued to be manufactured; *Moorfield Tile Works* of Kilmarnock who advertised in the *Carlisle Journal* in 1851 offered pipes 13 ½ inches long and tiles 12 inches in length. Pipes from *Sebergham Tilery* in 1852 measured 14 inches, shorter than those introduced at *Sandysike Brick & Tile Works* in 1864, which were 15 inches or upwards. The longer the tile, the fewer required to drain an acre, as illustrated in a publication of 1846, Table 8.1. Other advantages of the 15-inch size were considered to be ease of handling and stability in the drain. In other respects the 12-inch was superior, being less likely to twist in the kiln or be damaged in transit. Finally, for calculating tiles required for given lengths of drains, the 12-inch was obviously the most convenient.[5]

Table 8.1 Number of tiles of different lengths required per imperial acre at specified distances apart.

	12 in.	13 in.	14 in.	15 in.
Drains at 12 feet apart require	3630	3316	3111	2904 per acre.
... 15	2904	2681	2489	2323 ...
... 18	2420	2234	2074	1936 ...
... 21	2074	1914	1777	1659 ...
... 24	1815	1675	1556	1452 ...
... 27	1613	1480	1383	1291 ...
... 30	1452	1340	1245	1162 ...
... 33	1320	1218	1131	1056 ...
... 36	1210	1117	1037	968 ...

Source: Stephens (1846) *A Manual of Practical Draining* page 77

As previously discussed the price of tiles was determined by several factors in addition to labour costs. These included the expenditure on coal, and the cost of its carriage, which itself was influenced by the distance it had to be transported. The quantity of coal used was dependent on the qualities of the clay, which affected the time required to burn the tiles in the kiln. Clay itself quite often had costs in the form of royalties paid to the owner of mineral rights, who was not always the landowner or tenant. In 1835 Henry Nicholson and Joseph Pearson paid to the Earl of Egremont in respect of land at Embleton a yearly rent or royalty of £4 to cover the extraction of 240 cubic yards of clay, with a further charge of four pence for each additional cubic yard. These appeared to be the standard royalties charged by the Egremont estate, as the same amounts were applied in 1835 and 1837 for clay taken from lands in the parish of Dean. Clay royalty was charged by

General Wyndham on the basis of an amount per 1000 tiles manufactured, during the 1840s and 1850s. The *Curthwaite Tilery* and *Broughton Moor Tilery* both owned by Robert Lucock, paid in 1840 and 1857 six pence per 1000 for three-inch tiles, nine pence for four-inch, and one shilling for six- inch. Similar sums were remitted by *Bigrigg Tile Works* in the same period, including three pence per 1000 for 'twisted' tiles and from 1848 four pence per 1000 for two-inch tiles.[6]

Figures from *Culgaith Brick & Tile Works* between 1885 and 1896 when the royalty charge was six pence per cubic yard gave the quantity of clay required to make 1000 tiles of each size. One and a half yards of clay were needed to make 1000 two-inch tiles, with two and one half yards for three-inch tiles and corresponding amounts given for other sizes [see Appendix 5]. The figures for 1888 showed that 358,290 tiles and bricks were manufactured requiring 717 yards of clay.[7]

The price charged to the public for the three-inch arch-tile, or horseshoe drain-tile at Netherby in 1824 was 42 shillings per 1000, with the estate obtaining them for 24 shillings. They were widely produced in a number of sizes and often came out of the kiln in a variety of imperfect shapes as illustrated in, Figure 8.1 C & D.[8]

A Cumberland   **B** Furness & Cartmel   **C & D** Dumfriesshire

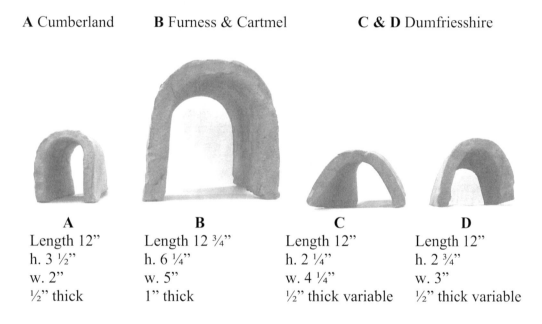

A	**B**	**C**	**D**
Length 12"	Length 12 ¾"	Length 12"	Length 12"
h. 3 ½"	h. 6 ¼"	h. 2 ¼"	h. 2 ¾"
w. 2"	w. 5"	w. 4 ¼"	w. 3"
½" thick	1" thick	½" thick variable	½" thick variable

Figure 8.1 Horseshoe tiles [internal height & width] [photographs S B Davis]

Following the introduction of machinery prices reduced dramatically as can be seen from this list of the *Eden Place Tilery* from 1852, Figure 8.2.[9]

TILES, HORSE SHOE SHAPE.

3	Inch by	2	per Thousand	...	...	19s.
3½	"	2½	"	...	...	21s.
5	"	3	"	...	...	26s.
6½	"	5	"	...	...	35s.

Figure 8.2 CAS (Carlisle) *Carlisle Journal* 15th October 1852

A list of the main sizes available up to 1862, with prices, is given in Table 8.2.

Table 8.2 Horseshoe-tiles:-sizes on sale in Cumberland with prices £ s d per 1000

Year	2 ½"	3"	4"	6"	Sources
1824		£2.02.00			Dickinson (1853) 83
1829		£2.02.00	£2.12.00	£4.04.00	Yule (1829) 394
1833		£1.10.00	£2.00.00	£3.00.00	*CJ* 2/2/1833
1834		*	*	*	*CJ* 11/1/1834, 6/9/1834
1835		*	*	*	*CJ* 31/1/1835, 1/8/1835
1836		£1.15.00	*		*CJ* 31/12/1836, CAS DCU/5/82
1837		*	*	*	*CJ* 30/12/1837
1840		*	*	*	CAS (W) D Lec/119
1841		£1.10.00	£2.00.00		CAS (W) D Lec/119
1842		£1.07.00	*	*	*CJ* 17/12/1842, D Lec/119
1843		£1.06.00	*	*	*CJ* 11/2/, 8/4/, 14/8/1843
		£1.08.00			*CJ* 12/1/1843, D Lec/119
1844		£1.02.06	£1.12.06	£2.05.00	CAS (C) D/Hud/17/158/1
1845		*	*	*	D Lec/119
1846		£1.07.06	*	*	*CJ* 12/12/1846, D Lec/119
1847		*	*	*	D Lec/119
1848		*	*	*	D Lec/119
1849		£1.01.00	£1.15.00	*	DUL Naworth C612/208
		£1.02.00			D Lec/119, *CJ* 6/4/, 21/9/1849
		£1.03.00			
		£1.05.00			
1850		£1.01.00	£1.10.00		DUL Naworth C612/208
1851	£1.02.06	19.00	£1.10.00	£1.15.00	*CJ* 18/7/, 17/10/1851
		£1.01.00	£1.15.00	£2.05.00	
		£1.05.00		£2.10.00	
1852	£1.00.00	19.00	£1.06.00	£1.15.00	CAS (W) D Lec/144
		£1.01.00	£1.15.00	£2.05.00	*CJ* 15/10/1852
		£1.02.06			
1853		£1.02.00	£1.15.00	£2.15.00	*CJ* 17/6/, 2/12/1853
		£1.06.00			Dickinson (1853) 83
1854		£1.07.06	£2.00.00	£2.15.00	*CJ* 16/6/1854
1856		£1.05.00	£1.12.06	£2.10.00	*CJ* 31/10/, 21/11/1856
			£1.15.00		
1857		£1.05.00	£1.12.06		*CJ* 9/1/1857
1858	*	*			D Lec/119
1859		£1.05.00	£1.15.00		*CJ* 4/3/1859
1860	*				D Lec/119
1861		*	*	*	*CJ* 27/12/1861
1862		£1.03.00		£5.00.00	*CJ* 19/9/1862

There were also two-inch, three-and-one-half-inch, five-inch and eight-inch diameter tiles occasionally offered for sale. The advertisement in Figure 8.3 for *Middlefoot Tile Works* still offered a horseshoe-tile, and an 'arch', the term often used for the larger diameter horseshoe shape, along with flat-bottomed pipes which were replacing them.

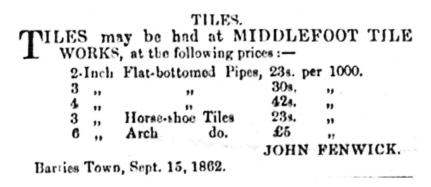

TILES.

TILES may be had at MIDDLEFOOT TILE WORKS, at the following prices :—

2-Inch Flat-bottomed Pipes, 23s. per 1000.
3   ,,   ,,   30s.   ,,
4   ,,   ,,   42s.   ,,
3   ,,   Horse-shoe Tiles   23s.   ,,
6   ,,   Arch   do.   £5   ,,

JOHN FENWICK.

Barties Town, Sept. 15, 1862.

Figure 8.3 CAS (Carlisle) *Carlisle Journal* 19th September 1862

When *Calthwaite Tile Works* closed in 1867 and all the equipment was sold, included in the auction was a quantity of horseshoe-tiles. It is possible they continued to be made and sold elsewhere after this date, as in 1873 draining-slates were still being advertised. Although these could have been used with tile-pipes, they were usually placed as soles under horseshoe-tiles.[10]

The purpose of soles, Figure 8.4, was to support the tile, particularly on soft ground, preventing it from sinking or becoming blocked with silt.

Tile on soles [D from Figure 8.1]
Sole length 12 ¾" x width 4 ½"
Thickness ½"

Flanged-tile length 14 ¼"
height 3 ¼" x width 2 ¼"
Base of each foot 1 ½"

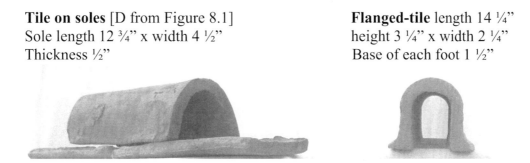

Figure 8.4 Horseshoe tile on soles and flanged-tile [photographs S B Davis]

Also in Figure 8.4 is a flanged-horseshoe-tile, used as an alternative to tile and sole but never very popular. The one illustrated is from Yorkshire. The only located advertisement in Cumberland for a flanged-tile was that of *Holme Cultram Tilery* in 1849, Figure 8.5.

2½ Inch do. with a flange 27s. 6d. per
3 Inch do. with   do.   30s.   per

Figure 8.5 CAS (Carlisle) *Carlisle Journal* 21st September 1849

Most writers on draining advocated the use of soles under horseshoe-tiles on both soft and hard ground. The usual objection to the use of manufactured clay soles was cost, and presumably for this reason only one tilery has been found in Cumberland which advertised soles, under the name of 'footing plates', Figure 8.6.

Figure 8.6 CAS (Carlisle) *Carlisle Journal* 22nd August 1840

They seem to have been more widely used in Scotland; one advertisement of 1851 by the *Moorfield Tile Manufactory* offered soles for each of their five common-drain-tiles (horseshoe tiles), a description also used by *Sebergham Tilery* in 1851. The prices of these at the works varied from eight to 20 shillings per 1000 dependent on tile size.[11]
Not all the soles used were of clay; one alternative was 'wooden soles of larch, alder and other low-priced kinds of wood', as advertised in 1839 by Carlisle Saw Mill, Figure 8.7.

Figure 8.7 CAS (Carlisle) *Carlisle Journal* 23rd February 1839

The most common substitute, as mentioned in the advertisement, was slate which was used by John Yule in 1830. In parts of the county where there were roofing slate quarries, thin offal slates provided an ideal sole. Longer lasting than wood, they were also economical to transport; it was suggested in 1842 that an ordinary cart could contain 2000. Throughout the 1850s there were numerous advertisements for drain-slates, particularly Welsh, Figure 8.8, with six by five and four by five the most common sizes.[12]

Figure 8.8 CAS (Carlisle) *Carlisle Journal* 10th March 1854

One of the first replacements for horseshoe-tiles was the small-bore-pipe with a collar, promoted strongly by Josiah Parkes, who presided over their manufacture from 1846 at *Hackthorpe Tilery*. Used widely by large estates, they replaced horseshoe-tiles in parts of Lancashire around 1846. Produced at *Lees Hill Tile Works* for the Naworth estate in 1849, in the same year they were offered to the public by *Holme Cultram Tilery*. In Furness and Cartmel they were sold by Armstrong & Hodgson at Sowerby Lodge.[13]

The pipe and collar shown in two views in Figure 8.9 were found in north Cumberland and probably date from the late 1840s or early 1850s.

Pipe & full collar – two views   **Location** Cumberland - Bewcastle
Pipe – length 13"   Collar – length 3"
Internal height1 ¼" x width 1 ½"   Internal height 2 ¾" x width 3"
Thickness of clay between ½" & ¾"

Figure 8.9 Pipe & collar [photographs S B Davis]

The illustration in Figure 8.10 depicts a pipe and half-collar from Dumfriesshire. This cross between a collar and a sole appears to be unusual, as no advertisements for this type have been found.

Pipe & half collar – two views   **Location** Scotland – Dumfriesshire
Pipe – length 13 ¼"   Collar – length approx 4"
Internal height 2" x width 2"   Internal height 2" x width 4"
                                                              Thickness of clay varies between ½"
                                                              and ¾" for both pipe & collar

Figure 8.10 Pipe and half collar [photographs S B Davis]

Pipes with collars were advertised in the Carlisle area during the 1850s by a number of works, particularly by the *Eden Place Tilery* Figure 8.11, and from 1852, by its associated works at Chapel Hill and Cocklakes.

EDEN PLACE TILERY, CARLISLE-
—
PRICES FOR THE ENSUING SEASON.
DRAINING PIPES, CIRCULAR OR WITH FLAT
BOTTOMS.

1 Inch, per Thousand...	...	...	...	12s.
1¼ „ „	...	...	...	15s.
2 „ „	...	...	...	19s.
2½ „ „	...	...	...	22s.
3 „ „	...	...	...	25s.
4 „ „	...	...	...	30s.
5 „ „	...	...	...	36s.
6 „ „	...	...	...	44s.
1½ Inch COLLAR, per Thousand	...	3s. 6d.
2 „ „	...	4s. 6d.
2½ „ „	...	5s. 6d.
2¾ „ „	...	6s. 0d.

Figure 8.11 CAS (Carlisle) *Carlisle Journal* 15th October 1852

The common sizes on sale in Cumberland between 1849 and 1865 are detailed in Table 8.3 with their prices. After this date the only located offers for sale are at the closure of tileries in 1867 and 1878, when the stock, including pipes and collars, was auctioned.[14]

Table 8.3 Pipes & Collars: – sizes on sale in Cumberland – prices £ s p per 1000

Year	1"	1 ¼"	1 ½"	2"	2 ½"	Sources
1849	£1.02.00	£1.05.00	£1.11.00			DUL C612/208
			£1.05.00	£1.15.00		*CJ* 21/9/1849
1850	18.00	£1.00.00	£1.02.00	£1.12.00		C612/208
1851			18.06	£1.03.06	£1.07.06	*CJ* 17/10/1851
	18.00	£1.00.00	£1.02.00	£1.12.00		C612/208
	£1.01.00		£1.05.00	£1.11.00		*CJ* 18/7/1851
1852			18.06	£1.03.06	£1.07.06	*CJ* 15/10/1852
			£1.02.06			*CJ* 5/11/1852
		£1.01.00	£1.05.00	£1.10.00		*CJ* 17/12/1852
1853	19.00		£1.03.06	£1.11.00		*CJ* 17/6/, 11/11/, 2/12/,
1854			£1.07.06	£1.15.00		*CJ* 16/6/1854
			£1.05.00	£1.12.06		*CJ* 15/12/1854
1855	19.00		£1.03.06	£1.11.00		DUL C612/209
			£1.05.00	£1.12.06		*CJ* 26/1/1855
1856			£1.05.00	£1.12.06		*CJ* 4/1/, 31/10/, 21/11/
1857			£1.05.00	£1.10.00		*CJ* 9/1/, 17/4/1857
1858			*			CAS (W) D Lec/119
1859			£1.05.00	£1.11.00		*CJ* 4/3/1859
1860			*			D Lec/119
1861			*			*CJ* 27/12/1861
1865				*		*CJ* 5/5/1865

Sources: CAS (Carlisle), CAS (Whitehaven), DUL Durham University Library

The period during which the tile evolved into the pipe produced a range of shapes from horseshoe-tiles with an integral sole to pipes with a slightly flattened base, Figure 8.12.

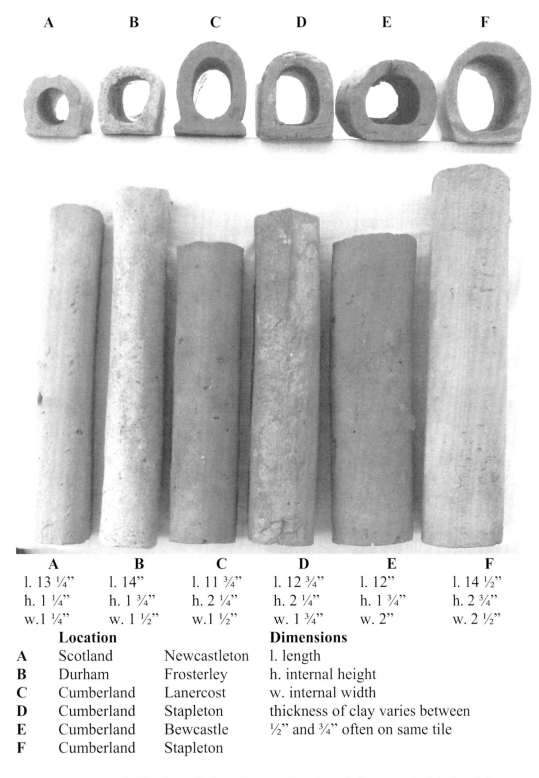

	A	B	C	D	E	F
l.	13 ¼"	14"	11 ¾"	12 ¾"	12"	14 ½"
h.	1 ¼"	1 ¾"	2 ¼"	2 ¼"	1 ¾"	2 ¾"
w.	1 ¼"	1 ½"	1 ½"	1 ¾"	2"	2 ½"

	Location		Dimensions
A	Scotland	Newcastleton	l. length
B	Durham	Frosterley	h. internal height
C	Cumberland	Lanercost	w. internal width
D	Cumberland	Stapleton	thickness of clay varies between
E	Cumberland	Bewcastle	½" and ¾" often on same tile
F	Cumberland	Stapleton	

Figure 8.12 Flat-based pipe-tiles or tile-pipes [photograph S B Davis].

These pipe-tiles were advertised either under that name or, by the 1860s, as 'pipes flat bottomed or circular'. In the USA tiles that were of a horseshoe shape with an integral sole were named 'sole-tiles' while round pipes with a flattened base were 'sole-pipes'[15]

In Cumberland the standard three-inch pipe-tile varied between one pound ten and one pound fifteen shillings per 1000 in the 1850s and 1860s, Table 8.4. The exception was 1851 when Joseph Rome at Stanwix sold that size at one pound five shillings per 1000.

Table 8.4 Pipe-tiles & pipes: – sizes on sale in Cumberland – prices £ s p per 1000

Year	2 ½"	3"	4"	5"	6"	Sources
1850		£1.15.00	£2.00.00			DUL C612/208
1851		£1.05.00	£1.10.00	£1.16.00	£2.04.00	CJ 17/10/1851
		£1.15.00	£2.00.00			C612/208
1853	£1.05.00	£1.10.00	£2.00.00	£2.10.00	£3.05.00	CJ 17/6/, 11/11/, 2/12/
1854		£1.12.06	£2.02.06			CJ 16/6/1854
					£4.04.00	CJ 15/12/1854
1855	£1.05.00	£1.10.00	£2.00.00		£4.00.00	C612/209
		£1.12.06	£2.02.06		£4.04.00	CJ 26/1/1855
1856		£1.12.06	£2.02.06	£2.10.00	£6.05.00	CJ 4/1/, 31/10/1856
			£2.02.00		£4.10.00	CJ 21/11/1856
1857		£1.12.06	£2.02.06		£6.05.00	CJ 9/1/1857
	£1.05.00			£4.00.00		CJ 17/4/1857
1858	*	*	*	*	*	CAS (W) D Lec/119
1859		£1.12.06	£2.02.06		£6	CJ 4/3/1859
1860	*	*	*	*	*	D Lec/119
1861		*	*		*	CJ 27/12/1861
1862		£1.10.00	£2.02.00			CJ 19/9/1862
1869	£1.02.06	£1.10.00	£2.00.00		£5.00.00	CJ 12/11/1869
1893	£1.10.00					Billhead
1900	£1.15.00	£2.05.00	£3.10.00		£7.00.00	CAS DBS/529/2/3

Sources: CAS (Carlisle), DUL Durham University Library, CAS (Whitehaven)

In Westmorland in 1860 at *Gaythorn Tilery* the three-inch pipes were two pounds five shillings per 1000, with the two-inch, here and at *Bleatarn Tilery,* sold at one pound five shillings. According to one writer, in the northern part of Westmorland in 1868, two-inch pipes cost about one pound two shillings and six pence per 1000, while in the Kendal district which contained no clay, tiles imported from Lancashire cost about twenty shillings per 1000. Prices in parts of Lancashire in 1851 were broadly similar to those in Cumberland, with the three-inch pipe-tile selling at thirty shillings per 1000 and the four-inch at forty shillings.[16]

During the 1850s several of types of tiles were available in Cumberland, as can be seen in an advertisement for the tileries owned by John Howe, Figure 8.13.

TILES AND DRAINING PIPES.
CHAPEL HILL, NEAR WREAY.
EDEN PLACE, STANWIX, CARLISLE.

List of Prices for this Season :—

6-inch Pipes (Flat Bottom) .... £6 5 0 per Thousand.			
4-inch ,, ,, ... 2 2 6 ,,			
3-inch ,, ,, ... 1 12 6 ,,			
2-inch ,, ,, ... 1 2 0 ,,			
1½-inch Pipe, with Collar .... 1 5 0 ,,			
3-inch Horse-shoe Tiles (Chapel Hill only) .... 1 5 0 ,,			
4-inch ,, ,, ... 1 12 6 ,,			

For Prices at the Railway Stations on the Lancaster, Maryport, Caledonian, Newcastle, Port Carlisle, and Silloth lines, apply to   **JOHN HOWE.**
Carlisle, October 30th, 1856.

Figure 8.13 CAS (Carlisle) *Carlisle Journal* 31st October 1856

Gradually the width of the flat-bottom was reduced to become only a very narrow strip, often hardly discernable, but sufficient to stop the pipe rolling, Figure 8.14.

NBL Blenkinsopp   CUL Stapleton   DUR Frosterley   SCT Dumfriesshire

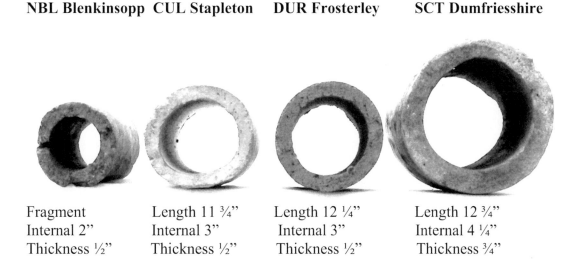

Fragment	Length 11 ¾"	Length 12 ¼"	Length 12 ¾"
Internal 2"	Internal 3"	Internal 3"	Internal 4 ¼"
Thickness ½"	Thickness ½"	Thickness ½"	Thickness ¾"

Figure 8.14 Pipes [photographs S B Davis]

A large variety of shapes and sizes of pipes were manufactured nationally; different tile-machine manufacturers, agriculturalists and drainers had their own preferred shapes and sizes. These authorities continued to promote alternative opinions throughout the nineteenth-century, helping to maintain the continued variety. One preference for the oval or egg-shaped pipe was rebutted in a book of 1870 whose writer considered wider bottoms superior, but the egg shape still found favour in 1911 when it was described 'as the most perfect form to adopt'. It was suggested that 'such a pipe being narrowest at the lowest point and gradually widening towards the top, the best possible flow of water is maintained, and the drain therefore has a better chance of clearing itself than if constructed of cylindrical tiles.[17]

An example of another design, a tapered pipe, not egg-shaped in diameter, is shown in Figure 8.15; this is from Ayrshire, although a similar shape of smaller diameter was also used in Durham.

Figure 8.15 Tapered pipe-tile 14 ¾ inches long, splayed end 2 ½ inches diameter, tapered end 1 ½ inches diameter [photograph S B Davis]

The tapered end of one tile would be inserted into the wider-splayed end of the next tile being laid. The narrowest end was always placed at the downward point of the drains incline. Tapered pipes were not included in a list of types available from the *Moorfield Tile Manufactory* in Kilmarnock, Figure 8.16, whose pipes were oval in shape. Still available from them in 1851 was an extensive range of horseshoe-tiles described as 'Common Drain Tiles'.

PIPE TILES, OVAL INSIDE, AND FLAT-SOLED.—Q Q Q

13¾ in. long, 4 x 3½ ....
13½   ,,   3 x 2½ ....
13½   ,,   2½ x 2 ....
13½   ,,   2 x 1¾ ....
13½   ,,   1½ x 1¼ ....

COMMON DRAIN TILES.

12 in. long, 6 in. deep, 5 in. wide—No. 1, or Mair
        Drain Tiles ....
    Soles to Ditto. ....
12 in. long, 5 in. deep, 4 in. wide—No. 2 Mains......
    Soles to Ditto. ....
12 in. long, 4 in. deep, 3 in. wide—No. 3, or Furrow
        Tiles ....
    Soles to Ditto. ....
12 in. long, 3½ in. deep, 3 in. wide—No. 4, Tiles ......
    Soles to Ditto. ....
12 in. long, 2½ in. deep, 2 in. wide—No. 5, or 2-inch
        Tiles ....
    Soles to Ditto. ....

Figure 8.16 CAS (Carlisle) *Carlisle Journal* 12th September 1851

In Scotland, as in Cumberland, the use of horseshoe-tiles continued alongside pipes. The *Mossneuk Tile-Works* of Beith in Ayrshire in 1862 was offering 'Common Tiles with Soles, Small Tiles with Soles and Large Tiles Nos. 1, 2 and 3 with Large Soles as well as Pipe-Tiles' in two sizes.[18]

Another tile with a distinct shape, most likely manufactured in Scotland but found in a drainage system in north Cumberland, is illustrated in Figure 8.17. No other 'square-pipe' has been located elsewhere in the county.[19].

Figure 8.17 'Square-pipe' personal collection [photograph S B Davis]

It was not the practice of manufactures to put their names on tiles, as many did with bricks- a reasonable decision as the articles were to be buried. This, coupled with the fact that with the opening of railways tiles were transported considerable distances, means that it is rarely possible to identify the works at which a tile was made. However, the types of tiles manufactured at a particular establishment can occasionally be identified by the rejects of kiln burnings - the burst, bent and twisted tiles found on the refuse mounds of a tilery site, Figure 8.18.

Threlkeld	**Kirkcambeck**	**Blenkinsopp**
Fragment of a pipe-tile	Fragment of pipe tile	12 ¾" long-curved
Flat base 2 ¾"	probably 2" internal	2" internal

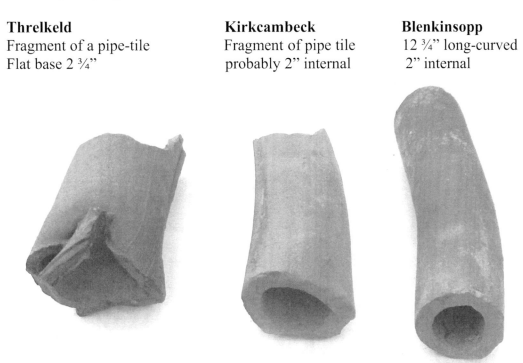

Figure 8.18 Misshapen rejects [photograph S B Davis]

In addition to tiles, most tile-works usually manufactured at least one type of brick, often for use in re-flooring and repairing their own kiln. In the western division of Cumberland a number of works utilised the local fire-clay to made fire-bricks. Throughout most parts of Cumberland and Westmorland two types of bricks were manufactured alongside tiles. These were perforated-bricks and hollow-bricks, Figure 8.19. The difference was that a perforated-brick had ten holes while the hollow-brick had only two, running lengthwise as seen in the illustration of the end view.

[a] Perforated-brick   [b] Hollow-brick

Figure 8.19 Perforated-brick & hollow-brick [photograph S B Davis]

As mentioned in the previous chapter, Thomas Nelson erected a manufactory in Carlisle to produce perforated-bricks. Hollow-bricks were also manufactured in the city, being offered for sale by *Eden Place Tilery* in 1853. A great advocate of the use of hollow-bricks when erecting farm buildings was John Grey of Dilston, agent for the northern estates of Greenwich Hospital. In a talk to the Hexham farmers' club in 1852, he referred not only to the importance of draining but encouraged the use of hollow-bricks and described buildings in which he had utilised them.[20]

Transporting the diverse range of pipes and tiles presented problems, with the quantity which could be carried by one cart determined in part by the condition of roads and tracks between the kiln and the lands to be drained. The weight of pipes (see Appendix 5) was dependent on the density of the clay; the widely-used three-inch diameter pipe weighed between 34 to 36 cwt per 1000, and the four-inch 45 to 47 cwt per 1000. In 1830 John Yule calculated that a single horse cart carried 250 tiles of various sizes. Comments from Scotland in 1847 illustrated the impact of distance on the quantity carried. When carrying 12-inch tiles from a kiln 20 miles away, using a single horse cart similar to those common in Cumberland, three journeys were required for 1000 tiles. Over a shorter distance, where the kiln was only one mile from the farm, a single horse cart could carry 450 tiles 15 inches in length together with 900 soles.[21]

The railways resolved the problem of moving tiles over longer distances, although tiles still had to be carried from station to field. Probably the first tilery in Cumberland to utilise it was the *Toppin Castle Tile Works* which in 1840 advertised that 'there is every facility for carriage along the railway'. It was from 1850 that some tile-works as a matter of course offered to deliver to railway stations. As to be expected from its location on the edge of Carlisle, the *Eden Place Tilery* at Stanwix was at the forefront and quoted prices for delivery to stations on 'the Lancaster, Caledonian, Dumfries, Newcastle & Maryport lines'.

A small number of tileries also used sea transport; one of these was *Brickhouse Tile Works* at Kirkbean, which had 'a shipping wharf within one hundred yards of the kiln where vessels drawing from eight to nine feet of water can load with safety'. Another Scottish tilery, *Moorfield Brick & Tile Manufactory*, advertised prices for tiles 'put on board in Troon Harbour'. In Cumberland, Joseph Lucock shipped bricks from Maryport in 1862, and the *Whitehaven Fire Brick Company* in 1869 advertised that field-drain-pipes could be forwarded by shipping to all parts of the United Kingdom.[22]

It is not possible to calculate the exact number of tiles that were being produced annually but some estimates and figures are available. According to William Dickinson in 1850, 27 tile manufactories in the western division of Cumberland made about ten million tiles per annum. Individual totals for a number of tileries are available from a variety of sources; Table 8.5 gives details of a number of these.

Table 8.5 Annual production of a selection of Cumberland tileries

Year	Quantity	Tilery	Source
1828	300,000	CUL Langrigg	*CJ* 5/4/1828-1/4
1836/7	114,719	CUL Winscales	CAS (W) DCu/5/82
1840	420.777	CUL Curthwaite	CAS (W) D/Lec 119
1840	307,273	CUL Broughton Moor	CAS (W) D/Lec 119
1841	316,149	DFS Woodhouse Lees	Bell (1843) 739
1842	243,000	DFS Woodhouse Lees	Bell (1843) 739
1842	320,327	CUL Westward Park	CAS (W) D/Lec 119
1854	300,000	CUL Brackenhill	*CJ* 10/3/1854-4/1
1883	250,000	CUL Broadfield	*CJ* 13/7/1883-7/8

Sources: CAS (Whitehaven), CAS (Carlisle) *Carlisle Journal*

Other tileries were producing much larger quantities. In 1846 *Toppin Castle Tile Works* advertised 'to be let the making and burning of 1,000,000 tiles'. *Sandysike Brick & Tile Works* in September 1864 had 400,000 tiles ready for the draining season. In Westmorland at *Hackthorpe Tilery* between April 1847 and April 1848 559,668 pipes of various sizes and 491,954 collars were made.

Other areas produced similar quantities. In Northumberland at Stanton near Morpeth, a tile-works was capable of manufacturing 700,000 to 900,000 annually, and another Northumberland tilery in 1856 required 500,000 tiles to be made and burned.

At Annan, in 1862 the *Whinnyrigg Tile Works* claimed that with three kilns operating for seven or eight months of the year, they produced 220,000 tiles and bricks per month.[23]

It was during this period, when these tileries were producing large quantities of tiles, that the peak in terms of numbers of tile-works was reached. The next chapter begins by describing the position in the late 1840s and through the 1850s when more tile-works operated in Cumberland than at any other time.

Notes

[1] Details of all Acts are listed in Appendix 2, Tullie House Museum Tile & Pipe Collection Horse-shoe Tiles marked DRAIN 1826, 1829, 1832, Museum of Scottish Country Life, Land Gallery, Completely Drained Exhibits No's 19 & 20, Museum of English Rural Life Objects 89/42/1-2

[2] Stephens (1846) 76-7, Hutchinson (1844) 191

[3] *CJ* 28/2/1835-3/4, 23/1/1836-2/4, 16/3/1844-1/3, 7/10/1837-2/7, 4/3/1843-2/6, 22/8/1840-2/3 Randall (1877) 224

[4] *CJ* 12/9/1851-2/1&2 with orders accepted by Thomas Thompson, Dockray Hall, Penrith, 12/11/1869-1/4, 1/3/1878-1/7

[5] Yule (1830) 66, Stephens (1846) 77, Hutchinson (1844) 197, Scot (1847) 156-7, Dickinson (1850) 34, *CJ* 4/3/1843-2/6, 12/9/1851-2/1, 17/12/1852-1/2, 30/9/1864-1/2

[6] CAS (Whitehaven) D Lec/219 Clay Royalty, Embleton 20/4/1835, D Lec/116 Dean 16/2/1835 & 6/2/1837, D Lec/119 Notebook Curthwaite & Broughton Moor 1840 & 1857, Bigrigg 1840-1850

[7] CAS (Carlisle) DB 74/2/41/21 Account of Clay used at Culgaith Tilery 1885-1896

[8] Dickinson (1853) 83, Yule (1829) 394, Phillips (1989) 159

[9] Dickinson (1853) 83, *CJ* 15/10/1852-1/2

[10] *CJ* 22/2/1867-1/6, 21/11/1873-8/1

[11] Stephens (1846) 75, *CJ* 22/8/1840-2/3, 18/7/1851-2/3, 12/9/1851-2/1&2

[12] *CJ* 23/2/1839-1/1, 30/8/1859-1/2 Norway Drain Battens, Yule (1830) 65, Dickinson (1850) 34, Stephens (1846) 75, *DT* 28/3/1842-1/C, *CJ* 11/5/1860-1/1, 10/2/1854-1/5, 10/3/1854-1/2, 16/6/1854-1/4, 15/9/1854-1/3, 18/1/1856-1/3, 5/12/1856-1/2, 26/10/1849-2/4, 8/11/1872-8/2, 21/11/1873-8/1

[13] CAS (Carlisle) D Lons L15/1/1/19, Fletcher (1962) 111, Durham University Library Special Collections Naworth C612/205, *CJ* 21/9/1849-2/3, *SUA* 22/2/1849

[14] *CJ* 22/2/1867-1/6, 3/5/1878-1/2

[15] *CJ* 18/7/1851-2/3, CAS (Kendal) WD DF Box 17/15 *Bleatarn Tilery*, *CJ* 30/9/1864-1/2, 21/9/1866-1/1, Weaver (1964) 125, 128

[16] CAS (Kendal) WD DF Box 17/15 *Gaythorn & Bleatarn Tilery*, Webster (1868) 25, Binns (1851) 17

[17] Laws (1850) Plate 5, Davison (1986) 19, Hozier (1870) 27, Harpur (1911) 67

[18] Tapered tiles from personal collection, Billhead *Mossneuk Tile-Works* 24/12/1862 in personal collection

[19] Douglas & Oglethorpe (1993) 17, with thanks to Alan Oliver for this square tile

[20] *CJ* 2/12/1853-1/4, 23/1/1852-4/4, Pevsner 91992) 252, 286, 372

[21] Mitchell (1894) 43, Yule (1830) 66, Scot (1847) 56-7

[22] CJ 5/9/1840-2/4, 17/10/1851-2/3, *DT* 9/6/1840-1/A, 14/6/1841-1/E, *CJ* 12/9/1851-2/1&2, 7/1/1862-2/4, Slater (1869) advert

[23] Dickinson (1850) 34, *CJ* 19/12/1846-2/2, 30/9/1864-1/2, CAS (Carlisle) D Lons L15/1/1/13 Pipe-tiles made,, *CJ* 23/9/1853-1/3, 4/1/1856-1/3, *D&GS&A* 9/7/1862-3/E

9

Tile-making at its peak c.1845-c.1869

At the end of 1837 there were 36 tileries operating in the county of Cumberland. Since that date the demand for tiles grew, as did the expertise of the tile-making industry, facilitated by the introduction of machinery in the mid-1840s. According to the section on agriculture in Mannix & Whellan's directory of 1847, the agriculture of Cumberland was in a 'high state of perfection' with 'that excellent system of tile-draining' assiduously attended to.

During the subsequent 10 years from 1845, the peak of tile-making, in terms of the number of tileries, was reached in Cumberland. Other northern counties experienced similar, although not identical, patterns of growth.

Tileries could be grouped into two broad categories. The first, estate and farm tileries, could be divided into those that manufactured exclusively for their own use and those which also sold tiles to the public. The second category was commercial tileries, whose customers were estates and farms without their own means of manufacture. These could also be split into two groups. The first were those who, although they produced some bricks, were essentially tileries. The second were commercial brick-works who also manufactured draining as well as other types of tiles, although usually only for a limited period.

It is impossible to know with certainty whether any one tilery, and particularly those in the first group, produced tiles every year. Many in both categories had dormant periods when for a variety of reasons manufacturing did not take place. The letting of a contract to make a quantity of tiles for a specific draining project could be followed by months when no further tiles were required. Accordingly it cannot be stated categorically that a given number of tileries were active in any one year. What can be determined by using the earliest and the latest date that each tilery appeared in a source was the period when a tilery existed, and therefore could have been manufacturing. In certain cases these sources record the actual commencement and closure of a tilery; in others the information is not as specific.

Using these earliest and latest recorded dates, it is possible to state that in Cumberland the 1850s was the period with the largest number of tile, and brick & tile-works operating. This peak of 75 works was preceded by 63 in the 1840s and followed by 62 in the 1860s with dramatic declines in numbers in subsequent decades.

The prominent writer on Cumberland agriculture, William Dickinson, who won prizes for his publications, was also a tile-manufacturer and joint owner of a number of tileries. His figures for the number of tileries in both the eastern and western divisions of Cumberland can therefore be accepted as authoritative. Using the earliest located dates, Table 9.1 gives a list of what are believed to be the 27 'drain-tile manufactories' described by William Dickinson as having been established in the western division by 1850.[1] Excluded from this list is Robert Smithson who appeared in Tables 3.1 and 5.1, but for whom no references after 1829 have been located.

Table 9.1 Tile-works in the western division of Cumberland before 1850

	Earliest Date	**Parish**	**Tile Works or Manufacturer**
1	1824	Bromfield	*Langrigg Tilery*
2	1829	Cockermouth	*Kirkgate Brick & Tile Works*
3	1829	"	William Mackreath Brick & Tile Maker
4	1830	Bridekirk	*Broughton Moor Brick & Tile Works*
5	1831	Westward	*Curthwaite Brick & Tile Works*
6	1835	Maryport	Nicholson & Pearson
7	1836	Plumbland	Robert Lucock
8	1836	Workington	*Winscales Tile Works*
9	1836	Dean	*High & Low Edge Tile Works*
10	1837	Camerton	*Seaton Tile Works*
11	1840	Egremont	*Bigrigg Tile Works*
12	1841	Arlecdon	*Dickinson & Dalzell*
13	1841	Aspatria	*Brayton Demesne Tile Works*
14	1841	Westward	*Westward Park Tilery*
15	1841	Bassenthwaite	*Bassenthwaite Tile Kiln*
16	1841	Bolton	*Bolton Tile Works*
17	1841	Bootle	*Bootle Tile Works*
18	1841	Irton	*Irton Tile Kiln*
19	1841	Millom	*Dickinson, Dalzell & Co*
20	1841	Brigham	*Jonah Dixon*
21	1841	Drigg	*Dickinson, Dalzell & Thompson*
22	1842	Isel	*Sunderland Tile Works*
23	1843	Caldbeck	*Caldbeck Tile Works*
24	1847	Workington	*Thomas Greggins*
25	1847	Brigham	*Hundith Hill Tile Works*
26	1847	Dearham	*Dearham Tile Works*
27	1849	Holme Cultram	*Abbey Tile Works*

Sources: *Gazetteer of Sites and Manufacturers*

The sources in the *Gazetteer* give the earliest date but only four of these refer to the actual year that the tilery opened. One of these was opened 1841 but for the remaining nine, the reason for citing 1841 was that tile-makers were living adjacent to the tilery site in the census of that year.. Similarly with 1847, a directory of that year provided the information regarding three works. These 13 tileries may all have commenced at an earlier date, although this would not necessarily alter the accuracy of the overall comparison with William Dickinson's figure.

Two individuals, as has been noted, were important in tile-making in the western division; the first was Robert Lucock, owner of numbers one, four, five and seven in the list. The other, William Dickinson had an interest in numbers 11, 12, 19 and 21. It can be seen in Figure 9.1 that compared to the late 1830s (Figure 5.7), not only had the number of tileries increased, but they had spread much further towards the south of Cumberland.

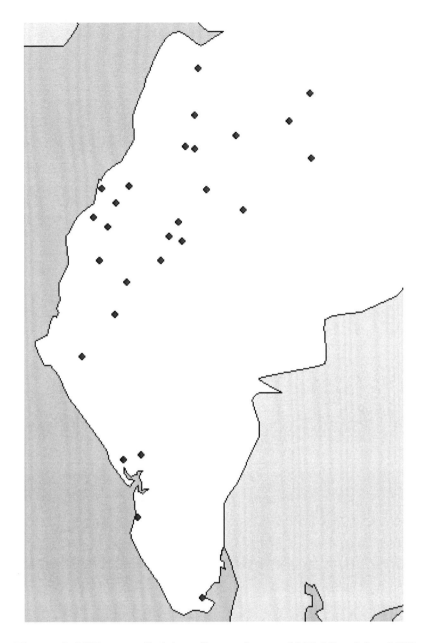

Figure 9.1 Western division tile-works pre 1850 [Gen Map UK]

William Dickinson in his *Essay on the Agriculture of East Cumberland* (Figure 9.2) also recorded the greater number of tileries in that division, totaling 42 in 1851.

In the Press, and nearly ready, DICKINSON'S
PRIZE ESSAY on the FARMING of EAST CUM-
BERLAND. THURNAM, Carlisle.

Figure 9.2 CAS (Carlisle) *Carlisle Journal* 6th May 1853

Using the same method as for the western division, Table 9.2 is an attempt to identify these 42 tileries which had been erected in the east of Cumberland by the end of 1851.

Table 9.2 Tile-works in the eastern division of Cumberland before 1852

	Earliest Date	**Parish**	**Tile Works or Manufacturer**
1	1821	Arthuret	*Sandysike Brick & Tile Works*
2	1821	Stanwix	*Linstock Tile Works*
3	1823	Rockliff	*Petersyke Tile Works*
4	1827	Brampton	*Middle Farm Tile Works*
5	1829	Bowness	Joshua Ward
6	1831	Burgh by Sands	John Glaister
7	1831	Sebergham	*Sebergham Tilery*
8	1831	Kirklinton	*Young's Close Tile Works*
9	1831	Castle Sowerby	*Lambfield Tile Works*
10	1833	Beaumont	*Beaumont Brick & Tile Works*
11	1833	Hayton	*Toppin Castle Brick & Tile Works*
12	1834	Wigton	*Parkgate Tilery*
13	1834	Kingmoor	Richard Wright
14	1834	Stanwix	*Eden Place Tile Works*
15	1834	Irthington	*Laversdale Lane End Tile Works*
16	1834	Bowness	*Millrigg Tile Works*
17	1835	Arthuret	*Netherby Tile & Brick Works*
18	1835	Stapleton	*Crossings Tile Works*
19	1835	Lanercost	*Kirkcambeck Tile Works*
20	1835	Carlisle	*Wragmire Tile Works*
21	1836	Kirkland	*Culgaith Brick & Tile Works*
22	1837	Stapleton	*Middlefoot Brick & Tile Works*
23	1837	Wreay	*Potter Pits Tile Works*
24	1838	Scaleby	*Longpark Tile Works*
25	1839	Stanwix	*Houghton Tile Works*
26	1839	Hesket-in-the-Forest	*Calthwaite Tile Works*
27	1839	Hesket-in-the-Forest	*New Inn Tile Works*
28	1840	Walton	*Leaps Rigg Brick & Tile Works*
29	1840	Kirkbride	*Pow Hill Brick & Tile Works*
30	1841	Kirklinton	*Newbiggin Tile Works*
31	1841	Hayton	*Allen Grove Brick & Tile Works*
32	1841	Wetheral	*Cumwhinton Tile Works*
33	1841	Penrith	Tile Works
34	1846	Greystoke	*Johnby Brick & Tile Works*
35	1847	Stapleton	*Cracrop Tile Works*
36	1849	Lanercost	*Lees Hill Tile Works*
37	1850	Irthington	*Glebe Farm Tile Yard*
38	1851	Greystoke	*Threlkeld Brick & Tile Works*
39	1851	Kirkandrews-upon-Esk	*Barns Tilery*
40	1851	Bowness	*Glasson Tile Kilns*
41	1851	Arthuret	*Brackenhill Tile Works*
42	1851	Carlisle	*Murrell Hill Brick & Tile Works*

Sources: *Gazetteer of Sites and Manufacturers*

The majority of the 36 tileries operating in the late 1830s (Table 5.1) were located in the eastern division of Cumberland; only 25% were in the western division. Therefore in 1839 there were 27 tileries in the east, mainly situated in the north of the division, around the area where tile-making began. Most of the 15 new works were in the same area, with one near Penrith and two in Greystoke Parish being the exceptions. The result is a very similar pattern in Figure 9.3 to that in Figure 5.7 which illustrated the spread in 1839.

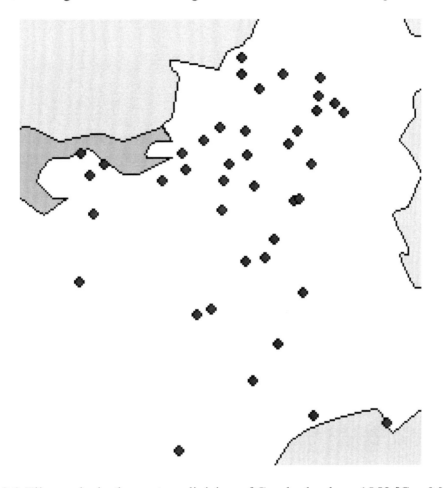

Figure 9.3 Tile-works in the eastern division of Cumberland pre 1852 [Gen Map UK]

This distribution of tile-works in both divisions was the result not only of demand for tiles in the area but also reflected the availability of the raw material for their manufacture. As previously mentioned, boulder clay was prevalent on the lower ground of both sides of the Pennines; it is the most extensive of the drift deposits of the Penrith district, although absent in some tracts. In the west of Cumberland, mudstones from the coal measures were a source of brick-clay at Whitehaven, and a sandy till was used for brick and tile-making at Drigg. Fire-clay, associated with coal seams, was used in brick-making, at separate establishments, such as Robert Lucock's *Broughton Moor Fire Brick Works*, which was adjacent to his tile-works. Fire-bricks were also manufactured at Maryport by Robert Hinde from 1856, where he also produced common-bricks and draining-tiles. It was in the western division of Cumberland that it was necessary to prefix 'tile' with 'draining', as other fire-clay blocks, described as 'tiles', were produced.[2]

Although Westmorland contained less than one tenth of the overall number of tileries in Cumberland, their rise and decline presented a later but very similar pattern. Tile-making did not arrive in the county until the 1840s when two tileries were constructed. During the 1850s the total increased to seven, with the peak of eight being reached in the 1860s, by which time one of the tileries opened in the 1850s seems to have closed. There followed a steady decline until by the early 1900s only two remained open.[3]

The account of agriculture in a Westmorland directory of 1851 included the comment that 'tile draining also has been introduced'. Another in 1860 described how towards the east and north of the county the soil was more inclined to clay which required draining. It then proceeded to recount how 'of late years considerable improvement has taken place in the cultivation of the county. Draining the heavy lands has been much attended to'. The narrative continued in 1868, when an article on 'The Farming of Westmorland' recorded that tile-draining had progressed considerably. There were then tile-works on the northern side of the county, although in the Kendal district where there was no clay, tiles were brought in from Lancashire.[4] The locations of these Westmorland tileries are shown in Figure 9.4.

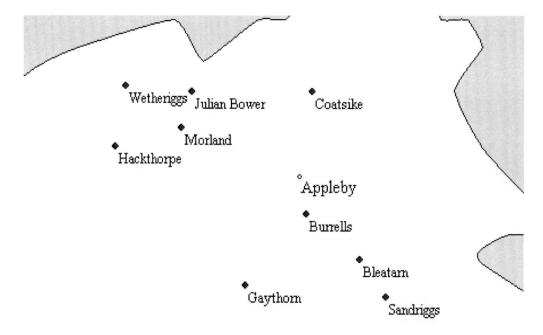

Figure 9.4 Westmorland tile-works [Gen Map UK]

In Lancashire by the 1850s it was reported that 'the demand for draining tiles is so great that they cannot be made fast enough at the numerous tile manufactories, which are now established in every part of the county'. Tileries were active in the 1840s on the Lytham estates of Thomas Clifton, and at Barton near Preston, where according to a report of 1849 'a large brickyard and tilery had been at work for more than 15 years'. During the 1850s tiles were being made at the *Hollowforth Tile Works* which advertised in the *Carlisle Journal* in 1859. On the Quernmore Park estate near Lancaster, a tilery was set up early in the decade to make tiles for the estate.[5]

North of the Sands, mention has already been made of the Earl of Burlington's tilery at Reake Wood, on his Holker Estate, and of two others in Low Furness. These and other locations where tiles are known to have been made are shown on Figure 9.5.

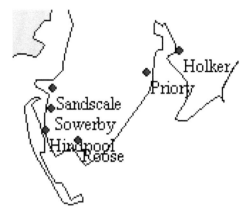

Figure 9.5 Tile-works in Furness & Cartmel [Gen Map UK]

The active period of all of these establishments was the 1850s and early 1860s; four were located in the parish of Dalton, one in Cartmel and one in Ulverston. There was also another possible manufacturer of draining-tiles in Ulverston; this was Isaac Ireland who was employed at the *Holker Tilery* in its early years. He later described himself in a directory of 1851 as 'a Brick & Tile Manufacturer of Ulverston', although in the census of the same year, he and his two sons gave their occupations as brick-makers.
During the rapid growth of Barrow there was huge demand for bricks, resulting in the setting up of many brick-works, some of which described themselves as 'brick & tile-works' although there is no indication whether these were making draining-tiles.[6]

In Northumberland there was a dramatic increase in the number of tile-works in the 1840s, with what appears to be a similar situation in County Durham. The peak in numbers in Northumberland occurred in the late 1850s and early 1860s akin, but not identical, to the pattern in Cumberland.[7]
Where the eastern boundary of Cumberland and the western boundary of Northumberland met there were periodic connections, in terms of ownership and labour migration, between tileries in both counties.
Thomas Nelson & Co of Carlisle erected and operated the *South Tyne Fire Brick Works* at Haltwhistle from 1846 until 1859, when it was offered for sale and purchased by William Hudspith. After the sale in 1860 T Nelson & Co acted as agent in Carlisle to receive orders for the works. It is not known if Nelson manufactured draining-tiles at Haltwhistle or restricted output to fire-clay products which included 'long bricks for Tile Kilns' A Northumberland entrepreneur with tile-works in both counties was Robert Wigham of Hargill House. He offered the *Allenheads Tile Works*, situated at Spartylea, to let in 1855, the same year that he advertised *Skelgill Tilery* at Alston for sale. This was not the end of his association with tile-making, as in 1865 he manufactured at *Featherstone Tile Works*. Near Greenhead, *Blenkinsopp Tilery* owned by the Naworth estate was operational in the 1860s with two tile-makers and a tile-burner employed in 1861.[8]

These tile-works, clustered around the border between the two counties, are identified in Figure 9.6.

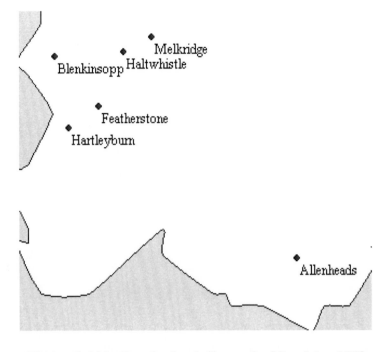

Figure 9.6 Northumberland tile-works [Gen Map UK]

In Scotland a number of the tileries established during the 1830s and early 1840s were sited close to the land border with Cumberland, with others along the coastal strip on the Scottish side of the Solway. This proximity resulted in a variety of relationships between these tileries and Cumberland, including movement of skilled workmen in both directions. From Scotland there was a much more positive marketing of tiles into Cumberland than appeared to happen in the opposite direction. This was confirmed in an 1868 article on earthenware manufacture in Scotland which stated that many millions of clay drain-pipes were produced every year for 'home use and exportation'.[9]

During the 1850s in the historic counties which now make up Cumbria, there were around 85 brick and tile-works in existence, although not all active at the same time. In addition, to the south, east and north, there were other works supplying tiles into the area. In terms of numbers of tileries, this period represented the peak and, possibly as suggested by the comments in Figure 9.7, the beginning of the decline.

**AGRICULTURAL REPORT FOR CUMBER-
LAND.**
Draining tiles have gone off rather slower of late ; this probably arises from two causes—first, because of the increased number of tile-yards ; and, secondly, from the great quantity of land already drained.—Dec. 28.

Figure 9.7 CAS (Carlisle) *Carlisle Journal* 6th January 1854

During this period of growth in the number of tileries, many of the key participants in the introduction of tile-making died, some to be replaced in the business by a family member. The Netherby agent, John Yule, had died in August 1847 at the age of 56 and been buried in Kirklinton churchyard. He had lived at Fergushill Cottage, close to the church since 1835, and in the years prior to his death had been secretary of the committee overseeing the rebuilding of the church. Another of the Netherby team, Robert Lucock, responsible for setting up a number of the Cumberland tileries, announced in June 1854 that his business would be carried on in future as R Lucock & Son, Figure 9.8.

R. LUCOCK returns his sincere thanks to the Public generally for their uniform patronage at his several TILERIES at LANGRIGG, CURTHWAITE, and BROUGHTON MOOR, during the long period of thirty years.

R. LUCOCK rests satisfied that he has never relaxed in keeping up to the mark of the most useful improvements, which opinion has been strengthened by the suffrages of the public; and he now solicits a continuance of their favours in behalf of R. LUCOCK & SON, in whose name all the above concerns will be carried on, at the following prices, after Midsummer day :—

Figure 9.8 CAS (Carlisle) *Carlisle Journal* 16th June 1854

Not long afterwards on the 6th of July, Robert died in his 69th year, (Figure 9.9), was buried in Aspatria churchyard and left his son Joseph to carry on the business.[10]

At Aspatria, on the 6th inst., Mr. Robert Lucock, fire-brick and tile manufacturer, in the 69th year of his age. Mr. Lucock was one of the first to introduce the manufacture of draining-tiles into the Western division of the county, in different parts of which he had extensive works. His uprightness and integrity of character had secured for him the esteem of a large body of agriculturists, by whom his loss will be deeply regretted.

Figure 9.9 CAS (Carlisle) *Carlisle Journal* 7th July 1854

In the 1841 census Robert Lucock had been the only individual described as a tile-manufacturer; in 1851 there were 12. The total number employed in tile-making in 1841 was 125, all in Cumberland; this had increased by two in 1851, with 119 in Cumberland and eight in Westmorland. In 1851 there was a dramatic reduction in the number described as 'tile-makers' - down from 104 in 1841 to 70, The increases which compensated for this were not only in tile-manufacturers, but a doubling from five to ten in tile-burners, and from three to six in tile-moulders. Tile-labourers increased from ten to 19, and runners from two to seven. Included in these totals for 1851 were 18 young people aged 15 and under, an increase of one, including a girl aged 11, three children aged 12 and three aged 14, most of whom were classed as tile-runners or labourers. Among the total in 1851 were 18 family groups accounting for 43 of the 127 workers, most born in Cumberland but three from other English counties, 11 from Ireland and seven from Scotland.

As well as being employed at tileries, boys were also used to carry tiles where draining was taking place. In 1850 around Whitehaven, and in 1857 outside Carlisle, the costs of draining included amounts for boys handling or spreading tiles.[11]

The 25 advertisements in the *Carlisle Journal* requiring tile workers between 1841 and 1850 was only a slight increase on the previous decade. There was a reduction in the number of burners and moulders needed, but an increase in the practice of letting by proposal or contract the making and burning of tiles. This would be either for a season at a price per 1000, or a fixed quantity of tiles, again at a price per 1000. In several of the advertisements requiring contractors or burners, the vacancies were at tileries in Northumberland or Scotland.[12]

During the period 1851 to 1860, there were 29 advertisements, with the number for contractors making tiles again increasing. Fewer burners were required, although this was balanced by an increase in the demand for individuals, skilled in both making and burning. Some advertisements were from outside Cumberland, including one from *Ovenstone Tilery* in Northumberland. Unexpectedly the need for moulders increased; 14 advertisements for them were placed, even higher than the period 1830 to 1840, Yet this was at a time when machine making was widespread, with some advertisements specifying 'making by machine'.[13]

During the 1860s there were fewer vacancies with just 16 advertisements, in which the greatest need was for contractors and burners. Only one moulder was required, presumably reflecting the almost universal use of machines by this date.[14]

There was a significant reduction in the numbers of tile-making workers at the time of the 1861 census, compared with 1841 and 1851. A total of 64 consisted of 47 in Cumberland, and 17 in Westmorland. This decrease was reflected in every tile-making occupation, although the decline in manufacturers, of which there were still ten all in Cumberland, was the smallest. Westmorland had one burner and 14 tile-makers, compared to 29 tile-makers, two burners and one moulder in Cumberland.[15]

Whether he was an owner, employee or contractor the key individual in a tilery had to be skilled in burning the kiln, as well as being capable of overseeing the other aspects of the operation. It appeared that the terms 'burner' and 'maker' were used synonymously, as with William Sanderson a tile-moulder in 1838, who by 1840 gave his occupation as 'tile-maker', changing it in 1853 to 'tile-burner'. Similarly John Law who was a tile-burner in 1862 described himself as a 'tile-maker' on moving to another tilery in 1866.[16]

In the early and peak years of the industry there was considerable movement of skilled workers, initially involving migration from the first group of tileries in the north of Cumberland. One example was William Witherington born at Mossband in Kirkandrews-on-Esk parish, who in 1833 aged about 28, was a tile-maker in Beaumont parish. He had moved by 1840, when he was advertising for tile-moulders to work at *Tarrasfoot Tile Works* just across the Scottish border in Canonbie parish. Still there in 1851, he employed six labourers and was described as a 'Tile Manufacturer'. His next move was to Drigg in south-west Cumberland, where in 1858 he was manager of the *Dickinson, Dalzell & Thompson Brick & Tile Works*. In 1861 he was still at the same works, describing himself as 'a burner'. Living in the same property was a tile-moulder, named George Elliot who had also moved from Canonbie.[17]

Tile-makers worked and moved as family groups; one such was Robert Irving and his sons. He was at *Calthwaite Tile Works* in 1849 as tile-maker, moving to *Ellerbeck Brick*

& *Tile Works* in 1851 where he and his two sons, Thomas aged 17 and Joseph aged 13 were all tile-makers. A year later, Robert was at *Bolton Tile Works* still a tile-maker, presumably his sons with him. Thomas, who by 1860 was married, moved to Abbey Town as a brick-maker, while his father Robert along with another son John living with him were at *Lees Hill Tile Works* in 1861.[18]

Obviously tile-makers moved to active tile-works. Robert Furness who was probably employed at *Winscales Tile Works* between 1846 and 1851, when lack of records suggest it ceased production, moved to Featherstone in Northumberland, remaining there from 1852 until at least 1861, a tile-maker at *Featherstone Tile Works*.[19]

The introduction of tile-making into Westmorland was based on migration of skilled workers from outside the county. Archibald Tweddle a tile-maker, moved from *Brackenhill Tile Works* in north Cumberland to the recently established *Wetheriggs Brick & Tile Works*. Two tile-makers moved from *Westward Park Tilery* in Cumberland: Thomas Edmondson to *Bleatarn Tilery* in 1861 and his son William to *Gaythorne Tilery*. Scotland provided tile-makers for *Burrells Tilery* near Appleby in 1851; both James Gass and James Jardine were from Troqueer and had probably worked at *Rydale Tile Works* in that parish. They subsequently moved to *Gaythorne Tilery* near Dufton in 1853.[20]

As well as the opening of new tileries and the flow of workers to them, the 1850s and 60s was the time when many of the pioneers of tile-making retired or died. The demise of John Yule and Robert Lucock, already noted, was followed in 1855 by the death of Joseph Rome, who had introduced machinery to *Eden Place Tile Works*, dramatically reducing the price of tiles sold from there. In 1860 died Halliburton Little, who in 1835 rented land from the Naworth estate and began *Kirkcambeck Tile Works*, and two years later opened *Middlefoot Tile Works*. Another stalwart of the early years, Emanuel Demain, retired in 1861 placing the business into the hands of his son James. The tileries operated by these individuals all continued after their death or retirement; unlike *Moorhouse Tilery*, of which no more was heard after the death in 1862 of Robert Richardson, who also owned *Cumwhinton Tile Works*. Similarly at Maryport the death of Robert Hinde in 1865 resulted in the closure of his tile works.[21]

These men were replaced by a new generation of manufacturers, one of whom, Samuel Taylor, was in the second-half of the century to become associated with several tileries. He originated from Patrington in Yorkshire and was employed initially at the largest and most important Westmorland tile-works, that of the Lowther estate. Erected in 1846 *Hackthorpe Tilery*, the name by which the estate tilery was known, continued operations until 1866 when it closed, with all the plant and machinery being sold by auction. As has been previously noted, during its lifetime millions of pipes were manufactured to drain the Lowther estate. The erection of the kiln and sheds was overseen by James Mawson, described as a 'builder and architect', who continued to be active, not only in new construction but also in the daily operations of the tilery. Also involved in the running of the works was Joseph Benn, land agent and subsequently principal agent to the Earl of Lonsdale. Josiah Parkes the drainage engineer, who purchased a tile-machine on behalf of the tilery, was also concerned in the negotiating of contracts with tile-burners and the setting of the prices to be charged for tiles to both the estate and others. This combination of expertise, both national and local, motivated by the interest, and as seen in correspondence, by the close monitoring of developments at the tilery by the Earl of Lonsdale, resulted in the manufacture of probably the largest number of tiles by any one tilery in the region. James Mawson provided the earl in London with regular reports of the progress of the tilery, together with accounts of production and stock. In return the earl offered his opinions and instructions thereby giving an illuminating record of the scale of the operation. On the 11th November 1847 Mawson reported that the large kiln was unloaded, the burning of the second kiln was finished and the construction of the large shed, built on stone pillars and heated, was complete. In his next letter Mawson wrote 'Regarding the drying of tiles by excess of heat, I have a great opinion of it', and then proceeded to describe how he had obtained lamps for the sheds, so that during the short days of winter the men could work longer hours to make the quantity of tiles required. According to Mawson's letter of 7th December the kiln was filled, burned and unloaded once every fortnight and approximately 150,000 pipes were on hand - sufficient to keep 100 men draining. Writing on the 11th February 1848 Mawson stated that 'last month the large Kiln burned twice and the small Kiln once'. Pipes taken out of the yard between 10th January and 10th February amounted to 190 cart loads- between 100,000 – 110,000 pipes, approximately 525 per cart load. He also noted that the 'Sheds were drying well and the flat flue was invaluable for drying'. Expansion and innovation continued, with the report of the 21st May 1848 announcing that a new kiln was nearly completed and that a railway to bring clay from the new pits to the sheds would be ready by the end of the week.[22]

The draining of the estate, using these pipes, was carried out under the supervision of Richard Miller, superintendent drainer, who arrived at Lowther from Surrey sometime between 1848 and 1850. Lodging with him in 1851 were four drainers from Surrey who may have been employees of Josiah Parkes, who was probably responsible for the seven drainers from Surrey at Hensingham in the same year. In 1851 the estate drainers laid 582,127 one-inch pipes, with the same number of collars, together with 254,475 one-and-one-quarter-inch pipes, again with the same number of collars. In addition, around 106 thousand pipes of various sizes up to five-inch diameter were used. Although tiles were also sold to others, the needs of the estate took precedence and outside sales were on occasions suspended, as in 1850 and 1855.[23]

The estate was also manufacturing at the *Greenbank Tilery*, Whitehaven, where between 1859 and 1862 over 500 thousand pipes were manufactured each year. In monetary terms during these years more were sold to the public than used by the estate. However, as the public was charged a higher price than the estate, it appears that the quantities were equally divided between estate and public. As well as obtaining tiles for the estate at a lower price than would have been paid at a commercial tilery, profits were made at both *Greenbank Tilery* and *Hackthorpe Tilery*. This was despite the expenditure on kilns, sheds and tramway, which at *Hackthorpe Tilery* amounted to £625 in initial costs, to be followed by further investments in more kilns and drying sheds to give the capacity to produce the quantities of tiles mentioned above.

The cost of erecting a tilery varied in different areas but was considered an expensive venture; during the late 1840s in Northumberland a tilery at Ponteland cost £698. In the 1860s in the same county at Melkridge, the cost was £747 although this included a cottage. These amounts were well in excess of the £300 or less estimated in the early 1840s as being required for a small kiln and shed, and reflected the higher costs of improvements in equipment and buildings required to produce larger quantities of tiles. This outlay could be funded by borrowings, as with the Lowther estate, which under the private money drainage acts, obtained £7000 in December 1859 and £10,000 in November 1862.[24]

A smaller version of the estate tilery could more appropriately be termed a 'farm tilery', of which there were a number in Cumberland. Less complex and often short lived they were set up to drain a specific property, although some also sold tiles. An example was *Glebe Farm Tile Yard* in Irthington parish, where, when the farm was to be let in December 1850, the advertisement proclaimed 'draining tiles made on the farm, part of which is already drained'. Less than two years later in October 1852, an advertisement stated that 'the sale of tiles will be discontinued'.[25]

Another farm where the progress of a 'Tile Kiln' is well documented was Leaps Rigg in Walton parish. In August 1839 the farm was to be let with every encouragement given towards draining; by December 1839 an advertisement noted that 'a Tile Kiln is proposed to be erected'. Still to let in August 1840, the tile-kiln was in the process of being erected, and by the following year was shown on a plan of the farm. When the farm was next offered to let in 1855, it was described as 'all tile drained'. No evidence has been found to suggest that tiles in excess of those required to drain the farm were ever manufactured and offered for sale.[26]

A similar development occurred on Sebergham Common where according to an advertisement of 1857, Figure 9.10, the proprietor of a farm being offered to let was erecting a tile kiln and would drain the property.

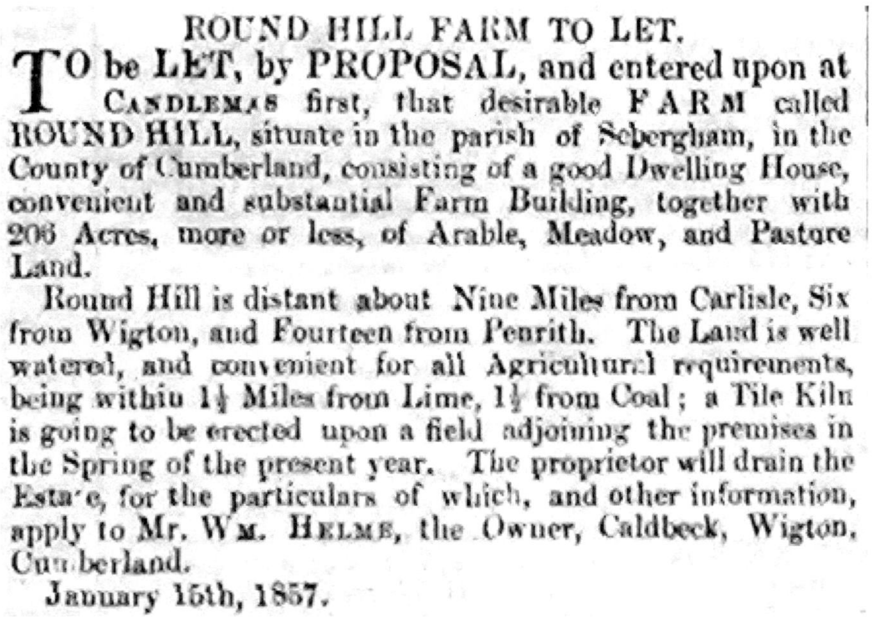
ROUND HILL FARM TO LET.

TO be LET, by PROPOSAL, and entered upon at CANDLEMAS first, that desirable FARM called ROUND HILL, situate in the parish of Sebergham, in the County of Cumberland, consisting of a good Dwelling House, convenient and substantial Farm Building, together with 206 Acres, more or less, of Arable, Meadow, and Pasture Land.

Round Hill is distant about Nine Miles from Carlisle, Six from Wigton, and Fourteen from Penrith. The Land is well watered, and convenient for all Agricultural requirements, being within 1¼ Miles from Lime, 1½ from Coal; a Tile Kiln is going to be erected upon a field adjoining the premises in the Spring of the present year. The proprietor will drain the Estate, for the particulars of which, and other information, apply to Mr. WM. HELME, the Owner, Caldbeck, Wigton, Cumberland.

January 15th, 1857.

Figure 9.10 CAS (Carlisle) *Carlisle Journal* 16th January 1857

In the same year William Helme the owner, a bobbin mill proprietor of Caldbeck, applied for a loan, Figure 9.11, to fund the enterprise.

THE LANDS IMPROVEMENT COMPANY
Hereby Give Notice, that application has been made by WILLIAM HELME, Esquire, of CALDBECK, in the County of Cumberland, for the advance of a Sum not exceeding that understated by way of Loan, under the Provisions of "The Lands Improvement Company's Act, 1853," and of "The Lands Improvement Company's Amendment Act, 1855," to be applied to Improvements on the Lands understated, and to be repaid with Interest by way of Rent-charge or Annuity, in the terms of the said Act.

Name of Estate.	Parish.	County.	Sum applied for — viz., the maximum amount proposed to be applied to the Improvements.	Term of years over which it is proposed the Rent charge shall be spread.
Round Hill	Sebergham	Cumberland	Six Hundred Pounds	Twenty-five Years

Figure 9.11 CAS (Carlisle) *Carlisle Journal* 29th May 1857

The construction had been completed by 1860, and in February of 1861 a brick- and tile-maker was required. The position was filled by William Richardson, a tile-maker previously employed at *Johnby Brick & Tile Works*. The tile-works was offered for sale in 1863, probably unsuccessfully, as no evidence has emerged of it being operational after that date. In 1872 described as *Goose Green Tile Works* it was again for sale or to let - obviously once more without response, as in 1877 the tile-making machines were to be 'sold cheap'.[27]

With the amount of draining taking place, and the number of tile-works operating - 63 during the 1840s, 75 in the 1850s and 62 throughout the 1860s- it was to be expected that there would be public interest in the industry. This was reflected in the publicity given to tile-making competitions, such as the challenge of 'Tiley Joe' in 1848, Figure 9.12.

CHALLENGE !
JOSEPH GALLAHAR, *alias* "TILEY JOE," of BURRELL'S TILERY, APPLEBY, is willing to MATCH himself to MAKE DRAINING TILES against any Man in the United Kingdom, for any sum between £20 and £50.
Burrells Tilery, 2nd August, 1848.

Figure 9.12 CAS (Carlisle) *Carlisle Journal* 4th August 1848

This challenge was accepted in an advertisement of the 11th with a match for £50 to be held at *Parkgate Tilery*, Wigton and arrangements to be finalised at the *Pack Horse Inn* in Plumpton. It is not clear if the match reported in October 1848, with a prize of £5, was a continuation of this contest as Joseph Gallahar was not a finalist. The protagonists in the encounter were Joseph Hodgson of *Parkgate Tilery*, incorrectly described as 'Aikbank Tilery', and John Kennedy, an employee of Robert Lucock's tilery at Sunderland. The 'Tiley Joe' who won this event was Joseph Hodgson, who, in two five-hour sessions over two days, made 2391 tiles, 111 more than his opponent.[28]

Another feature of this period was the awareness of landowners that tile-making presented opportunities when selling or letting land, as in an advertisement of 1857, when a field was described as suitable for 'Crop or Tile Works', Figure 9.13.

TO be SOLD, an excellent FIELD, good Three Acres, useful for Crop or Tile Works; the better half Meadow; near Mr. HODGSON's, Houghton House, in the Parish of Stanwix.—Apply to Miss STEELL, the Owner, Greymoor Hill.
February 18, 1857.

Figure 9.13 CAS (Carlisle) *Carlisle Journal* 27th February 1857

As with many other aspects of society, the expansion of the railway network brought about very important changes to the structure of the tile-making industry. All of the major Cumberland tile-works were from the early 1850s offering delivery to railway stations. These included John Howe's group of three works at Stanwix, Wreay and Cocklakes, from all of which prices were quoted for deliveries to 'the various stations on the Lancaster, Maryport, and Newcastle Railways'. Many works were connected by a siding to main lines, such as that of Joseph Sheffield, Figure 9.14.

2,500,000 Superior DRAINING TILES in Stock, sizes ranging from two to twelve inches diameter. Prices quoted on application. The Works are connected by a siding to the line of the Maryport and Carlisle Railway. One mile west of Wigton.
Proprietor: JOSEPH SHEFFIELD.

Figure 9.14 CAS (Carlisle) *Carlisle Journal* 17th November 1865

The first works to have opened in Cumberland, *Sandysike Brick & Tile Works,* was in 1862 moved to a new site a short distance from the original to facilitate access to the *Border Union Railway*. This enabled it to advertise pipes 'delivered into trucks and forwarded to any other railway out of Carlisle'. The situation was the same in Westmorland, where both the *Julian Bower Brick & Tile Works* and *Wetheriggs Brick & Tile Works* had their own sidings connecting them to a main line. In 1856 Joseph Hall, an agent for the sale of coal and lime at his Wigton railway station depot, also stated that pipe and horseshoe-tiles could be 'had at shortest notice'.[29]

Railways also gave tile-works outside of Cumberland and Westmorland the opportunity to sell into these counties. There were occasional advertisements placed in Carlisle newspapers by Lancashire tileries such as that in 1859 by *Hollowforth Tile Works* of Broughton near Preston, which offered tiles delivered to Carlisle Station, but it was Scottish businesses which were the most assertive. The activities of *Moorfield Brick, Pipe*

& Tile Manufactory have been already noted, and they were followed by others who appointed agents to solicit orders. In 1859 Richard Wright, a Carlisle builder who in the 1830s and 1840s had also been a brick and tile manufacturer, was appointed agent for *Sanquhar Brick & Tile Works*. Notices appeared in the *Carlisle Journal* on the 20th and 27th May advising that Mr Wright held samples of tiles and could quote prices.

In December 1856 *Wishaw & Coltness Tilery* advertised sizes of tiles with prices and gave their Carlisle representative as Rowland Boustead. The agent in the city had changed by 1859, Figure 9.15, although only samples were held there with tiles being dispatched from Lanarkshire.

ARMSTRONG & GRAHAM,
TIMBER AND SLATE MERCHANTS, LONSDALE-ST.,
ARE AGENTS for the SALE of WISHAW PIPE, and PIPE and COLLAR TILES, SEWAGE PIPES, CHIMNEY CANS, &c., which are of very superior quality. Samples can be seen on application as above.

Figure 9.15 CAS (Carlisle) *Carlisle Journal* 11th November 1859

This may have altered by 1863, when the slightly ambiguous wording of an advertisement seemed to suggest that stock was held in Carlisle, Figure 9.16. However, holding stock by merchants did not become a general practice until the 1870s.

WISHAW AND COLTNESS TILERY.
A PLENTIFUL SUPPLY of those celebrated PIPES and TILES of all sizes up to 18 inches now in Stock, and can be supplied immediately on receipt of order.—Apply to
JAMES GRAHAM,
Timber and Slate Merchant,
Sole Agent for Cumberland and Westmorland.
Lonsdale Street, Sept. 24th, 1863.

Figure 9.16 CAS (Carlisle) *Carlisle Journal* 13th November 1863

In 1860 John Jackson, a railway contractor, took over *Whinnyrigg Tile Works* at Annan, where by 1862 there were three kilns operating. An agent was appointed for Carlisle in 1864 to receive orders for delivery to any railway station in Cumberland, Figure 9.17.

TO LAND PROPRIETORS, LAND AGENTS, AND FARMERS.
JOHN JACKSON begs respectfully to intimate that he has appointed Mr. W. KIRKUP, Auctioneer, 13, SPENCER STREET, Carlisle, as his AGENT for the SALE of DRAIN TILES, for which he will be glad to receive Orders. J. J. has always on hand a good Stock of all sizes, which he will deliver at Moderate Prices at any Railway Station in Cumberland. For Price, &c., apply to W. KIRKUP, who has Samples for inspection; or at the Works.
Winnerigg Tile Works, Annan, Oct. 12, 1864.

Figure 9.17 CAS (Carlisle) *Carlisle Journal* 21st October 1864

In the same year an agent was also appointed in Silloth who held samples and could arrange for orders to be delivered at any station on the Silloth line.[30]

Tileries in Northumberland do not seem to have attempted to sell their products into Cumberland, as no advertisements have been found in local newspapers.

Although the period 1840 to 1870 contained the greatest number of operational tileries of the nineteenth century, not only in Cumberland but also in Westmorland, the total figures do not present the full picture. Using the categories described at the beginning of this chapter, it is possible to elaborate on what was actually occurring. During the 1840s, included in the total number of tileries working at some point during the decade, there were seven estate or farm tileries; commercial operations included 46 tileries, nine brick & tile-works and one brick-works which also manufactured tiles. Contained in these figures were 28 businesses which opened within the period, and 11 which closed.

During the 1850s, the ten years which contained the largest number of active works, 23 commenced operation and 22 ceased. The next decade had nine openings, which were cancelled out by 26 closures, with the highest figures provided by commercial tileries.

Statistics for the century of tile-making 1820 to 1920 are analysed in a future chapter, placing each decade in the context of the rise and decline of the industry.

The pattern beginning in the 1860s of closures exceeding openings had its own narrative at individual level. Firstly a works would be offered either for sale by private treaty or to be let. On receiving no response the next step was to try a public auction of the works, either as a going concern or involving the disposal of the machinery and the dismantled structures. Examples include *Bassenthwaite Tile Kiln* to let in April 1854, auctioned in July and August 1854 and with nothing further recorded regarding this works. In December 1854 the *New Inn Tile Works* was offered to let as a going concern; in August of the following year the machinery and buildings were auctioned to be sold either together or in lots. *Skelgill Tilery* near Alston was offered for sale in December 1855, obviously unsuccessfully, as in November 1856 the machinery together with the slates, timber and bricks of the dismantled buildings were auctioned. This trend continued. In 1865 *Maryport Brick & Tile Works* was to let in March but again no tenant must have been forthcoming as the machinery, plant and stock-in-trade were auctioned in May. At Wigton *Parkgate Tilery* was for sale by private contract in July 1868, followed very swiftly by an auction in August. Others did not attempt to sell privately but proceeded straight to an auction sale, as with *Calthwaite Tile Works* in February 1867, and *Brownrigg Tilery* in November 1869.[31]

These are examples of closures which usually took place for one of three reasons: the death of the proprietor; the exhaustion of a convenient bed of clay; or lack of demand for tiles within the immediate area of the works as local draining was completed. This latter would of course be the reason why it was virtually impossible to sell, or let a tilery as a going concern. This situation was not restricted to Cumberland, as in Ayrshire where tile-making had also commenced in the 1820s the history of one estate tilery, *Fergushill Tileworks*, illustrates the same characteristics. Erected in 1831 it sold tiles to estate tenants and the public but by the end of 1852 demand for tiles had fallen, as it had at other local tile-works. An unsuccessful attempt was made to let the works; it was then dismantled and the material and machinery sold and the site levelled.[32]

Among the works which did not close, many increased their production of bricks, possibly encouraged by the abolition of duty in 1850, and in a small number of instances they diversified into other products manufactured from clay. The description of a business, either as a 'Brick & Tile Works', or a 'Brick Works', could change between advertisements, reflecting the product which was predominant at that time. In 1861 a brick-maker was required for *Longlands Head Brick Works*, a business which employed tile-makers in 1861 and was described as a 'Tile Works' in 1866. The title changed from the late 1870s to become *Longlands Head Brick & Tile Works*.[33]

Similarly, one of the Lucock businesses, *Curthwaite Tilery* which was described as a 'Tilery' from its beginnings in 1830 until the 1850s, was in 1865 styled a 'Brick & Tile Works' and continued to be so named in the 1870s. The figures in accounts prior to the 1860s showed the products to be almost exclusively tiles and pipes.

At Broughton Moor where there were two Lucock operations, one initially a tilery, and the second a fire-brick works, only 5100 bricks were produced in 1840, rising to 16,000 in 1844. This had increased to 210,000 in 1847, when 185,000 tiles were also made. Ten years later in 1857 a total of 214,000 tiles, pipes & collars, along with 350,000 common-bricks, flooring-tiles and sewerage-pipes plus 175,000 fire-bricks, flags and chimney-pots were manufactured. In 1858 the 96,000 pipes accounted for only a small part of production, with 425,000 common-bricks etc and 168,000 fire-clay products providing the majority of the output.[34].

It is apparent that by the mid-1860s the decline in the number of Cumberland tile-works, which was to continue to the end of the century, had begun. As a rural industry there were seasonal factors which affected tile-making, as illustrated on 2nd April 1847 when John Barker land agent at Greystoke wrote to Joseph Benn his counterpart at Lowther 'There is no appearance of tile-making going on soon for at present we have deep snow and bitter hard frost'.[35]

The impact of animal disease could have a far-reaching effect on daily activity. An outbreak of rinderpest, commonly called 'cattle plague', began in 1865 and by January 1866 movement restrictions of cattle and people were in place in Cumberland. Notices appeared in newspapers prohibiting travellers and others from calling at farms and forbidding trespass on land. These conditions must have been a deterrent to draining, as during the first nine months of 1866 only one advertisement offering draining-tiles appeared in the *Carlisle Journal*. These embargoes were not lifted until November 1866 some months after Cumberland was declared free of the disease. Rinderpest was completely eradicated in Britain by 1871, although not internationally until 2010, but foot-and-mouth disease remained prevalent with severe epidemics in 1869 and 1870, which again curbed freedom of movement.[36]

Weather, animal disease and the effect on prices of international trade were all influences resulting in the reduction of the number of tileries in Cumberland. The other major reason was the completion of many local draining projects which left isolated rural enterprises without accessible customers and unable to compete with larger brick & tile-works which were connected by sidings to a railway. The next chapter explores the impact of these factors on the industry during the remaining years of the nineteenth century.

Notes

[1] 'Agriculture of Cumberland' *The Farmers Magazine* (1838) 135, Mannix & Whellan (1847) 35, Dickinson (1850) 33, Dickinson (1853) 22

[2] Arthurton, R S & Wadge, A J (1981) *Geology of the Country around Penrith* HMSO, Akhurst, M C et al (1997) *Geology of the West Cumberland District*, British Geological Survey 12, *CJ* 30/3/1844-1/5, CAS (Carlisle) D HUD 3/66/2 1845, *CJ 14/11/ 1856-1/2*

[3] Sources of individual tileries in *Gazetteer of Sites and Manufacturers* Westmorland

[4] Mannex (1851) 47, Whellan (1860) 704, Webster (1868) 25

[5] Binns (1851) 17, Garnett (1849) 23-4, 46, Mannex & Co (1851) 592, Garnett (1849) 20-1, *CJ* 9/9/1859-4/6, Hudson (2000) 57

[6] Sources of individual tileries in *Gazetteer* Furness & Cartmel, LRO (Preston) DDCa 13/299 Payments-Isaac & Thomas Ireland, Mannex (1851) 452, Census 1851 HO107/2274/386/5, Marshall (1958) 287, OS Lancashire 1889 Sheet XXI-7 *North Lancashire Brick & Tile Works*

[7] Davison(1986) 20, Phillips (1981) 163, DCC (1969) *The Londonderry Papers* 36

[8] *CJ* 7/2/1846-2/5, 13/2/1847-2/3, 4/11/1859-1/6, 18/5/1860-8/3, Bulmer (1886) 654, *CJ* 5/1/1855-1/4, Whellan (1855) 820, *CJ* 28/12/1855-1/5, 8/12/1865-8/1, DUL Archives & Special Collections Naworth C631/58, Census 1861 RG9/3866/577/19

[9] Scottish tileries in *Gazetteer* Scotland, Bremner (1869) 400

[10] *CJ* 11/7/1835-2/3, 11/1/1845-1/4, CRO (Carlisle) PR156/22 Kirklinton Burial Register 31/8/1847, *CJ* 16/6/1854-1/4, 7/7/1854-8/6, CAS (Carlisle) PR154/4 Aspatria Burial Register 10/7/1854

[11] 1851 Census Returns in sources of tileries *Gazetteer* Cumberland & Westmorland, Dickinson (1850) 36-7, CAS (Carlisle) D ING 23 Draining Hill House Nook Farm 1857

[12] *CJ* 9/1/1841-1/4, 6/2/1841-1/2, 29/4/1843-1/3, 2/12/1843-1/2, 9/12/1843-2/5, 17/2/1844-1/2, 24/2/1844-2/5, 15/2/1845-2/5, 22/3/1845-1/7, 12/7/1845-2/5, 13/12/1845-2/5, 28/3/1846-2/7, 18/4/1846-2/5, 27/6/1846-2/3, 19/12/1846-2/2, 26/12/1846-2/4, 27/3/1847-2/4, 31/12/1847-2/1, 14/4/1848-1/1, 23/2/1849-1/5, 25/1/1850-1/7, 26/4/1850-1/6, 14/6/1850-1/2

[13] *CJ* 24/1/1851-2/1, 18/4/1851-1/8, 23/5/1851-2/1, 16/1/1852-1/7, 6/8/1852-2/1, 22/4/1853-4/1, 20/5/1853-4/1, 5/8/1853-4/1, 28/10/1853-1/4, 3/3/1854-4/1, 10/3/1854-4/1, 26/1/1855-4/1, 2/3/1855-4/1, 13/4/1855-4/1, 4/5/1855-4/1, 21/12/1855-1/4 [repeated], 4/1/1856-1/3, 26/12/1856-4/1, 13/2/1857-1/5, 3/4/1857-1/4, 10/4/1857-4/1, 1/5/1857-4/1, 22/1/1858-4/3, 2/4/1858-4/1, 13/5/1859-4/3, 20/5/1859-4/3, 6/1/1860-4/1, 13/7/1860-4/1

[14] *CJ* 5/2/1861-1/1, 26/4/1861-8/1, 16/5/1862-8/1, 16/9/1862-1/1, 27/3/1863-8/4, 10/4/1863-8/1, 10/6/1864-4/3, 9/9/1864-4/1, 8/12/1865-8/1, 26/6/1866-1/1, 21/12/1866-8/1, 15/2/1867-4/1, 27/12/1867-8/1, 31/1/1868-8/4, 10/4/1868-8/1

[15] 1861 Census Returns in sources of tileries *Gazetteer* Cumberland & Westmorland

[16] CAS (Carlisle) Camerton Baptism Register PR143/3 August 5th 1838 July 12th 1840, PR143/4 November 15th 1853, 1851 Census HO107/2435/19/30, CAS (Carlisle) Wigton Baptism Register PR36/263 May 11th 1862, PR36/264 May 27th 1866

[17] CAS (Carlisle) PR106/8 Beaumont Baptism Register 12/4/1833, *CJ* 1/2/1840, Census 1851 Canonbie 814/6/15, Kelly (1858) 160, Census 1861 Drigg RG9/394/42/6

[18] CAS (Carlisle) PR35/10 Hesket-in-the-Forest Baptism Register 28/4/1849, Census 1851 Caldbeck HO107/2433/423/12, CAS (Carlisle) PR158/6 Bolton Baptism Register 14/5/1852, PR122/458 Holme Cultram Baptism Register 10/3/1860, Census 1851 Kingwater RG9/3909/33/6

[19] Census 1851 CUL Winscales HO107/2435/67/15, Census 1861 NBL RG9/3866/85/8

[20] *Gazetteer of Sites and Manufacturers*, Appendix 4 Edmondson, *D & G S* 28/8/1850-1/E

[21] *CJ* 21/3/1856-1/6, Durham University Library, Special Collections Naworth C612/250, *CJ* 25/2/1837-1/4, *CJ* 27/12/1861-4/5, CAS (Carlisle) PR43/10 Wetheral Burial Register 5/9/1862, *CJ* 26/9/1862-8/1, *CJ* 5/5/1865-8/2

[22] Samuel Taylor see Appendix 4, CAS (Carlisle) D Lons L 15/1/1/1-31, L 15/1/2/1-6, L 15/1/3/1-6, James Mawson Census 1851 HO107/2440/204/2, Mannex (1851) p.230, Census 1861 RG/3962/30/2, Joseph Benn P & W (1829) p.595, Census 1851 HO107/2440/204/1, Mannex (1851) p.230, Josiah Parkes D Lons L 15/1/1/27, Phillips, ADM (2004) 'Parkes, Josiah (1793-1871) *ODNB*, Minutes of Proceedings (1872) 'Mr

Josiah Parkes' *Institution of Civil Engineers* Vol XXXIII, 231-236, CAS (Carlisle) D Lons L1/2/178 11th November 1847, L15/1/3/4 15th November 1847, L1/2/178 7th December 1847, L1/2/178 11th February 1848, L1/2/178 21st May 1848

[23] Richard Miller Census 1851 HO107/2440/206/6, Census 1861 RG9/3962/31/4 (Richard was the father of Philip Miller who operated *Troutbeck Brick & Tile Works)*, CAS (Carlisle) D Lons L 15/1/1/19 Stock Account Year ending 13th April 1851, D Lons L 15/1/2/178, *C & W A* 6/11/1855-1/5

[24] CAS (Carlisle) D Lons W3/61 *Greenbank Tilery*, CAS (Carlisle) D Lons L15/1/1/29, Day & Charlton (1981) p.289, *CJ* 9/12/1859-2/1, 7/11/1862-8/1

[25] *CJ* 6/12/1850-1/2, 1/10/1852-2/1

[26] *CJ* 10/8/1839-2/4, 14/12/1839-2/5, 15/8/1840-1/2, CAS (Carlisle) DB3/244 Leapsrigg Plan 1841, *CJ* 3/8/1855-1/3

[27] *CJ* 16/1/1857-1/2, *Gazetteer* Caldbeck, Whellan (1860) 248, *CJ* 5/2/1861-1/1, Census 1861 RG9/3931/33/4, *Gazetteer* Greystoke, *CJ* 21/8/1863-1/5, 2/2/1872-8/6, 20/3/1877-1/2

[28] *CJ* 4/8/1848-2/2, 11/8/1848-2/3, 20/10/1848-2/6

[29] *CJ* 20/12/1850-2/2 [repeated], 17/10/1851-2/3, 15/10/1852-1/2, 17/6/1853-1/3, 11/11/1853-2/4, 15/12/1854-1/3, 26/1/1855-4/4, 31/10/1856-1/2, 17/11/1865-8/7, 21/9/1866-1/1, OS 6" WES Sheet VIII, *C & W A* 6/11/1866-2/4, *CJ* 18/12/1863-1/2, 5/12/1856-4/2

[30] *CJ* 9.9.1859-4/6, 12/9/1851-2/1&2, 20/5/1859-1/1, 27/5/1859-1/1, 5/12/1856-4/4, 11/11/1859-1/2, 13/11/1863-1/2, *Annan Observer* 20/9/1860, *D & G S A* 19/7/1862-3/E, *CJ* 21/10/1864-1/2, 23/12/1864-1/1

[31] *CJ* 14/4/1854-1/4, 21/7/1854-1/5, 8/12/1854-1/5, 3/8/1855-1/, 28/12/1855-1/5, 14/11/1856-1/6, 24/3/1865-1/5, 5/5/1865-1/6, 24/7/1868-1/5, 21/8/1868-1/4, 22/2/1867-1/6, 5/11/1869-1/7

[32] Hawksworth, C (2006) 'Fergushill Tileworks – a short lived industrial concern on the Eglinton Estate' *Ayrshire Notes* No.32 pp21-25

[33] Census 1861 RG9/3928/76/1 Longlands Head, *CJ* 14/3/1862-8/1, OS 1st edition 6" Sheet XXI surveyed 1866, *CJ* 1/8/1879-1/4

[34] *CJ* 12/2/1831-2/6, OS 1st edition 6" Sheet XXIX surveyed 1865/6 , *CJ* 3/5/1872-1/5, 14/2/1873-8/3, CAS (Whitehaven) D/Lec 119 Curthwaite Tiles 1844-1858, *CJ* 30/3/1844-1/5, OS 1st edition 25" Sheet XLV-13, XLV-9, CAS (Whitehaven) D/Lec 119 Broughton Moor Tiles 1844-1858

[35] CAS (Carlisle) D Lons L15/1/3/4

[36] Ernle (1936) 375, *CJ* 23/1/1866-1/3, 26/1/1866-8/6, 6/11/1866-1/3, Stratton & Brown (1969) 114-117

10

Years of decline c.1870-c.1900

As described previously the decline in the number of operational tile-works in Cumberland began during the 1860s, with 26 closures compared to 11 openings. This, however, still left 62 in operation, making the decade numerically the third highest in terms of functioning tileries. During the next 30 years, between 1870 and 1900, closures exceeded openings in every decade, with the number of working tileries consequently diminishing. There were 43 tile-works active during the 1870s, reducing to 32 in the 1880s, and with a further decline to 26 making tiles at some point in the 1890s. Another five closures during the 1890s were followed by 11 during the 1900s, with even more occurring as the new century progressed.[1]

These dwindling figures can only be explained by a combination of different circumstances, most of which, locally, nationally and internationally, related to the revolutionary improvements in transport and technology.

During the 1850s and 1860s agriculture was in a period traditionally regarded by historians as a 'golden age' of 'high farming'. This changed during the 1870s when farming in the United Kingdom entered an era of depression, which extended to the end of the century and into the 1900s. The reasons for this included the long-term fall in prices: 'wheat and wool prices fell by half between the early 1870s and the mid-1890s and cattle and sheep prices by one-quarter to one-third'. Although these reductions varied between markets and years, they do indicate the broad trend of the times. Lower prices coincided with a run of exceptionally wet weather in the late 1870s, which continued into the 1880s and resulting in a succession of poor harvests. On previous occasions low yields brought high prices, but this no longer applied as imports of grain from the USA and other countries more than compensated for the shortfall. This was made possible by the extension of railways, particularly into the wheat-growing plains of North America, and by the development of steam ships which reduced the cost of maritime freight. Freezing plants and refrigerated ocean transport brought about the same ingress of meat and other perishable foods.[2]

There were, of course, regional variations in the impact of the recession. This led to an opinion that the years from 1850 until 1914 were 'generally a successful time for the north's agriculturalists'. These sentiments were based on comments such as the one expressed in 1882 that 'agricultural recession does not exist in Cumberland and Westmorland'- a sentiment with which farmers at the time would not necessarily have concurred![3]

The reason that the depression had a lesser impact in Cumberland, can be attributed to the fact that it was largely a grazing county, producing meat and dairy products, particularly fresh milk for which there was no foreign competition. Demand for these items was increasing and the expanding rail network facilitated their speedy delivery. In 1878 James Caird commented that, 'thirty years ago probably not more than one third of people of this country consumed animal food more than once a week, now, nearly all of them eat it, in meat or cheese or butter, once a day'. In Cumberland and Westmorland the practice of domestic dairying, carried out by farmer's wives and daughters in response to this demand, helped alleviate the effects of the recession.

Dairy farmers were also assisted by the establishment of enterprises such *Carrick's Cumberland Dairy*, founded at Low Row near Brampton in 1881. Supplies of milk were obtained from 60 to 70 farms in the stock-raising districts around Carlisle. The dairy had a retail business in Newcastle-upon-Tyne and also sold milk through agents, as well as butter, some cheese and cream in pots, Figure 10.1. Some indication of the impact of this business can be ascertained from production figures for the 15-month period prior to 1883 when 482,371 gallons of milk, 175,407 lbs. of butter and 361,779 lbs. of cheese were processed.[4]

Figure 10.1 *Carrick's Cumberland Dairy* cream pot [personal collection]

The effects of the agricultural depression on drainage, and consequently on tile-making, are not always apparent. While there was obviously a detrimental effect as attempts were made to economise, some other estates actually increased drainage in a bid to assist tenants augment their yields and also to provide employment.

Since the 1850s there has been speculation about how much agricultural land required draining and how much had been drained. Attempts have been made to calculate the total acreage underdrained, using different statistic but without reaching a definitive universally-accepted outcome. One theory is that by the mid-1880s most cost-effective drainage had been completed, especially of pastureland. This inability to accurately determine the extent of land drained also applies regionally and locally.[5]

Nationally there were two peaks of activity for draining under the land improvement acts, one in the 1850s and 1860s, and a second on a much smaller scale in the 1880s. The supply of draining loan capital between 1847 and 1899 does give some indication of draining activity. In Phillips (1969) the sums each county borrowed by decade are expressed as a percentage of the total. Figures for Cumberland, at 36% for the 1850s and 24% for the 1860s, are consistent with the numbers of operational tileries benefiting from this expenditure. At 8% the 1870s do appear to have been affected by the recession, with the 19% of the 1880s probably reflecting an attempt by landlords to ameliorate the impact. Although both Lancashire and Westmorland show considerable borrowing in the 1880s, there was no uniformity in expenditure patterns by decade among the north-western counties. When the figures are taken for 1847 until 1879, there is consistency between Cumberland at 76% followed by 19% in the 1880s, and Lancashire with 77% and then 21%. Westmorland does not conform to this trend; here 63% of the total borrowing was between 1847 and 1879, succeeded by 35% in the 1880s. [6]

Throughout the 1870s and into the 1880s, 'The Land Loan and Enfranchisement Company', which was to be amalgamated with 'The Lands Improvement Company' advertised in the *Carlisle Journal* offering loans. Among the sums borrowed was £3000 in 1878 by the Earl of Lonsdale for improvements to part of his Whitehaven estate. 'The Lands Improvement Company', which had made numerous loans in Cumberland during the late 1850s and 1860s, advertised locally only infrequently during the 1870s. Regular notices appeared during the early 1880s placed by 'The General Land Drainage and Improvement Company', which accepted repayment over 31 years. What all had in common was that loans could be made not only for drainage but also other improvements such as farm buildings and cottages, and even for the construction of railways and canals. [7]

Despite the fact that James Caird was still advocating in 1878 in his book *The Landed Interest and the Supply of Food*, which by 1880 was in its fourth edition, that 'the first improvement, in all cases where it is required, is drainage', the economic reality was being reassessed. In 1873 a committee of the House of Lords concluded that improvement of land as an investment was not lucrative and that in particular borrowing to finance draining did not pay. A landlord who raised rents after installing field-drains could have obtained a better financial return on investments elsewhere, although this view did not take into account the improvement to the agricultural potential of the land. [8]

Draining appears to have been offered as an alternative to reduced rents and an incentive to retaining tenants or encouraging new ones. In his 1895 *Report on the Agriculture of the County of Cumberland*, Wilson Fox gave details of the effect of the depression upon landowners and confirmed that in the early years some landlords increased their outlay on drainage and other improvements with the object of maintaining rents. [9]

The approach and timing of actions to assist tenants varied between estates. At Netherby annual expenditure on draining, which had been in the region of £2000 annually in the 1860s, fell to an average of £946 from 1879 to 1894. As £240,000 had been invested between 1822 and 1894, the bulk of draining had probably been completed by the 1880s, making extensive new projects not an option. Rent reduction appears to have been the preferred subsidy at Netherby, with an abatement of 10% every year from 1880 to 1886, made permanent in 1887. An additional decrease of 10% from 1889 to 1893 became permanent in 1894. [10]

In 1892 Lady Carlisle, who had from 1888 undertaken the administration of the Naworth estate and had after 1890 sole responsibility for management, wrote to tenants informing them of a 10% abatement in rent to help them to cope with the exceptionally depressing agricultural conditions.[11]

On the smaller Greystoke estate, where gross rental was less by 17% in 1894 compared to 1879, expenditure on draining in 1893 and 1894 was high at £285 and £280, compared to the following years. Total outlay on draining between 1893 and 1902 amounted to £2053, using tiles from *Johnby Brick & Tile Works* on the estate.[12]

Commenting specifically on draining, Wilson Fox wrote that 'in some cases it was said that draining had been somewhat neglected in recent years, but generally speaking, it has been well maintained on good land'. He went on to describe how an agent to a tile manufacturing company, unfortunately not named, informed him that 'his average yearly sales of tiles had been greater since the depression than before'[13]

A report of 1897 described how, on the 22,000 acre Underley estate in Westmorland, despite the spending of £102,000 on repairs and improvements over the preceding 28 years, annual rental income had fallen from £24,000 to £20,000. The same source concluded that in Northumberland 'even in the bad times the heavy expenditure of landlords in improvements had helped to mitigate loss'. Comments relating to Lancashire summarise the general situation: the 'loss of the last few years has not fallen exclusively on the tenant, although remissions of rent have fallen far short of a fair proportion to depreciation of produce. On many estates a heavy outlay has been maintained to keep tenants going'. One other factor touched on above in relation to domestic dairying was the importance of the labour of 'farmers' sons and daughters who have suffered rather than the land, for they have been and are giving their best energies towards its cultivation, receiving no reward in the present, and with but little prospect for it in the future'.[14]

This was the environment in which tile-making was operating during the last three decades of the nineteenth century. Not only were there fewer tileries but the remaining ones were changing, with improved technology and a new generation of manufacturers.

The 1870s began with two deaths in the county's principal tile-manufacturing family. Joseph Lucock, who with his brother Robert, already deceased, was at Netherby when tile-making was introduced into Cumberland, died in 1871 aged 81, at the home of his son James. He was buried at Curthwaite where he had managed the tilery since its opening in 1831, having prior to that worked with Robert in the first Lucock tilery at Langrigg.[15]

James Lucock, who was a beneficiary with his sisters under Joseph's will, ran *Curthwaite Brick & Tile Works* between 1872 and 1874, offering bricks and pipe-tiles for sale. In August 1874 there appeared the first of a number of advertisements, continuing until 1881, offering the tilery initially for sale by private treaty, then by auction, and then changing from 1876 to either 'for sale or to let' with James described as owner of the premises. A fifty-year involvement of the Lucock family with Curthwaite ended in 1881, when James was living with his daughter in Carlisle. The following year the business re-opened with the same name, but under the ownership of James Beaty, a builder, who was to become an important figure in brick-making in Carlisle.[16]

The second bereavement in the Lucock family was more tragic and unexpected; Roberts's son, also named Joseph, had taken over the family business on his father's death in 1854. On the 7th June 1871, aged only 36, Joseph died from an attack of measles and smallpox. His death is recorded, along with those of other family members, on a Lucock memorial in Aspatria churchyard, Figure 10.2.

DEATH OF MR. LUCOCK OF BROUGHTON MOOR.
—We regret to have to announce the death of Mr. Joseph Lucock, tile manufacturer, which took place at his residence at Broughton Moor, near Maryport, on Wednesday morning last. Mr. Lucock was one of the elected trustees of the town and harbour of Maryport; he was a large employer of labour, a kind-hearted and genial man, and was respected and esteemed by every one who had the pleasure of his acquaintance. As a member of the Trustee Board, he brought to bear upon all public questions an ability of no ordinary kind; and above all and before all he had at heart the interests of the rate-payers whose representative he was. Mr. Lucock was first attacked with measles and then with small pox, and died of the latter disease after a short illness. He was only 36 years of age at the time of his death. He has left a widow and seven children to mourn the sad loss which they have experienced.

Figure 10.2 Lucock Memorial [photograph S B Davis] - *Carlisle Journal* 9th June 1871

Joseph who at 17 years of age was described as an 'Assistant Brick & Tile Manufacturer' proved, on taking over the businesses, to be just as enterprising as his father. In addition to carrying on with the existing tileries, he invented and improved tile and pipe-making-machines. In distributing bricks from Broughton Moor, he not only utilised rail but also shipped them from Maryport harbour. At the time of his death he was involved in the planning and construction of a new brick-works at Gillhead colliery, which he also owned.[17]

All of his estate was left to his wife Mary, who in a directory of 1873 was described as a 'Brick-maker, Fire-brick-maker and Colliery proprietor'. This was only temporary as she soon divested herself of the businesses; *Broughton Moor Brick & Tile Works* was sold to a new company in 1873, with the sale of *Langrigg Tilery*, and the brick-works and colliery at Gillhead following shortly afterwards. The latter two were purchased by Henry Graves of Aspatria, a builder who was to have extensive involvement in brick and tile-making into the early 1900s. No longer involved in the industry, Mary Lucock had by 1881 retired to Carlisle.[18]

Mention must be made of a second Robert Lucock, who spent his entire working life at one tilery at Carleton, the *Wragmire Tile Works*, which appears to have been a small enterprise. Both Roberts were born at Irthington, although any relationship is unclear. Beginning work at Wragmire in 1835, Robert remained there until his death in 1877. He left the whole of his property consisting of the plant and machinery at the works to his illegitimate son. Also included in the bequest was the interest due to him from Mary Lucock of Hartington Place, Carlisle, who was the widow of Joseph Lucock.[19]

The earliest tile-maker on the Naworth estate, Emanuel Demain, who subsequently founded the *Allen Grove Brick & Tile Works,* passed on the management of the operation in 1861, after a total of 42 years in tile-making, to his son James. Emanuel died aged 86 in 1871, to be followed in 1874 by James, aged 55, who had combined the trade of inn-keeper with tile-manufacturing. The business described as a 'Brick and Tile Shed and Yard' was left to another Emanuel, nephew to James, son of his brother William and grandson of the original Emanuel.[20] Trading continued with bricks becoming the most important product. Tiles were still made, Figure 10.3, although in declining quantities until 1891. Finally in March 1895, the business ceased trading.[21]

TILES.—For Sale, at Allan Grove Brick and Tile Works, near Warwick Bridge, 2 inch, 3 inch, and 4 inch Tiles of superior quality. Also a quantity of well-burnt Common Bricks.—Apply to E. Demain on the premises.

Figure 10.3 CAS (Carlisle) *Carlisle Journal* 14th March 1879

On land owned by the Greystoke estate *Johnby Brick & Tile Works* was operated by members of the Pickering family. Jane Pickering was the first; she moved there in the late 1850s from Annan, where her deceased husband Joseph had owned the *Howgill Tile Works*. In 1871 aged 70, she still described herself as a 'Tile Manufacturer', with her son James as a tile-maker. He continued with the business until 1906, in the latter years as manager following his sale of the tilery in 1900. Two of his sons, John and Joseph, also worked there in the late 1880s and early 1890s, at a period when it was also a 'Saw Mill', Figure 10.4[22].

JAMES PICKERING,
Tile and Brick Manufacturer,
SAWYER & WOOD MERCHANT,
JOHNBY WYTHES TILERY AND SAW MILL.

Figure 10.4 Porter (1882) *Postal Directory of Cumberland*

One establishment, *Troutbeck Tilery* links three families-Tweddle, Miller and Taylor-, all of whom played significant roles in tile-making. It is not known exactly when production began there, but James Tweddle was a tile-maker at Troutbeck in 1862 and 1865. It appears that the tilery, but not the land, was owned and founded by a member of the Miller family, and may have been planned as a result of the closure of *Hackthorpe Tilery*. Samuel and George Taylor, who had both worked at Hackthorpe, were tile-makers at Troutbeck, Samuel in 1866 and 1867, and George his brother in 1870 and 1871. The owner was a Mr Miller, first mentioned in 1868, at which time Phillip Miller described in 1876 as 'Brick & Tile Manufacturer' was only 17. It was probably either Richard Miller, Phillip's father, previously mentioned as superintendent drainer of Lowther estate, or an

Isaac Miller who purchased many of the tile-making machines and other equipment at the auction sale of the contents of *Hackthorpe Tilery* in 1866. The owner wished to leave in 1879 when the 'Brick and Tile Works and Saw Mill' was offered to let as a going concern with entry on 25th March 1880, Figure 10.5, but this did not happen.

BRICK AND TILE WORKS AND SAW MILL.—To be Let, the Current-going Brick and Tile Works and Saw Mill at Troutbeck, with entry at 25th March, 1880. The Works adjoin the Cockermouth, Keswick, and Penrith Railway, a Siding from which goes into the yard; there is a large field of clay. The Works are fitted up with steam machinery, and are capable of turning out a large quantity of Drain Tiles and Building Bricks annually. There is also a Saw Mill connected with the works, at which a great amount of sawing has been done for a number of years. The machinery and such erections as belong to the present tenants to be taken at a valuation. The present tenants, Messrs. Miller, will, on application, show the premises, and give any further information.—Offers will be received by Thos. Robinson, Esq., Whitbarrow Hall, the owner; or Philip Miller, at the Works.

Figure 10.5 CAS (Carlisle) *Carlisle Journal* 19th December 1879

The ownership of Phillip Miller & Co finally ended in 1888 when the tilery, described as being in the occupation of Messrs Miller, was to let. The new tenants were Messrs Ridley of whom nothing is known; they relinquished it in 1896 when it was again advertised to be let. In the following year it re-opened under the ownership of Samuel Taylor, who in the intervening years had managed *Threlkeld Tile Works*, Figure 10.6.

THRELKELD BRICK AND TILE WORKS.

WM. JACKSON begs to call the attention of Farmers and others to his extensive STOCK of BRICKS and PIPE TILES.

He is now prepared to supply a first-class article to all Stations on the Cockermouth, Keswick, and Penrith Railway, or at the Works.

Orders may be addressed to S. TAYLOR, Manager, Threlkeld; or W. JACKSON, Coal Agent, Keswick, Proprietor.

Figure 10.6 CAS (Carlisle) *Carlisle Journal* 8th December 1871

He had left there in 1874 for a similar position at *Culgaith Brick & Tile Works* where he was to remain, even after his purchase of *Troutbeck Brick & Tile Works.* Family involvement in tile-making continued into the 1900s with a number of his sons playing an active part at both Troutbeck and Culgaith.[23]

Also at Troutbeck in the early years was James Tweddle, a member of an extended family with many of their number prominent in tile-making. James was born on 22nd April 1830 at Mossthorn in Stapleton parish, close to Netherby, as were a number of other family members who became involved in the industry. In 1852 James was at Holme Cultram where he probably worked at *Abbey Tile Works* as a tile-maker. The following year he had moved northwards, crossing into Scotland to *Tarrasfoot Tile Works* in Canonbie; he was initially described as a tile-maker and later, in 1857, as 'Tile Manufacturer'. He was in Troutbeck by 1862 remaining there until at least 1871 when he again described himself as a tile-manufacturer, with his two sons as tile-labourers. Although still in Greystoke parish, by 1881 he was living at Field House employed as a general labourer. This brief description of James Tweddle's progress between works illustrates a practice common to many tile workers. They not only changed location, but also the method of working. Rather than being employed as a tile-maker, they contracted with a tilery owner to make a given number of tiles for a fixed sum per 1000, thereby acting as a self-employed tile-manufacturer.

There were at least ten tile-workers named Tweddle, including a number of fathers and sons. Joseph Tweddle, born in Stapleton parish, worked at *Sandysike Brick & Tile Works* from 1847 until 1884 when he was succeeded by his son Joseph, who worked with Alexander Tweddle, Figure 10.7.

Sandysyke Steam Brick & Tile Works,
J. & A. Tweddle, managers

Figure 10.7 Bulmer (1884) page 382

The family tradition continued into the 1890s when three of Alexander's sons were also employed at Sandysike. Connections with *Tarrasfoot Tile Works* extended into the 1880s when William Tweddle, probably a son of the first Joseph of Sandysike, was a 'Master tile-maker' employing seven men and one boy.[24]

As well as these families who were prominent in the industry, there were many others- tile-burners, makers and labourers who moved around the county. One such family was that of Joseph Wallace, an agricultural labourer in 1841, who in 1851 was a tile-burner at Castle Sowerby. Ten years later, he was still there with his 20 year-old son, also Joseph, a tile-maker. The elder Joseph was in Cumwhinton as a tile-maker by 1871, with another move in 1881 to Troutbeck with the same occupation. That year, the younger Joseph was in Dalston as a tile-maker, as was his brother Frank who was back at Cumwhinton in 1891as a brick-field labourer. Still there in 1901 he then described himself as 'a tile and brick-maker'.[25]

What all of these individuals had in common was the relationship between themselves, their place of employment, and agriculture. Robert and Joseph Lucock had been drainers before commencing tile-manufacture, as had Emanuel Demain. The site of the Pickering tilery was on a farm, which they also worked, and which was later to be named 'Tilery Farm'. The various tileries which employed the Taylors and Tweddles were in rural locations, and many of the family members had been, or became, agricultural labourers. With the new generation of manufacturers, many of them builders, it was this connection with agriculture that was broken. Obviously tiles were still sold to farmers, but the tile-works were no longer situated close to the land to be drained. An important factor was the link between the rail network and the works, which had to be adjacent to a main railway line, connected by its own siding.

One such works on the outskirts of Wigton was *Sheffield's Brick & Tile Works*. The founder Joseph Sheffield, a timber merchant and builder, died aged 76 in 1872, at which time his executors, together with his son Thomas, a joiner, managed the business. This situation lasted only a few years, as Thomas also died. From 1877 it was his trustees who were in charge on behalf of his widow Dinah. In 1882 and 1884 she was described in directories as 'proprietress', one of a small group of women to be acknowledged as owners. For the remainder of the century, it was the trustees who advertised large stocks of 'Bricks and Draining Pipes' for immediate delivery by rail, Figure 10.8.[26]

Wigton Brick and Tile Works.

BRICKS, &c.—Large Stocks of Machine-made Building Bricks and Draining Pipes, from 2½in. to 12in. diameter, for immediate delivery by rail. Works connected by private siding with the M. and C. Railway.—Manager: J. Salisbury Mark, Wigton.

Figure 10.8 CAS (Carlisle) *Carlisle Journal* 20th October 1893

Henry Graves, a builder and quarry owner of Aspatria, has already been mentioned as a purchaser of two businesses from Mary Lucock. The first, *Gillhead Brick Works* managed by his son Richard, he continued to own until 1897. *Langrigg Tilery* which he also acquired remained in production throughout the 1870s; by 1880 due to the supply of clay running out, part of the site was being levelled. His next enterprise was *Old Domain Brick & Tile Works* near Aspatria, which had been erected about 1876 on the site of two collieries which had closed in 1875 - an ideal location for transport, Figure 10.9.[27]

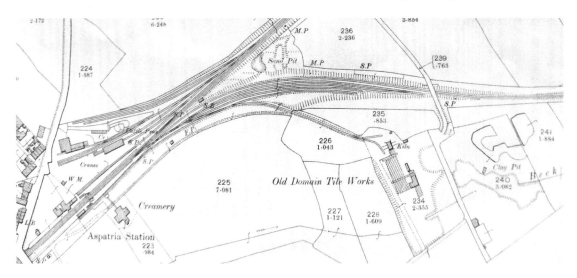

Figure 10.9 CAS (Carlisle) OS 2nd edition 1899, 25" Sheet XXXVI-9

In and around Carlisle, brick and tile-making was controlled by builders. *Botcherby Brick & Tile Works* operated by Thomas Mowbray during the 1870s was taken over by James Metcalfe, builder in 1880. The tradition continued when in 1897 the works was in the hands of James Baty & Son builders. The firm of J & W Laing, who manufactured bricks in Blackwell Road from 1874, also made and sold draining-tiles in 1880 and 1881. During the same period and into the 1890s, the building firm of Beaty Bros. was also producing tiles, as well as bricks at Upperby.[28]

Stockholding merchants were new entrants into the distribution of bricks and tiles from the late 1870s. In Carlisle it was the firm of P.J.G. Dixon, coal merchants, whose first advertisement, for Wishaw tiles, appeared in 1877, Figure 10.10.

TILES.—About 1,500 2½ inch Wishaw Tiles for Sale, of first-rate quality.—Apply P. J. G. Dixon, Coal Merchant, 25. English Street, Carlisle.

Figure 10.10 CAS (Carlisle) *Carlisle Journal* 30th March 1877

Their advertisements continued frequently from that date onwards - in 1882 for 'Scotch Drain Tiles', then regularly from 1890 and into the 1900s for 'Drain Tiles - large stocks, all sizes' at Caledonian Yard.[29]

As tileries closed, there was a continuation of the same cycle - of unsuccessful attempts to sell or to let, followed by an auction of the plant, and often the material of the dismantled structures, Figure 10.11 and 10.12.

TILE AND BRICK WORKS, HAYTON, MARYPORT.—For SALE, by PRIVATE TREATY, all the WORKING PLANT, MACHINES, PLANKS, BARROWS, &c.—Apply JOSEPH BROUGH, Crossrigg, Aspatria.

Figure 10.11 CAS (Carlisle) *Carlisle Journal* 8th July 1881

HAYTON TILE WORKS, NEAR ASPATRIA.
MR. R. DUGDALE has been instructed to SELL, by AUCTION, on FRIDAY, OCTOBER 14 1881, the WHOLE of the PLANT of the above Tile Works. Sale to be for Ready Money and to commence at Three o'Clock.

Figure 10.12 CAS (Carlisle) *Carlisle Journal* 7th October 1881

Some tileries sold in this manner did survive for a further period; one such was *Longlands Head Brick & Tile Works* which having failed to sell as a going concern in August 1879 saw its plant and materials auctioned in October. What occurred between 1879 and 1894 is not known, but from that year it traded under a new owner until his death in 1902. The fact that the works had a siding on the Silloth and Carlisle railway may account for its extended life.[30]

Westmorland experienced a similar decline, leaving the county with only three tileries in the 1880s and virtually no tile-making capacity by the end of the century. In Warcop parish, *Bleatarn Tilery* was advertised to let in 1882, 1883 and 1885, Figure 10.13.

TILERY WITH LAND IN GRASS TO LET.
TO be LET, about 30 Acres of GRASS LAND and a TILERY at BLEATARN, near Warcop, Westmorland.—Apply to W. HOWSON, Appleby.

Figure 10.13 CAS (Carlisle) *Carlisle Journal* 11th December 1885

From 1871 the tile-maker there had been William Elliot, also a farmer, and working with him from 1881 were his sons John and William. The last record of a tile-maker was in a directory of 1885 which listed William Elliot as tile-maker and Thomas Bell as owner. In 1891 William and John Elliot were farmers at Bleatarn; this suggests that despite the fact that the tilery appeared on both the 1897 and the 1913 editions of OS maps, tile-making had most likely ceased in the mid-1880s.[31]

There is no doubt regarding the closing date of *Julian Bower Brick & Tile Works*. It was offered 'to let as a going concern' in 1888, obviously unsuccessfully, despite its railway siding, as in 1891 an auction of all the plant and machinery was held. In this the boards and roofing timber of dismantled drying sheds were sold in lots. [32]

This left *Wetheriggs Pottery & Tilery* where, although it has been stated the last tiles were manufactured in 1902, they were certainly being sold in 1905, and as late as 1922 the works was still described in a directory as producing drain-pipes.[33]

In contrast to Scotland, where many tileries also manufactured pottery on the same site, in Westmorland only one tile-works also described itself as a 'pottery'. In the 1850s *Wetheriggs Pottery & Brick & Tile Works* manufactured 'Milk Bowls, Cream Pots, Tea Pots, Garden Vases, & Flower Pots' also 'Chimney Tops, Solid and Hollow Bricks, Sewerage Pipes, and every size and variety of Tiles' After production of tiles ceased the trading name changed to the well-known *Wetheriggs Pottery*.

In Cumberland it was *Carlisle Brick & Tile Works* which on occasion included 'Pottery' in its title, Figure 10.14. They had an extensive range from the early 1890s, produced under the management of William McMorran, with his son William having responsibility for making the moulds for the pottery items.[34]

THE CARLISLE BRICK, TILE & POTTERY WORKS,

TRADE MARK   CARLISLE.   OFFICE : 25, LOWTHER STREET.

MANUFACTURER OF ALL KINDS OF BRICKS, DRAINAGE AND ROOFING TILES (INCLUDING THREE NEW REGISTERED DESIGNS OF THE LATTER); RIDGE, FLOORING AND GARDEN EDGING TILES; FLOWER AND CHIMNEY POTS.

Figure 10.14 Kelly (1894) *Directory of Cumberland*

Other companies were also diversifying in the 1890s, including *Seaton Fire Brick Co.* at Camerton. Their merchandise included bricks of all varieties, furnace-blocks and flooring-tiles and also draining-pipes, chimney pots, flower pots and other fancy goods.

In the western part of Cumberland a number of other brick and tile-works further extended their range of articles, mainly goods made from fire-clay. The previous chapter has described how in the late 1850s *Broughton Moor Brick & Tile Works* had both a tilery and a fire-brick works. Flooring-tiles, sewerage-pipes, chimney tops and flags were manufactured, in addition to both bricks and fire-bricks. At Whitehaven in 1869 the *Whitehaven Fire Brick Company* advertised vases and 'field drain pipes' as well as a range of fire-clay products. Sewerage-pipes and chimney tops were also produced by Thomas Nelson at Murrell Hill in Carlisle in the late 1850s and early 1860s.[35]

Changes, other than diversification of products, had been taking place at the brick and tile-works which were surviving. The difference between many of the small rural tileries which were the first to close, and the brick and tile-works which survived for longer, was the use of steam-power. Although steam-engines had been introduced in the late 1850s, it was from the later years of the 1860s through the 1870s that they were used as the prime source of power. Despite the introduction of steam, works still closed, and it is from the auction details that information is gleaned. Steam-driven machinery was used at *Longlands Brick & Tile Works,* where they had a 10 horse-power engine. *Kirkgate Brick & Tile Works* where the plant and machinery were auctioned in 1873 had a four-horse-power steam-engine with boiler attached. The largest engine appears to have been at *Sandysike Brick & Tile Works,* which in 1873 boasted a '18 horse Horizontal Steam Engine' with Cornish boiler. When J & W Laing offered 'Steam Brick making Plant' for sale in 1884, the information furnished showed that this consisted of a '12 Horse Horizontal Engine, Tubular Boiler, double tubed, 18ft long by 7 ft. diameter, with iron tank', along with a '8 Horse Engine, with Vertical Boiler'. How the power was used was illustrated in detail from an advertisement of 1874 when *Curthwaite Tile Works* was offered for sale by auction, Figure 10.15.[36]

> Storing Sheds, with iron tramways extending from the Kiln, which is lined with fire bricks, to the Pug Mills, and thence to the first Clay Pit.   A Six Horse Power Steam Engine, sustained by an 8-horse Boiler, drives the Saw Benches, Pug Mill, and Tile Tables, and draws the loaded waggons from the Clay Pit to the Pug Mill. The Tile Kiln, which is a very superior one, will burn from 35,000 to 40,000 at once.   The Engine and Boiler Houses. with tall stone chimney shaft, are conveniently

Figure 10.15 CAS (Carlisle) *Carlisle Journal* 2nd October 1874

Attached to *Curthwaite Tile Works* and utilising the steam-power as at Troutbeck and Johnby was a sawmill. This was not the only similarity; at all three works steam also provided the power to draw loaded wagons from the clay-pits to the pug-mill. The line of the waggon tramway at Johnby was illustrated on the 1st edition OS map, Figure 10.16.

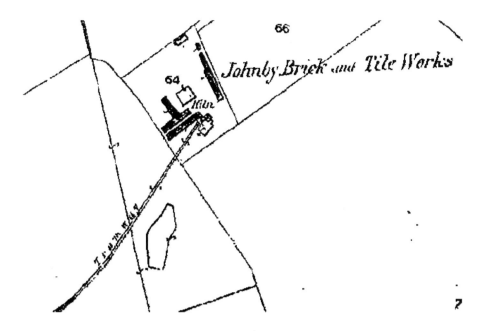

Figure 10.16 CAS (Carlisle) OS 1st edition 1860 25" Sheet XLIX-9

When *Johnby Tilery* was sold in 1899, the valuation included an embankment and culvert, two clay waggons, 478 sleepers and 956 lineal yards of iron rails. The quantity of rails suggested that the length of the embankment was approx. 478 yards. The tramway did not appear on the second edition OS Map, possibly because it was not in use due to its poor condition. Two of the first actions of the purchasers were to instigate repairs to the 'structures supporting the elevated tramway' and to order new stronger rails.[37]

The embankment of the tramway at Johnby Wythes, Figure 10.17, would seem to be the only one extant in Cumberland.

Figure 10.17 Remains of embankment of tramway [photograph S B Davis 15/1/2001]

Other tileries with tramways included *Hackthorpe Tilery,* which at the disposal auction in 1866 had 1500 lineal yards of iron rails used for tramway along with a turntable and four 'clay wagons'. At Cockermouth, *Kirkgate Brick & Tile Works* had in 1873 what was described as 'Grant's Patent Railway (about 40 yards), with Turn Table, two tipping waggons' and 'about 40 yards of ordinary tramway rails, 8 drying waggons constructed to hold 800 two inch tiles'.[38]

These works with steam-engines and boilers also required chimneys. At *Kirkgate Brick & Tile Works* in 1873 there were '2 large brick chimneys, recently erected'. In 1874 at *Curthwaite Tile Works*, a 'tall stone chimney' was connected to the engine and boiler house. The heights of these structures were not given, but in 1899 the chimney at Johnby was 45 feet high and was valued at £42, and the boiler house including boiler at £33.[39]

Drying sheds, although structurally improved with slate or tile roofs and louvered sides, were basically similar to those in earlier tileries. One more sophisticated drying shed at *Hackthorpe Tilery* has already been described, and others will feature in Chapter 11. Also to be discussed will be improvements to kilns, the capacity of which determined the output of the tilery. The tile-kiln in Figure 10.15 is described as being capable of holding 35,000 to 40,000 tiles. Unfortunately very few production figures are available for tileries. Two works, *Sandysike Brick & Tile Works* in 1873 and *Bonshaw Tile Works* at Annan in 1892, advertised that they could manufacture one and one-half million bricks and tiles annually. In the south west of the county, *Silecroft Brick & Tile Works* in 1883 was stated to be capable of manufacturing 9000 bricks and tiles per day.[40]

At the other end of the spectrum, production at smaller tileries such as *Allen Grove Brick & Tile Works* had not risen. In 1878 they sold 175,863 tiles of various sizes, plus 87,053 bricks; sales in 1891 amounted to 60,294 tiles and 132,905 bricks. During its later years bricks were the predominant product, but production was not sustained, as the works closed in 1895.[41]

Among the named tile-making machines in closure advertisements in Cumberland and Westmorland, Whitehead's remained predominant. At national level this had competition, such as J D Pinfold's, Figure 10.18, whose machine was considered superior to Whitehead's by a narrow margin at the RASE show at Oxford in 1870.[42]

Figure 10.18 *JRASE* 2nd Series Vol.6 Trial of Implements, pp 510-512

THE YEARS OF DECLINE c.1870-c.1899

An evocative description of the demise of a rural tile-works in Northumberland, which appeared in a book published in 1909, reflects the situation in the north-western counties. The author, Hastings M Neville, rector of Ford, based his account of what was *Flodden Brick & Tile Works* on observation and information supplied by a man who had worked there. His first comments are on the effect on a rural community of the coming of a railway: 'No doubt our railways, indispensable as they are in many ways, must bear no small part of the blame of destroying our country industries. They centralize, instead of localizing, trade.' He went on to relate this to the tile-works, describing how 'at one point on our section of the London Edinburgh road, there may be seen an extensive range of red tiled buildings and a tall chimney'. Redundant for a number of years 'the place is called the tile shades, because, besides bricks, and the dear old roofing pantiles, a very large quantity of drain pipes were made there. In those days much money was spent in draining the land.' He hoped that demand for drain-pipes would return. 'But now all is silent and deserted; outside, only stacks of unsold bricks, and inside the drying sheds only the ghosts of the freshly made tiles, and bricks and flower pots, which during the latter days of the industry one used to see.' The author goes on to relate how 'the man is dead who told me of the busy days of the tile shades, the days before the railways'. He had described how 'eighty men were employed, forty by night and forty by day.'[43]

The decline in numbers of rural tileries over three decades was not helped by yet another outbreak of foot-and mouth-disease in 1881-3, and was to continue into the new century. The remaining works in Cumberland were now largely located adjacent to railways and dependent on steam power. In Westmorland production of tiles continued at only one site, and that was soon to cease.[44]

Notes

[1] *Gazetteer of Sites and Manufacturers* earliest date and latest date

[2] Perry, P J (1974) 40, Jones (1962) 102-3, Mingay (1994) 197, Perren, R (1995) 1, 7

[3] Hallas, C (2000) 409

[4] Perren R (1995) 13, Jones (1962) 110, Humphries, A (1996) 23, Fussell (1966) 298, Bulmer (1884) 424, *The Cumberland News* 9th January 2009 'The Dairy Empire that spawned a café culture'

[5] Phillips (1969) 45, Green (1980) 130, Holderness (2000) 890-1

[6] Phillips, A D M (1969) 124-6

[7] *CJ* 24/9/1869-8/2, 28/1/1870, 7/4/1874-8/4, 12/4/1878-1/7, 12/7/1878-1/5, 2/6/1882-1/6, 23/11/1883-1/5, 12/4/1878-1/7, 2/6/1882-1/6, 23/11/1883-1/5, 27/1/1888-4/2

[8] Caird (1878) (1880) 87, Thompson (1963) 251, Perren (1995) 4

[9] Royal Commission on Agriculture of England (1895) *Cumberland* 25

[10] Ward (1967) 70, Royal Commission 27

[11] Roberts (1962) 136-42

[12] ibid. Royal Commission 26, CAS (Carlisle) D/HG 214, Davis (2002) 265

[13] ibid. Royal Commission 23

[14] Channing (1897) 15-16, 124, 139

[15] Appendix 4 Lucock, Lonsdale (1868) 39, *CJ* 11/8/1871-3/7, CAS (Carlisle) PR56/21 Westward Burial Register 6/8/1871

[16] CAS (Carlisle) 1871 Joseph Lucock W642, *CJ* 8/2/1872-8/1, 3/5/1872-1/5, 14/2/1873-8/3, 13/6/1873-1/2, 6/2/1874-8/2, 21/8/1874-1/7, 2/10/1874-1/2, 23/6/1876-1/5, 19/1/1877-8/3, 11/5/1877-8/3, 26/10/1877-

8/3, 24/11/1878-1/1, 17/6/1879-1/1, 27/2/1880-8/3, 12/3/1880-8/2, 14/5/1880-1/5, 16/7/1880-1/4, 21/6/1881-1/2, Census 1881 RG11/5155/19/30, *CJ* 25/8/1882-1/1

[17] Census 1851 HO107/2433/213/28, *CJ* 16/6/1854/-1/4, 2/3/1855-1/5, RASE (1855) *Catalogue of the Various Agricultural Implements* Stand No.78, Kelly (1858) 114, 126, 256, Census 1861 RG9/3929/56/35, *CJ* 7/1/1862-2/4, 9/6/1871-4/6, 19/1/1872-1/1

[18] CAS (Carlisle) 1871 Joseph Lucock W501, Kelly (1873) 855, 818, *Gazetteer* Bromfield, Bridekirk, Flimby, Aspatria, Census 1881 RG11/5158/7/7

[19] *Gazetteer* Carlisle *Wragmire Tile Works,* CAS (Carlisle) 1877 Robert Lucock W377, Census 1881 RG11/5158/7/7

[20] *Gazetteer* Brampton, Hayton, Appendix 4 Demain, CAS (Carlisle) Emanuel Demain Will 1872, James Demain Will 1874

[21] *Gazetteer* Hayton, CAS (Carlisle) DX558/77 (With thanks to Dennis Perriam)

[22] *Gazetteer* SCT Annan, Census 1871 RG10/5204/78/5, *Gazetteer* Greystoke, Appendix 4 Pickering

[23] *Gazetteer* Greystoke, *Gazetteer* Lowther, Appendix 4 Tweddle and Taylor, CAS (Carlisle) D Lons 15/1/1/12, *Gazetteer* Kirkland

[24] *Gazetteer* Holme Cultram, *Gazetteer* SCT Canonbie, Appendix 4 Tweddle, Census 1891 RG12/4283/49/5, *CJ* 23/4/1878-1/1, Census 1881 SCT 814/2/4/ DFS Canonbie

[25] Census 1841 HO107/165/8/17 Sebergham, Census 1851 HO107/2426/149/12 Castle Sowerby, Census 1861 RG9/3903/59/13 Castle Sowerby, Census 1871 RG10/5215/52/13 Cumwhinton, Census 1881 RG11/5144/20/4 Troutbeck RG11/5163/88/7 Dalston, Census 1891 RG12/4277/23/6 Troutbeck

[26] *Gazetteer* Wigton

[27] Bulmer (1883) 350, *Gazetteer* Flimby *Gillhead Brick Works*, Bromfield *Langrigg Tilery*, Aspatria *Old Domain Brick & Tile Works*

[28] *Gazetteer* Carlisle, Botcherby, Blackwell, Upperby

[29] *CJ* 30/3/1877-8/2, 1/3/1878-8/1 [repeated throughout 1878], Porter (1882) 54, Slater (1884) 59, *CJ* 21/2/1890-8/2

[30] *Gazetteer* Aspatria *Hayton Tile Works*, Newton Arlosh *Longlands Head Brick & Tile Works*

[31] *Gazetteer* WES Warcop, *Bleatarn Tilery*

[32] *Gazetteer* WES Brougham, *Julian Bower Brick & Tile Works*

[33] *Gazetteer* WES Clifton *Wetheriggs Brick & Tile Works*

[34] *THASS* (1851 Plan of Works Plate 1, *CJ* 7/2/1873-1/5, *Gazetteer* Wetheral *Carlisle Brick & Tile Works*

[35] *Gazetteer* Camerton, *Seaton Fire Brick Co*, Bridekirk *Broughton Moor Brick & Tile Works*, Whitehaven, *Whitehaven Fire Brick Works*, Carlisle *Murrell Hill Brick Works*

[36] *CJ* 4/4/1873-8/3, 5/12/1873-2/3, 1/8/1879-1/4, 30/5/1873-8/3, 25/7/1884-8/2, 2/10/1874-1/2

[37] OS 1st edition 1860 25" Sheet XLIX-9, OS 2nd edition 1898 6" Sheet XLIX-SW, CAS (Carlisle) Johnby Wythes Tilery Co D/BS Boxes 528/529 Valuation for Sale 1899, Minute Book of Board of Directors page 21 3rd December 1901

[38] *C&WA* 20/11/1866-2/2, CAS (Carlisle) D Lons L15/1/1/12 Prices achieved at sale by Auction 29th November 1866, *CJ* 5/12/1873-2/3, 19/12/1873-8/3

[39] *CJ* 19/12/1873-8/3, 2/10/1874-1/2, ibid. CAS (Carlisle) Johnby

[40] CAS (Carlisle) DBS 529/221, *CJ* 30/5/1902-8/5, 29/8/1873-8/2, 11/3/1892-8/5, Bulmer (18830 445

[41] CAS Carlisle DX558/77 with thanks to Dennis Perriam

[42] *CJ* 18/3/1870-1/4, 20/3/1877-1/2, 24/4/1891-1/3, *JRASE* 2nd Series Volume VI (1870) 510-12

[43] Neville, H M (1909) *A Corner in the North* Reid, Newcastle upon Tyne 83-84, Whellan (1855) 701

[44] *CJ* 11/2/1881-8/2, 1/5/1883-8/4, 18/9/1883

11

The early 1900s

Agriculture during the early 1900s experienced a continuation of the depression of the final quarter of the previous century. Improvements in shipping, coupled with the needs of industry to sell abroad, often with the necessity of importing food in return, depressed the home agricultural market. Farmers in this country could not compete on price with this overseas produce. This resulted in a vicious circle of lower income with less money to spend on labour and improvements. Consequently, the gains made by nineteenth-century drainers were being lost, with ditches choked, outlets blocked and tile-drains silting up.[1]

A reduction in draining naturally caused a decrease in demand for tiles, which was followed by a further loss of tileries. This was exactly the situation in Cumberland during the first decade of the new century, when a number of works ceased production. When recording the demise of a business, it is not always possible to determine the final year of production. Some closures can be chronicled precisely because of a displenishing sale of plant and machinery. Where this kind of information is not available, the last located reference has been substituted.

One in this category was *Kinkry Hill Drain Tile Works* situated in Bewcastle, the most isolated parish in north Cumberland. Operations had begun in 1864 and had been in the hands of the same owner, Robert Douglas, from that date. Manufacturing seems to have ceased by 1901 when he was no longer described as a proprietor of the works. The statement in a directory of 1901 to the effect that clay at Kinkry Hill was used to manufacture drain-tiles was a repetition of the one in the 1884 edition. There is no other evidence from that date to suggest continuing production.[2]

Another works with its last date being in a directory, also of 1901, was *Camerton Brick & Tile Works* which during the 1880s had advertised as a brick & tile company, although without specifying the type of tile.[3]

Operated by Beaty Brothers, builders and contractors, *Upperby Brick & Tile Works* was offered 'to be let' several times in the 1890s - obviously unsuccessfully, as again the last located reference is in a 1901 directory, when the manager was John Taylor.[4]

At the other end of the county, 1901 was also the final directory entry for William Bradley of Millom who in 1894 was described as a drain-pipe manufacturer as well as a builder and contractor.[5]

Although not a notice of closure, an advertisement of 1901 offered a cottage, land and buildings to let at *Wigton Brick & Tile Works*, which was another name for *Sheffield's Brick and Tile Works*. After that date no further mention of the works, previously a frequent advertiser, suggests that it also had ceased operations.[6]

There is no doubt about the sequence of events during the last months of *Toppin Castle Brick & Tile Works*. In September 1901 it was offered to let with the tenancy to begin the following year, Figure 11.1.

TOPPIN CASTLE TILEWORKS.

TO Let, with entry at Candlemas, 1902, the above TILEWORKS, with Engine, all Machinery, Sheds, &c., situated about 1 mile from Heads Nook tation (N.E.R.) and 6 miles from Carlisle ; also 4 FIELDS

Figure 11.1 CAS (Carlisle) *Carlisle Journal* 27th September 1901

No tenant was found and the final act took place in May 1902 when it was advertised for sale with the buildings to be dismantled and taken away, Figure 11.2.

FOR Sale, the TILE SHEDS and BRICK KILNS (Engine House only reserved) at TOPPIN CASTLE, near How Mill, with all Fittings, except Machinery, to be taken down and cleared away. The Sheds are covered with some excellent Blue Slates and Red Tiles, and contain a quantity of very good Shelving Boards.

Figure 11.2 CAS (Carlisle) *Carlisle Journal* 30th May 1902

As previously described, *Longlands Head Brick & Tile Works* had been auctioned in 1879, following which there may have been a dormant period. At some point in the early 1890s, it was taken over by Thomas Longcake and under his ownership continued until his death in 1902, when it finally closed. The notice of the auction gives a picture of an establishment with the situation and equipment, which should have enabled it to survive. Adjacent to the North British Railway, with a siding owned by the works, the four-acre site contained four drying kilns, drying sheds and a drying shelter. The equipment included two sets of brick & tile-making machines, a brick & tile-cutting machine, pressing machine and pug-mill all driven by a 20-horse-power horizontal engine and boiler. On the site there was also a blacksmiths and joiners shop and two cottages. [7].

There is also no doubt about the date of closure of *Kingstown Brickworks*, acquired in 1888 by James Beaty after he left *Curthwaite Brick & Tile Works*. In January 1909 an article in the *Carlisle Journal* described how the works 'closed at the end of last year' and it never reopened.[8]

Two works with speculative dates for the cessation of manufacture included *Silecroft Brick & Tile Works* where an entry in a directory of 1910 appears to be the last reference. It was owned by William Walker and managed from 1881 by James Lings, aged 57 in that year, who was still in control in 1901, assisted by his son Thomas. A second enterprise, for which its final year can only be surmised, was *Old Domain Brick & Tile Works*. Its name did not appear in a 1910 directory; this suggests that an advertisement of 1911 was the last occasion on which drain-pipes were offered for sale, presumably selling off stock.[9]

THE EARLY 1900s

Despite the uncertainty with regard to the final year of production for some of these brick and tile-works, this reduction of ten active concerns illustrates how the demand for tiles must have declined. Among this group were establishments with a link to railways, demonstrating that it was not just isolated rural enterprises which were suffering. During the period up to 1911 there were three other works, which obtained a reprieve due to change of ownership. This was only temporary, even though two had railway sidings; after a brief revival all three succumbed to the inevitable and trading ended.

The rural tilery in this group, *Johnby Brick & Tile Works*, was sold in 1899. The purchaser was a new company, *The Johnby Wythes Tilery Company Limited*, created by Henry Howard of Greystoke, who owned the land on which the tilery stood. The first meeting of the directors was held on the 24th July 1900 at which Henry Howard, the major shareholder, was confirmed as chairman. A manager of the tilery was also appointed; this was James Pickering the previous owner. During the next few years, despite considerable expenditure, production and sales never reached economical levels. The outlay on refurbishment and equipment included boiler repairs, a new tile-machine and new rails for the tramway. Many of the regular meetings of the directors were devoted to disputes with James Pickering over remuneration. Finally, a decision was taken in September 1905 to terminate James Pickering's employment as manager with effect from March 1906

Production of various sizes of tiles, plus a small quantity of bricks, reached a very modest total of around 200,000 units, resulting from 15 kiln burnings in the season 1904/5. Annual sales at their peak only reached around 160,000 units, and after Pickering left no further tiles were produced. Attempts were made to let the tilery in 1906 without success, and during 1907 the remaining tiles, followed by the plant and machinery, were offered for sale. At the final directors' meeting on 2nd February 1909, it was noted that Henry Howard had settled the deficit at the bank, and that the company had been voluntarily wound up

Prior to this, the buildings belonging to the company, together with the bed of clay, had been purchased by Mrs Popham of Johnby Hall. In 1909 she was described as the occupier of the tilery building and land, which in a directory of 1910, was listed as *Johnby Brick Tile & Pottery Works*. This is the last located reference to tiles at Johnby Wythes following a period of around 65 years of manufacturing.[10]

Also mentioned previously, *Troutbeck Brick & Tile Works* had been taken over by Samuel Taylor around 1897 but did not survive his death in 1905. Operated by three of his sons, one of whom was manager, it benefited from access to the rail network with a siding at Troutbeck Station. It was offered for sale in 1905 by the owner of the land, after which date there are no further references to tile-making on the site. The involvement of the Taylor family (see Appendix 4) with tile-making did continue at Culgaith and elsewhere[11]

A works, whose existence was initially extended following the death of the proprietor, was *Cumwhinton Brick & Tile Works*. It was owned from the late 1870s by Thomas Hamilton who was also the proprietor of *Braidwood Tile Works*, and, possibly, of *Lampits Tile Works*, both of which were in Lanarkshire. It was at the latter that William Hamilton, who came to Cumwhinton to manage *Cumwhinton Brick & Tile Works* in about 1883, had previously worked. Coincidentally William McMorran, already noted as manager of *Carlisle Brick & Tile Works,* also at Cumwhinton, had been employed at *Lampits Tile Works.* Thomas Hamilton had intended retiring in 1902 and announced the works 'to sell or let'. Figure 11.3.

TO Sell or Let, CUMWHINTON BRICK and TILE WORKS, near Carlisle, so long carried on by Mr. Thomas Hamilton, the proprietor, who is retiring. The Works are about 1 mile from Cumwhinton Station and 4½ miles from Carlisle, on the Midland Railway, and there is a private siding for them.

Figure 11.3 CAS (Carlisle) *Carlisle Journal* 28th February 1902

Sadly, retirement did not happen, as by August of the same year he had died, Figure 11.4.

NOTICE. — All Persons having CLAIMS against the late Mr. THOMAS HAMILTON, Brick and Tile Maker at Cumwhinton, near Carlisle, and Braidwood Works, Lanarkshire, who resided at PARK HOUSE, CARSTAIRS, are requested to lodge the same, duly vouched, with the Subscriber, within fourteen days from this date, and all Persons Indebted to the said Thomas Hamilton are requested to make payment of their accounts at the Cumwhinton and Braidwood Works within the same period.

Figure 11.4 CAS (Carlisle) *Carlisle Journal* 22nd August 1902

Exceptionally *Cumwhinton Brick & Tile Works* acquired a new owner, Nicholas Wright, who between 1906 and 1908 regularly advertised drain-tiles of all sizes delivered to the nearest railway station. In 1910 he was still listed in a directory as a brick & tile-maker of Cumwhinton, but by the 1914 edition his occupation had changed to market gardener. After 1910 nothing has been located to indicate that the works was active.[12]

Remarkably, in 1912 a new works commenced manufacturing on an old site, Figure 11.5.

OLD BRICKWORKS TO BE REVIVED.
It has been decided by a number of Whitehaven gentlemen to restart the old brickworks on the Low Road, and it is stated that the undertaking will be in the hands of a private company, steps for the formation of which were taken at a meeting last week. The works have been standing idle for a number of years.

Figure 11.5 CAS (Carlisle) *Carlisle Journal* 3rd December 1912

This traded as *Whitehaven Brick & Tile Company Ltd* which in 1928 was producing 'Agricultural Field Drain Tiles' in various sizes.[13]

During the 1920s Cumberland had nine brick and tile-works which were active for some period during the decade, Figure 11.6.

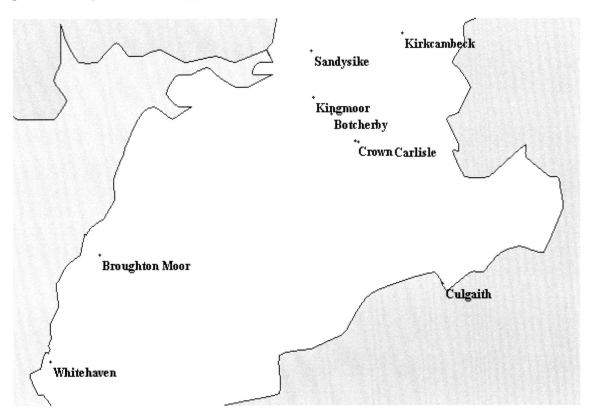

Figure 11.6 Brick & tile-works in Cumberland 1920-29 [Gen Map UK]

Interestingly, a century after tile-making was introduced into Cumberland, there were the same number of sites manufacturing tiles in the 1920s as there had been in the late 1820s. Also, a comparison of the locations on the above map with Figure 3.7 illustrates a very similar geographical spread.

Only one, from the original group had survived; that was *Sandysike Brick & Tile Works*, the pioneering Netherby estate tilery. This was still producing tiles on a site only a few hundred yards from where it began. Operated until the early 1900s by Joseph and Alexander Tweddle, the contracting manufacturer in 1909 was one of Samuel Taylor's sons, John Thomas Taylor. Born at Troutbeck, where he worked in the tilery as a boy, he was in Derbyshire in 1901, employed as a wood sawyer. He remained at Sandysike as a manufacturer until at least 1914, with his son Harold as a tile-maker, thus continuing the family tradition. A new occupier was required for the works in 1919, when it was taken by Joseph and William Pigg, under whose stewardship it remained until 1938 when it was again advertised for sale.[14]

Samuel Taylor had managed *Culgaith Brick & Tile Works* prior to his death in 1906, at which point his sons Clement and John Fallowfield took over, and regularly appeared in directories from 1910 until 1925 as brick-makers. When the baptisms of John Fallowfield Taylor's children were recorded between 1908 and 1914, he always gave his occupation as tile-maker. The business was taken over in 1926 by Joseph Stamper and from then traded as *Culgaith Brick & Tile Company Ltd.*[15]

One of the works remaining in the 1920s was Robert Lucock's 1830 enterprise, opened initially as a tilery, with a fire-brick works added in the 1840s. After being taken over in the 1870s, it became *Broughton Moor Fire Brick Works* and continued production until at least 1921. Also begun in the 1830s in Carlisle, *Botcherby Brick & Tile Works* had passed from J Baty & Sons around 1920 to Forster Ridley & Sons, who continued throughout the 1920s and 1930s. The demolition and clearance of the site finally took place in 1947.[16]
On the opposite side of Carlisle *Kingmoor Brick & Tile Company* was offered for sale in 1920 but continued to be listed under the same name in directories into the 1930s.[17]
At Cumwhinton where there had been three adjacent businesses, all with railway sidings, one, as noted above, had closed in 1910. The next to succumb was *Crown Brick & Tile Works,* described in 1908 as the largest manufacturer in the north of agricultural drain-tiles with immense stocks. It was offered for sale by private treaty in 1919, followed in 1921 by an auction sale. The most enduring was *Carlisle Brick & Tile Works,* possibly because of its diversification into other products which included also a T-shaped chimney pot. Examples of these could at one time be seen on many roofs around Carlisle.[18]

Features common to those businesses that survived the longest were not only the rail link but also improved technology, details of which can be gleaned from sale advertisements. One example described *Sandysike Brick & Tile Works* as having 'six Kilns and large Drying Sheds heated by steam' Figure 11.7.

BRICK & TILE WORKS FOR SALE.—
Comprising SIX KILNS, large Drying Sheds heated by steam, good Boiler and 16 h.p. Engine etc.; Workman's Cottage (4 Rooms), and large valuable Field of Clay, the whole extending to 26.358 Acres, adjoining main North British Railway (Waverley Route), 7 miles north of Carlisle with siding running alongside Yard. Good road access. Possession could be had in three months, or earlier by arrangement.
For particulars to view apply
J. W. BATY,
Netherby Estate Office.

Figure 11.7 CAS (Carlisle) *Carlisle Journal* 14th February 1919

Similarly, in the same year the plant and machinery at *Crown Brick & Tile Works* included a 'Belgian Continuous Kiln' of 16 chambers, as well as the ubiquitous 'Scotch Kiln'. There were two steam-engines, one of five, and another of 25 horse-power, a 'Lancashire Boiler', and a 120 feet high chimney. The three drying sheds had a capacity of around 70,000, and on the 18-acre site there were still ample stocks of clay.

The *Culgaith Brick & Tile Works* also had a landmark chimney, erected in 1926 reaching a height of 90 feet and demolished in 1981. At this works a former ship's boiler was used to dry the bricks and tiles.[19]

Among the survivors there was one isolated rural tilery still being listed in directories until 1914. This was *Kirkcambeck Brick & Tile Works,* founded in 1835. It was occupied from 1901 until 1914 by John Tweddle, who described himself in 1901 as 'labourer at the Tilery on his own account' but was listed in directories as a tile-maker.[20]

Stockholding and distribution of tiles by merchants became commonplace as in Carlisle by P J G Dixon, Figure 11.8, and others around the county.

DRAIN TILES.—Stock of all sizes on hand at Caledonian Railway Yard.—P. J. G. Dixon, 25, English Street, Carlisle.

Figure 11.8 CAS (Carlisle) *Carlisle Journal* 3rd March 1911

In Wigton J G Frizzel & Co, Figure 11.9, in Workington E. Burrow & Son, in Penrith J & M Fidler and in Carlisle, Walter Wood all of whom stocked tiles of various sizes.[21]

Figure 11.9 Billhead [Personal Collection]

Although later in the century mention must be made of another new entrant; *Kirkhouse Brick & Tile Works* was opened in Farlam parish in 1934 and was manufacturing field drain-pipes during the 1940s and early 1950s. [22]

Tile-making was now an industry in the hands of a small number of manufacturers with their products also being sold through merchants, who could of course, by utilising the rail network, source the same articles from anywhere in the country. In contrast, previously tile-making had been a by-product of agriculture, close to the land which was to be drained, employing workers who had been, and might again be, agricultural labourers.

Reluctance on the part of agriculturalists to spend money on improvements meant that, by the late 1930s, 'the amount of intensive tile draining which was being undertaken was negligible'. For some soils 'mole drainage' by tractor was being used as a relatively cheap alternative, which could be repeated as necessary. Eventually the entire process was mechanised using perforated plastic pipes.[23]

Notes

[1] Livesley (1960) 7-8

[2] *Gazetteer of Sites and Manufacturers* Bewcastle, *Kinkry Hill Drain Tile Works*, CAS (Carlisle) DW9/51 4th April 1864, Bulmer (1884) 392, 394, Bulmer (1901) 136, 138

[3] Slater (1884) 203, Bulmer (1901) 685

[4] *Gazetteer* Carlisle *Upperby Brick & Tile Works*, Bulmer (1901) 287

[5] *Gazetteer* Millom *William Bradley Brick & Tile Maker*, Kelly (1894) 204, *Directory of Clayworkers* (1901) 18

[6] *Gazetteer* Wigton *Sheffield's Brick & Tile Works*, CJ 1/3/1901-1/5

[7] *Gazetteer* Newton Arlosh *Longlands Head Brick & Tile Works*, CJ 24/10/1879-1/4, Kelly (1894) 165, *CJ* 14/11/1902-1/2

[8] *Gazetteer* Kingmoor *Kingstown Brickworks*, CJ 1/1/1909-4/5

[9] *Gazetteer* Whicham *Silecroft Brick & Tile Works*, Census 1881 RG11/5197/91/119, Bulmer (1901) 629, Kelly (1910) 348, *Gazetteer* Aspatria *Old Domain Brick & Tile Works, CJ* 3/3/1911-8/1

[10] Davis (2002), *Gazetteer* Greystoke *Johnby Brick & Tile Works*, CAS (Carlisle) DBS 529 *Johnby Wythes Tilery Co Ltd*, *CJ* 16/1/1906-1/4, *Penrith Observer* 2/4/1907-4/2, *CJ* 9/8/1907-8/3, , CAS (Carlisle) TIR/4/15, Kelly (1910) 162 & 348

[11] *Gazetteer* Greystoke *Troutbeck Brick & Tile Works*, Kelly (1897) 155/6, 338, Census 1901 RG13/4856/21/4, *CJ* 21/7/1905-8/8, Appendix 4 Taylor

[12] *Gazetteer* SCT Carnwath *Lampits Tile Works*, *Gazetteer* Wetheral *Cumwhinton Brick & Tile Works*, *CJ* 28/2/1902-8/4, 22/8/1902-8/5, 6/3/1906-1/2, 1/12/1908-1/2, 15/12/1908-1/2, Kelly (1910) 131, 348, Kelly (1914) 13

[13] *Gazetteer* Whitehaven *Whitehaven Brick & Tile Company*, CJ 3/12/1912-5/5, 14/12/1928-1/5

[14] *Gazetteer* Arthuret *Sandysike Brick & Tile Works*, Appendix 4 Taylor, Census 1901 RG13/3251/119/55 Brimington, Derbyshire

[15] *Gazetteer* Kirkland *Culgaith Brick & Tile Works*, Appendix 4 Taylor

[16] *Gazetteer* Bridekirk *Broughton Moor Brick & Tile Works* Kelly (1914) 352, Kelly (1921) 347, *Gazetteer* Carlisle *Botcherby Brick & Tile Works*, CN 6/9/1947-5/4

[17] *Gazetteer* Kingmoor *Kingmoor Brick & Tile Company Ltd*

[18] *Gazetteer* Wetheral *Crown Brick & Tile Works, Carlisle Brick & Tile Works* CAS (Carlisle) DX 50/2

[19] *CJ* 14/2/1919-10/2, 16/5/1919-12/1, Cumbria Libraries (Penrith) Cutting in Culgaith File *CWH* 18/7/1981

[20] *Gazetteer* Lanercost *Kirkcambeck Brick & Tile Works,* Census 1901 RG13/4860/40/2, Bulmer (1901) 119, Kelley (1910) 197

[21] *CJ* 3/3/1911-8/1, 6/12/1907-8/2, 3/3/1911-8/1, *Whitehaven News* 15/11/1928, J.G.Frizzel & Co Billhead 22/5/1905, Kelly (1894) 340

[22] Kelly (1934) 336, Kelly (1938) 344, Davison (1986) 119

[23] Harpur (1911) 108, Nicholson (1944) 64, Livesley (1960) 64

12

The rise and fall of a rural industry

It is a statement of the obvious that not only the rapid rise in the number of tileries but also their very existence was a result of the use of tiles as a conduit in underdraining. During the mid-nineteenth century there was what can only be described in modern terms as a 'boom' in agricultural drainage. This was the result of a belief on the part of agriculturalists, in particular the owners of large estates, that action must be taken to revive, assist and stimulate agriculture. This brought about the concept of 'high farming' which required a high input of fertilisers to obtain a high yield from land. To achieve this, improvements had to be carried out, and the first, and, and to many the most important, was drainage. Among the numerous vocal advocates of this was Philip Pusey, a 'progressive and practical' farmer, who wrote in 1842 that 'all acquainted with improved husbandry are now agreed that on wet land thorough-draining is to a farm what a foundation is to a house'.[1]

It was widely accepted that nationally, draining was in a poor backward state, either badly done or not done at all. This made extensive and effective underdraining a necessity, desired by both landlords and tenants. Also promulgated was the concept that the best materials for draining were tiles.[2]

These principles were expounded through the pages of the *Journal of the Royal Agricultural Society of England*, volume one of which was published in 1840. Its first editor was Philip Pusey who remained in the post until 1854, and during his tenure a stream of articles on draining appeared. Every aspect of the topic was examined from reports on improvements in yields following land drainage to the most economical methods of manufacturing tiles. Articles discussed tile-making machines and the most suitable depth and distance apart for tiles to be laid.[3]

In the Scottish equivalent *Prize Essays and Transactions of the Highland Society of Scotland*, subsequently renamed *Transactions of the Highland and Agricultural Society of Scotland*, there was also a spate of articles extolling the merits of tile-drainage. One of the earliest of these was John Yule's account of the introduction of tile-making at Netherby, Figure 12.1.

AN ACCOUNT OF THE MODE OF DRAINING, BY MEANS OF TILES, AS PRACTISED ON THE ESTATE OF NETHERBY, IN CUMBER-LAND, THE PROPERTY OF SIR JAMES GRAHAM, BART. M. P. *Communicated by* JOHN YULE, *Esq. Glingerbank.*

Figure 12.1 *Prize Essay & THASS* New Series Vol.1 (1829)

Among the many pamphlets and books published, mention has been made in earlier chapters of those of James Smith and Josiah Parkes. It was the theories of these two individuals which were combined to produce what became the accepted system of thorough-draining. Many books on land drainage appeared during the 1840s setting out approved principles; these included in 1844 a work by Henry Hutchinson, a land-agent and authority on draining, entitled *A Treatise on the Practical Drainage of Land*. A chapter on draining-tiles contained advice on selecting the best quality, an important concern at that time. Another small publication of 1847 contained the opinions on draining of agriculturalists and practical drainers who had appeared before a committee of the House of Lords in April and May of 1845. Evidence was taken on the benefits that could be obtained from legislation to enable the owners of estates to charge the cost of money borrowed for draining against their property. The result of this was eventually the passing of various public and private money drainage acts, another major factor in the expansion of underdraining.

Also in 1847 a new edition of a book by Henry Stephens, author of the influential *Book of the Farm*, was published and advertised locally in the *Carlisle Journal*.[4]

An environment was created nationally in which landowners were made to feel that if they were not draining, their tenants would suffer through not being able to obtain the maximum yield from their farms. At the same time landlords were considered to be depriving themselves of the higher rents more productive farms could generate. Draining was essential, tiles were the best medium with which to drain, and they must be made available to tenants. Therefore it was imperative for every improving estate to have a kiln, enabling it to be supplied with tiles at a lower price than that charged by the many commercial tileries being set up by enterprising individuals

As noted in earlier chapters, the controversy over the appropriate depth and distance apart of drains rumbled on for many years. The debate over the best diameter for tile-pipes, driven by the insistence of Josiah Parkes on the use of small-bore pipes, was resolved more quickly in favour of a larger diameter. Even on the Netherby estate, drains had initially been made too shallow and in the 1850s were being taken up and relaid at a greater depth. In the west of Cumberland, many drains had been set at 18 to 30 inches and they too were relaid at three-to five-feet deep. It was there that Lord Lonsdale had employed Josiah Parkes to superintend drainage of his estates, and this work was carried out at an appropriate depth. It was also there that the distance apart of drains was too great; as account had not been taken of the very high rainfall in that area. The remedy was to lay new drains between the old, using a larger diameter pipe.[5]

The emphasis being placed on tile-draining in Cumberland can be followed in the advertisement pages of the *Carlisle Journal*. In 1847 the sale notice for farms near Annan described the arable land as being 'tile-drained', and in the same year a tile-maker was wanted to take a clay-field to manufacture tiles for the Applegarth estate in Annandale.[6]

Tenants of farms to let at Workington in 1849 were to be supplied with tiles, while two farms to be let in Stapleton parish had been thoroughly tile-drained. Askrigg Hall in Skelton parish, to let in December 1849, was to have an agreed number of acres tile-drained every year by the owner.[7]

Skilled individuals were required to supervise this type of work, as illustrated by an advertisement in April 1848 for a land agent 'experienced in Stone and Tile Draining', although that description also shows that tiles had not completely replaced stones in draining.[8]

During the early 1850s there was a regular demand for draining contractors to quote for the cutting and filling of a given number of roods of draining; there was also a requirement for drainers to carry out the work.[9]

The importance attached to draining, and the interest in it of owners of major estates, was demonstrated by such events as the match, in 1859 on the estate of the Duke of Sutherland at Trentham, Staffs. Here, 75 drainers in the employ of various estates in different counties worked in teams of three to cut forty yards of drains in a workmanlike manner in not more than four hours. Although the first prize was awarded to men from the Earl of Ellesmere's estate for digging the length in three hours 56 minutes, three drainers from the Earl of Carlisle's Naworth estate, -Joseph Little, Thomas Davidson and John Gulliver- were a close second, completing the work in three hours 59 minutes.[10]

Following the introduction of tiles on the Netherby estate, of which the ancestral seat was Netherby Hall, Figure 12.2, the number of tileries in Cumberland increased rapidly.

Figure 12.2 Netherby Hall [post card n.d.]

The enthusiasm for draining of Sir James Graham, and his agent John Yule, must have stimulated others to emulate the actions of the Netherby estate. This created a demand for tiles which resulted in 37 tileries, many in the northern part of the county, being set up during the 1820s and 1830s, thus pre-dating the national promotion of underdraining with tiles which did not gain momentum until the 1840s.

Clay was the essential requirement for manufacturing tiles, and its wide availability around Carlisle, throughout the Eden valley, and in the western coastal belt has already been described. The locations of beds of clay would have been known from the sites of coarse pottery manufacture such as at Dearham and Little Broughton, both recorded in 1794.[11] These were both areas which were to become centres of agricultural tile-making. The spread of tileries throughout the region is illustrated in the frontispiece, and the commencement dates of tileries in Cumberland are given in Table 12.1

Table 12.1 Commencement dates of Cumberland tile-works by decade

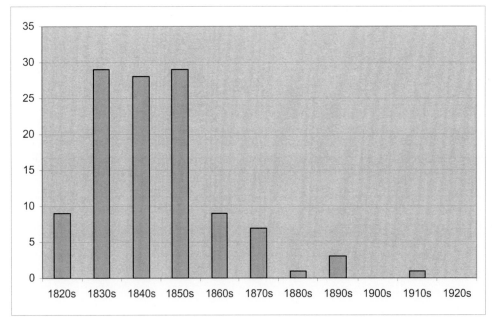

Sources: - *Gazetteer of Sites and Manufacturers*

The importance of the three decades from 1830 in terms of the dates of opening of new tileries is paralleled by a similar predominance of the three decades from 1840 in terms of operational tileries, Table 12.2.

Table 12.2 Cumberland tile-works operating by decade 1820-1920

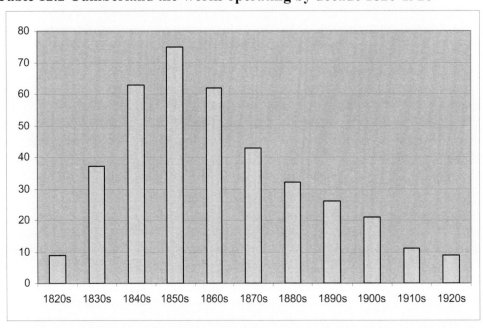

Sources: - *Gazetteer of Sites and Manufacturers*

There was a limited number of defined occupations within tile-making, and as has been noted earlier, the job descriptions 'tile-maker' and 'tile-moulder' could describe the same function. Similarly, the terms 'tile-burner' and 'tile-maker' were often used by the same individual in different sources. Taking these factors into account the data within Table 12.3 derived from occupations in census returns does not claim to be definitive.

Table 12.3 Occupations in tile-making in Cumberland 1841-91

Occupation	1841	1851	1861	1871	1881	1891
Tile Manufacturer	1	12	10	5	4	2
Tile Works Manager			1		2	1
Tile Works Foreman		1				
Tile-burner	5	10	2		1	
Tile-maker	104	64	29	21	12	13
Tile-moulder	3	6	1	1		
Tile-labourer	10	19	4	7		1
Tile-runner	2	7				
Total	125	119	47	34	19	17

Sources Census returns 1841-91

Presenting this information in a different form, Table 12.4 gives the number of tile-workers decade by decade.

Table 12.4 Workers in the tile-making industry 1841-91

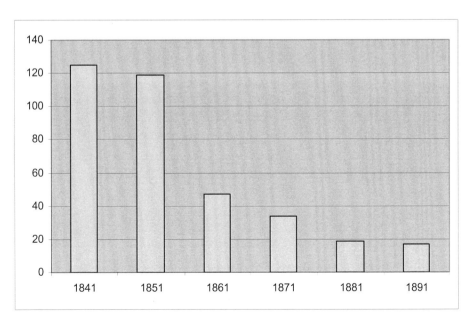

Sources Census returns 1841-1891

The 1841 and 1851 columns in Table 12.4 are similar to those decades in Tables 12.1 and 12.2, while the 1861 columns only show the same pattern in Tables 12.1 and 12.4. What appears to have occurred was firstly the reduction in the number of tileries opening, and secondly the widespread use of tile-making machines. This resulted in a reduction in the numbers of workers describing themselves as 'tile-makers' or 'moulders'.

The rise of tile-making in Westmorland lagged behind Cumberland and was a much smaller industry. Therefore despite the migration of some workers into Westmorland the numbers are not significant enough to make up the deficit, Table 12.5.

Table 12.5 Occupations in tile-making in Westmorland 1861-91

Occupation	1861	1871	1881	1891
Tile Manufacturer		2		
Tile Works Manager			1	2
Tile-burner	1			
Tile-maker	14	3	3	
Tile-labourer	2			
Total	17	5	4	2

Sources Census returns 1861-91

Much of the work within a tilery would fall within the category of labouring. The fact that a labourer was working at a tilery was noted in some Cumberland census returns but not as conscientiously as in Scotland. There, it was common practice to append the industry in which the labouring was being carried out. In Westmorland in 1848 returns of workmen employed at the *Hackthorpe Tilery* regularly included 15 to 18 - well in excess of the numbers detailed in other sources.[12]

The businesses at which these workers were employed can be divided into four broad categories- estate, including farm tileries; commercial tileries set up to manufacture drainage tiles; brick and tile-works producing a wider range of products than the 'pure' tileries; and finally brick-works which also made tiles. These groupings are not absolute, and, as already noted, did alter as diversification took place. What the exercise does do is confirm that within the overall totals over the around 100 year period of 11 estate, 68 commercial, 25 brick and tile-works and nine brick-works there was a distinguishable pattern. This was the more rapid rise and demise of the rural farm and commercial tileries as compared to the longer life of the brick and tile-works.

Overall estate and commercial tileries accounted for 23 of the total openings of 29 in Cumberland in the 1830s. The 1840s included 26 in the total of 28 and the 1850s 16 out of 23 new works.. As illustrated above in Table 12.1, commencement of new works dramatically reduced in the 1860s, and only four of the nine were commercial tileries.

Closures occurred as soon as the industry began: three in the 1820s and 1830s, followed by 11 in the 1840s, all in the estate and commercial tilery category. The decades containing the most activity were the 1850s and 1860s, when openings peaked, the greatest number of tileries was operational, and closures escalated, Table 12.6.

Table 12.6 Closure dates of Cumberland tile-works by decade

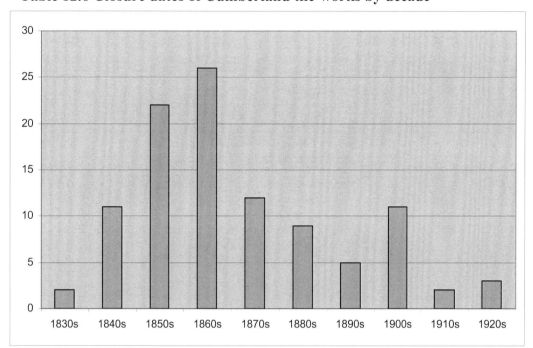

Sources: *Gazetteer of Sites and Manufacturers*

The intensely active period for tile-making was from early 1830 to late 1860, when many tile-manufacturers were also farmers and when rural tileries were being established to drain a specific area. This was often to provide the tiles to drain a particular property or group of properties, in reality what was a small estate. An example of this was the Cracrop or Stapleton estate comprising six properties totaling 1162 acres, drained between 1847 and 1860. To fund the scheme, a loan of £1000 was obtained under 'The Drainage Act' of 1846, and a tilery was set up on one of the farms to provide tiles. On completion of the project, as in many other similar situations, there was no further production at the tilery. [13]

Throughout the north of England in the mid-nineteenth century extensive land drainage was taking place. On the Teesdale estate of Lord Barnard, by 1866 most of Ettersgill had been underdrained. In Northumberland, the number of tileries had increased dramatically in the late 1840s and all through the 1850s, and had peaked in the early 1860s. During the 1870s about 60 remote rural tile-works closed. [14]

Nationally the position was that from the 1870s Britain was largely an industrial country rather than the agricultural one it had once been. Food could be imported from the rest of the world more cheaply than British farmers could produce it. Consequently, the period

1880 to 1939 was largely one of agricultural depression and decay. One of the first causalities was the system of field drainage. Not only did new drainage work cease but old schemes were neglected, therefore reducing the demand for tiles[15]

The previous chapter detailed the situation in the early 1900s; Westmorland had only *Wetheriggs Pottery & Tilery* which may have manufactured tiles in the first few years of the century. In Cumberland during the 1920s there were only nine establishments likely to have been producing tiles, the same number of works as in the 1820s, although markedly different in terms of size, production capacity, ownership and location. The close links with agriculture had been severed; the works were industrial sites linked by sidings to railways. Only seven operated during the 1930s, the result of three further closures and one opening.

Some agricultural drainage continued to be carried out during the twentieth century, particularly from 1929 when grants were available for schemes which provided employment. Then again, during the Second World War, subsidies were made available to drain land which could be brought into food production. Following that conflict, mechanisation and the more recent use of continuous perforated plastic pipes, have become the norm. Traditional clay-pipes are now only the preserve of farmers who are prepared to lift, clean and relay old drainage systems, - one element of the legacy of tiles which will be discussed next.[16]

Notes

[1] Thompson, F.M.L. (2004) 'Pusey, Philip (1799-1855)' *ODNB*, Pusey, P (1842) 'On the Progress of Agricultural Knowledge during the last Four Years' *JRASE* Vol.3, 170

[2] Burke (1841) 273, Wiggins (1847) 9, Pusey (1842) 173

[3] Thompson (2004) *idem, JRASE* Vols 1 (1840)-14 (1853)

[4] Hutchinson, H (1844), Wiggins, J (1847) Stephens, H (1846) *CJ* 23/1/1847-2/7

[5] Caird (1852) 354, 362

[6] *CJ* 27/2/1847-1/3, 15/5/1847-1/1

[7] *CJ* 6/7/1849-1/2, 6/7/1849-1/3, 7/12/1849-1/3

[8] *CJ* 28/4/1848-1/5

[9] *CJ* 9/1/1852-2/1 Cutting & Filling, 26/1/1855-4/1 Wanted 40 Drainers, 10/2/1854-4/1 Drainers Wanted, 17/3/1854-1/3 Draining to let, 3/11/1854-1/3 22,000 Roods of Drains

[10] *CJ* 14/1/1859-5/4

[11] Hutchinson (1794) Vol. II 265

[12] Census 1851 DFS Canonbie, Dumfries Archive Centre Transcript 45-46, CAS (Carlisle) D Lons 15/1/1/29 Return of Workmen Employed at Tile Works November-December 1848

[13] Farmers who were also tile-manufacturers included Robert Douglas, John Storey, John Murray, Peter Hindson, John Johnston, John P. Wells, P.H. Dodgson, James Pickering, *Gazetteer of Sites and Manufacturers* Stapleton *Cracrop Tile Works, CJ* 13/3/1847-1/7, 6/1/1860

[14] Roberts (1978) 158 in Clapham (1978), Davison (1986) 20

[15] Harvey (1956) 35-6

[16] Nicholson (1944) 7, Livesley (1960) 8-9

13

The legacy of tiles

Tiles were made to be buried in the ground, and so, unlike other products manufactured from clay such as bricks, there are no visible monuments constructed from them. The most enduring and discernable memorial to drainage tiles is one which symbolises the purpose of their manufacture. That is the quality and dryness of land, beneath which lies a pattern of still-functioning drainage tiles.

It is rare that the tiles used in a drainage scheme can again be seen over a wide area, but this has occurred on the Mersehead nature reserve, which is in the parish of Kirkbean, Kirkcudbright. On farmland lying on the edge of the Solway coast, the erosion by the sea of the top soil has exposed the tiles The farm of Mersehead was offered to let in 1857, and at that time it was said that 'a considerable portion' had been drained 'during the last 18 years'. This information, as well as the type of tiles, Figure 13.1, gives a reliable date of late 1830s to early 1840s for when they were laid.

Figure 13.1 Exposed tiles at Mersehead, KKD [photograph S B Davis 2004]

Two different tiles are visible: a horseshoe, in Scotland called a 'mug' or 'mugg-tile', complete with sole, and also a pipe with half-collar. It was common to use more than one type and size of tile for main and lateral drains.

In all there are several different shapes and sizes of tiles visible over the wide area of previously productive land now lost to the sea, Figure 13.2.

Figure 13.2 Beach at Mersehead, KKD [photograph S B Davis 2004]

Tiles were readily available from two tile-kilns in the parish of Kirkbean from the late 1830s. *Southcarse Tile Works* advertised large stocks in 1839, and *Brickhouse Tile Works* was doing the same in 1840. Both tileries were only a short distance by land or water from Mersehead farm.[1]

With many of the tiles still lying firmly in position, were it not for the action of the sea this drainage would probably still function. This would have more than met the expectations reiterated in 1911 that 'where the larger pipes are used, and the drains well laid, the system should remain in an active condition for upwards of one hundred years'.[2]

The effect of systematic underdraining on the appearance of the landscape can be best appreciated when a comparison is made between drained fields which have been maintained and those which have been neglected.[3]

An indication of the need for remedial work is the appearance of small lush hollows, Figure 13.3, - evidence of a blocked pipe often the result of the use of heavy machinery.

Figure 13.3 The first sign of a blocked pipe [photograph S B Davis 2001]

Frequently several such depressions appear in a row; the remedy is to dig down and locate the blockage, clear the pipe, and re-lay, Figure 13.4.

Figure 13.4 Lift, unblock and re-lay [photograph S B Davis 2001]

Observation of such an exercise on well-maintained land in Stapleton parish in 2001 confirmed that the original drains parallel to the hedges utilised horseshoe-tiles. These were set at some point after 1835 when the first of the two local tileries commenced production. The line of the drains, which were seven yards apart, followed the slope of the land and were overlaid with a second line of pipes at an angle.[4]

Some distance away, land on another property illustrates neglect; the first and most obvious indication of lack of draining is the prevalence of rushes, Figure 13.5.

Figure 13.5 Incursion of *Juncus effusus* [photograph S B Davis 2001]

Once *Juncus effusus*, the common rush and other bog-plants start growing, the absolute deterioration of the land soon follows, Figure 13.6.

Figure 13.6 Invasion by rushes almost complete [photograph S B Davis]

It is not only the appearance of well-drained land that is an asset; there are many other benefits, expounded over the years by agriculturalists, and still relevant. Dry and therefore warmer land enabled ploughing to begin earlier in the spring and later in the autumn, thus extending the growing season. Yields from drained lands increased dramatically; on the farm belonging to Holme Eden, production between 1838 and 1851 almost doubled following draining.[5]

Draining also had an improving effect on the atmosphere, as supported by this comment in 1838: it 'must be much more pure and healthy when the water is drawn from the surface of the ground; every body knows how unhealthy low, fenny, marshy districts are'. Very similar sentiments were expressed in 1888 about the climate of Alston Moor where extensive draining had taken place. This involved not only open channels but also tile-drainage with tiles from two tileries at Alston as well as from works near Haltwhistle.[6]

Conversely agricultural drainage has in the past, and more recently, been erroneously blamed for being one of the causes of flooding. It was suggested in 1883 that as a consequence of tile-draining and the associated clearing of ditches, rainfall was more rapidly discharged. This resulted in rivers receiving a larger quantity of water in less time producing flooding. The contra argument was that the flooding was the result of inadequately maintained rivers and waterways. These were no longer used for transport and therefore there was no incentive, or funds, to keep them clear. Floods, of course, predate tile-drainage and over the centuries have usually been as a result of a combination of factors involved in our complex weather system.[7]

The physical remains on sites of the majority of tileries are very limited, particularly for small rural operations. Erected where a bed of clay was available, the structures required were limited in number and of a simple construction. In Cumberland the location on the ground of a site is usually the result of prior knowledge of its existence from a map reference. The landscape illustrated in Figure 13.7, the site of *Eller Beck Brick & Tile Works,* which commenced in 1850, contains only a series of small mounds and hollows, similar to myriads of others in similar terrain.

Figure 13.7 Site of *Ellerbeck Brick & Tile Works* [photograph S B Davis 2002]

A slightly less isolated rural site, *Crossings Tile Works* which began in the mid-1830s is again represented only by rough mounds and hollows, the latter water-filled following wet weather, Figure 13.8.[8]

Figure 13.8 Site of *Crossings Tile Works* [photograph S B Davis 2000]

When disturbed and their thin coverage of wiry grass removed, some of these mounds reveal broken bits of brick and tile. Such spoil heaps exist at all sites, although not as visible as the one at *Blenkinsopp Tilery,* just across the county boundary in Northumberland.[9]

More substantial remains are rare; just a few sites contain tumbled blocks of stone, brick or masonry. One of these is *Johnby Brick & Tile Works* where substantial blocks, some with bolts projecting, can be seen on the surface, Figure 13.9. Also exposed at this location is a single course of bricks which outline the base of the chimney.[10]

Figure 13.9 Site of *Johnby Brick & Tile Works* [photograph S B Davis 2001]

Within Cumberland there appears to be only one relatively intact kiln surviving; this is fighting a losing battle with a tree on the site of *Kirkcambeck Tile Works*, Figure 13.10.

Figure 13.10 Chimney at northern-end of kiln [photograph S B Davis 1998]

144

It is a Newcastle kiln; a type commonly used in many rural tileries in Northumberland and at brick-works on Tyneside. A bank of three, modified for use as agricultural buildings, is visible from the road at Belsay in Northumberland. Also still standing, and again within view from a public road is a double-chambered version with a central chimney on the site of the *Tarras Foot Tile Works* at Canonbie in Dumfriesshire.[11]
At *Kirkcambeck Tile Works* the kiln was constructed using bricks, and both side walls were reinforced with three sloping buttresses, Figure 13.11 and Figure 13.12.

Figure 13.11 Eastern elevation of kiln [photograph S B Davis 1998]

Figure 13.12 Western elevation of kiln [photograph S B Davis 1998]

At the south-end, the front of the kiln, are the entrance and two fire-holes, Figure 13.13.

Figure 13.13 Front, southern end, of kiln [photograph S B Davis 1998]

After filling the kiln the central entrance, Figure 13.14 [B], could be either bricked up for the duration of the burning or used as a third fire-hole. All apertures were arched using wedge-shaped bricks, as can be seen in the detail of the left-hand side fire-hole [A].

[A]   [B]

Figure 13.14 [A] Left-hand side fire-hole [B] Entrance [photographs S B Davis 1998]

Overall, excluding buttresses the kiln is almost square, being approximately 19 feet long and 21 feet wide. At the chimney end there is an iron girder resting on corbels and bolted to the wall; the chimney itself is approximately seven-feet wide. The three sloping buttresses on each side are just under three-feet wide and approximately seven-feet high. There are four frontal buttresses, two with similar dimensions to those on the sides and two narrow ones either side of the entrance. Across the front elevation there is also a girder at a height of nine feet. The entrance is five-feet high and three-feet wide and the two arched opening are both approximately 15 inches wide. With parts of the kiln, particularly at the front, distorted by the ingress of tree roots, and with the side buttresses crumbling, these dimensions are not exact.

Internally the walls and vaulted roof are in better condition, Figure 13.15.

Figure 13.15 Interior of kiln [photograph S B Davis 1998]

At the base of the rear internal wall of the chimney, there are four arched flues at ground level, two of which are illustrated in Figure 13.16.

Figure 13.16 Interior showing flues [photograph S B Davis 1998]

In Westmorland the only known remains of a kiln are blocks of stone on the site of *Gaythorn Tilery*. On the Holker estate in Cartmel there are the partial remains of a Scotch kiln. On private land, and not freely accessible, it has been surveyed and recorded by members of the Cumbria Industrial History Society and the results published in *The Cumbrian Industrialist*.[12]

The reason for the paucity of kiln remains was the practice, on closure of a tilery, of selling the structure as building material, with the purchaser demolishing and removing the contents. Boards and timber of drying sheds were dealt with in the same manner, Figure 13.17.

> GOOSE GREEN TILERY, SEBERGHAM.
> TO be SOLD, by PUBLIC AUCTION, at the
> above WORKS, on WEDNESDAY, JULY 18th,
> 1877. Large KILN, suitable for Building Purposes.
> 3 000 FEET of INCH BOARDS. 7 to 9 feet long ; OAK
> PILLARS, suitable for Gate Posts ; 8 000 1½ INCH
> PIPE TILES, with Collars ; 1,000 BRICKS, Lot of

Figure 13.17 CAS (Carlisle) *Carlisle Journal* 13th July 1877

Until a few years ago a drying shed still stood on the site of *Tarrasfoot Tile Works* at Canonbie [see *Gazetteer*] but this has now been demolished.

The most numerous and extensive reminders of tile-making are the hollows, formed by the extraction of clay, now water-filled in wet weather Figure 13.18. In areas of rough fell pasture these clay-pits are not the only quarries and without prior knowledge of the existence of a tilery are difficult to identify.

Figure 13.18 Old clay-pits at Johnby [photograph S B Davis 2001]

In some areas excavations for clay were deeper and resulted in permanent ponds, often designated for fish or wildfowl and appearing on maps as such. In Carlisle the prime example is Hammond's Pond on the site of old flooded clay-pits, now a local amenity. Not only in Cumberland but country wide this was the destiny of many of the surviving redundant clay-pits of the nation's tile-works.[13]

Not all the depressions resulting from clay extraction still exist. One of the principal reasons for this was the inclusion in agreements for taking clay of a stipulation that the ground should as far as possible be returned to its original condition. In 1825, the seven-year lease for *Petersyke Tile Works*, Rockliff (e), contained the provision that the lessee should 'from time to time replace the surface soil where such clay may have been excavated so as to make a regular uniform surface'. Similarly in 1864 at Bewcastle, Sir F U Graham of Netherby required ground from which clay had been taken to be re-soiled and restored. The 'clay quarries' at Stanwix used by *Eden Place Tile Works* were levelled in 1862, and in 1880 the contract for the levelling and soiling of *Langrigg Tilery* at Bromfield was advertised, Figure 13.19.

TO be LET, at LANGRIGG TILERY, on
TUESDAY, FEB. 3, the LEVELLING and SOILING
of a PORTION of the OLD WORKINGS.—For particulars
apply to the FOREMAN, on the Works : or to

Figure 13.19 CAS (Carlisle) *Carlisle Journal* 27th January 1880

With kilns and drying sheds removed for building materials, and most of the sites levelled and re-soiled, it is not surprising that in Cumberland as in the north-east 'most brick and tile yards have been swept away without trace'.[14]

While physical remains have disappeared, other reminders exist. In rural areas many of what were tile-making sites are now covered by small plantations of trees, resulting in one of the most common tile-related place-names, Table 13.1.

Table 13.1 Drainage-tile related place-names in Cumberland and Westmorland

Place-name	Parish	Source
Brick Kiln Wood	Cockermouth	OS 1:25000 1998
Brick Kiln Wood	Wetheral	OS 6" 2nd edition Sheet XXIV-SE rev 1899
Brickfield Plantation	Kirklinton	OS 6" 2nd edition Sheet X-SW rev 1899
Kiln Wood	Arthuret	OS 6" 2nd edition Sheet VII-SW rev 1899
Potterpits Plantation	Wreay	OS 6" 2nd edition Sheet XXX-NE rev 1899
The Tilery	Warcop	Modern house name
The Tilery Farm	Greystoke	OS 1:50000 1976
Tile Kiln Wood	Beaumont	OS 1:25000 1973
Tile Kiln Wood	Hutton/Forest	OS 1:25000 1998
Tile Sheds Cottage	Lanercost	OS 6" 2nd edition Sheet XII-NW rev 1924
Tilekiln Cottage	Arlecdon	OS 6" 2nd edition Sheet LXVIII-NW rev 1898
Tilekiln Cottage	Aspatria	OS 6" 2nd edition Sheet XXXV-SE rev 1898
Tilekiln Field	Greystoke	CAS (Carlisle) TIR/4/5
Tilekiln Plantation	Hutton/Forest	OS 6" 2nd edition Sheet XLIX-NE rev 1923
Tilekiln Wood	Arthuret	OS 6" 2nd edition Sheet VI-SE rev 1899
Tilekiln Wood	Kirkandrews	OS 6" 2nd edition Sheet VI-NE rev 1899
Tilery Cottages	Greystoke	Existing property name

The cottage occupied by the tile-maker often survived the demise of the tilery and a number still exist as private houses using 'Tilekiln' or 'Tilery' as their house-name.

Another common place-name related to clay diggings was 'Clay Dubs', combining the dialect term 'dub', a small but deep pool or pond, with extraction of clay. This use was normally connected with brick-making, as at Brampton where it dates back to 1778. There was also a 'Clay Dubs' at Wigton in 1865 and a 'Brick Dubs' at Dalston in 1893.[15]

Using tiles for purposes other than drainage probably dates back to when they were first made. Their use for ventilation purposes in the walls of farm buildings is one of the most visible alternative uses, common throughout the north of England, Figure 13.20.

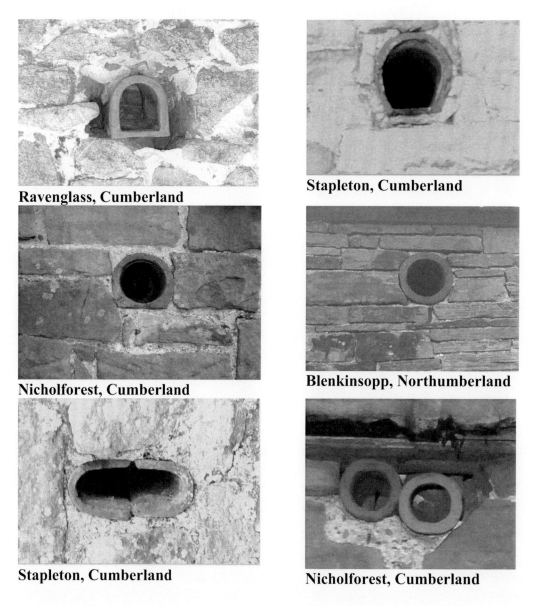

Ravenglass, Cumberland

Stapleton, Cumberland

Nicholforest, Cumberland

Blenkinsopp, Northumberland

Stapleton, Cumberland

Nicholforest, Cumberland

Figure 13.20 Tiles used for ventilation in farm outbuildings [photograph S B Davis]

This practice was advocated in Westmorland in 1868 for farm buildings: 'by perforating the walls in proper places ventilation without draughts and cold might be secured, the common draining tile, inserted in the wall, answers very well for this purpose'.[16]

As time passes these few physical remains of tile-making will continue to deteriorate and eventually collapse and be dispersed, just as tile-affiliated place-names will be dropped from modern maps as has already occurred with many of them.

The story of individual local tileries lives on through the historical sources, newspapers, OS maps, census returns and parish registers, together with the limited extant manuscript archives. Nationally, 'thorough-draining' and the manufacture and use of tiles were extensively chronicled through the agricultural journals and the manuals on draining, which are still accessible.

It was not only in these practical publications that tile-draining appeared but also in works of fiction; this suggests that its importance was widely recognised. In *Wives and Daughters* by Mrs Gaskell it was said that the squire 'had taken the lead among the neighbouring landowners, when he first began "tile-drainage'.[17]

A mention of drainage and tiles in a local historical novel, *Thorston Hall* by O.S. Macdonell published in 1936, relates the problems associated with digging trenches in wet weather. It goes on to describe going to Wheyrigg to see the clay for the drain-pipes. However while the location is a feasible one, the novel was set in a period several decades earlier than pipe manufacture in Cumberland![18]

Major repositories of the history and use of tiles are exhibits in museums and in private hands. Tullie House Museum and Dumfries Museum both hold examples of tiles, although with only a limited number on view. The most complete presentation is in the Museum of Scottish Country Life, which in its Land Gallery has a fascinating display covering every aspect of tiles and draining. At Reading, the Museum of English Rural Life holds the most comprehensive collection, much of which can now be accessed on-line. All four institutions include in their collections tiles marked 'DRAIN' - dating them to the period from 1826 when such stamped tiles were exempt from duty to 1850 when all duty on bricks and tiles was removed.[19]

Finally there remain the collections in private hands, such as that accumulated by the authors while researching this work, Figure 13.21.

Figure 13.21 Personal collection -with thanks to all who have contributed to this study

The preceding pages illustrate the dangers (and the joys!) of asking, and trying to answer the questions 'what is that and what was it for?' described in the introduction. Almost thirteen years later we have produced some at least of the answers and provided the sources for further research, which we shall now leave to others, and the sites to the sheep!

Notes

[1] *Mersehead Nature Reserve: A Solway Gem* RSPB Leaflet (n.d.) [Our thanks to Geoff Brambles for drawing this to our attention], OS 1st edition 6" Sheet 47, surveyed 1851, *CJ* 19/6/1857-1/4, *DT* 24/7/1839-1/A, 9/6/1840-1/A, 14/6/1841-1/E

[2] Harpur (1911) 83

[3] Fenton (1976) 18

[4] With thanks to Mr Calvert who allowed us to observe, and photograph this remedial work in May 2001.

[5] Farey (1813) 362, Lovat (1831) 70, Dickinson (1853) 16, 19

[6] *Farmers Magazine* (1838) 335, Nall (1888) 7-8 [My thanks to Peter Wilkinson for this reference], *Gazetteer of Sites and Manufacturers* Alston *Skelgill Tilery* & *How Hill Tile Works*

[7] Wheeler, W H (1883) 'On River Conservancy and the Cause and Prevention of Floods' *JRASE* 2nd Series Vol.19 393, 396, Watkins, S & Whyte, I (2009) 103

[8] Raistrick, A (1973) *Industrial Archaeology* 75-6, *Gazetteer* Caldbeck *Eller Beck Brick & Tile Works*, Stapleton *Crossings Tile Works*

[9] *Gazetteer* NBL Haltwhistle *Blenkinsopp Tilery*

[10] *Gazetteer* Greystoke *Johnby Brick & Tile Works*

[11] *Gazetteer* Lanercost, Askerton *Kirkcambeck Tile Works* [Permission was given to photograph this kiln which is on private land], Hammond (1977) 171, Day & Charlton (1981) 289, Northumberland *Belsay Tilery* NSMR 03-10938, *Gazetteer* SCT Canonbie *Tarras Foot Tile Works*

[12] *Gazetteer* Lanercost *Tile Works*, *Gazetteer* WES Crosby Ravensworth *Gaythorn Tilery*, *Gazetteer* LAN (F&C) Cartmel *Holker Tilery*, Keates, T (1998) 'Reake Wood Tile Kiln' *The Cumbrian Industrialist* Vol.1, 21-43

[13] Carlisle City Council 'Doorstep Walks' No.5 Hammond's Pond, OS 2nd edition 25" Sheet XXXIX-14 *Calthwaite Tile Works* Fish Pond covering part of site, Ayrshire Fergushill *Tileworks* 'The clay pit --- is now a large pond – home to waterfowl' *Ayrshire Notes* (12006) 24

[14] *Gazetteer* Rockliff *Petersyke Tile Works*, CAS (Carlisle) DMH 5/2/2 February 1825, *Gazetteer* Bewcastle *Kinkry Hill Drain Tile Works*, CAS (Carlisle) DW 9/51 April 1864, *CJ* 17/1/1862-8/3, 27/1/1880-1/2, Davison (1986) 279

[15] Dickinson, W (1859) *A Glossary of the Words and Phrases of Cumberland*, Whitehaven 33, CAS (Carlisle) QRE/1/76 Brampton, OS 1st edition 1865/6 25" Sheet XXIX-6, Wigton, *CJ* 29/12/1893-8/2

[16] Webster C, (1868) 27

[17] Mrs Gaskell (1866) *Wives and Daughters* cited in *OED* under 'tile' as one of the sources for 'tile-drainage'

[18] Macdonell, O S (1936) *Thorston Hall: A Tale of Cumberland Farms in Old Days*, Selwyn & Blount, London 213-239

[19] Appendix 2 Acts relating to Duty on Bricks and Tiles

Appendix 1

Places, dates, money, weights and measures

Places

The names used for areas and places are those relevant to the period. Counties are known by their historic names, as are ancient parishes and their constituent townships. This provides a structure for the *Gazetteer*, based on information from mid-nineteenth century directories, which allows direct comparison between contemporary sources.

Dates

Candlemas – February 2nd

In farming, the day on which new engagements were entered into for the twelve months following the next Lady Day.

Lady Day – March 25th

Michaelmas – 29th September

Two of the quarter-days on which rents were paid; these were also the days when the contract period for taking a tile-works often began.

Money

Prices throughout the period researched were in pounds, shillings and pence. These have been retained and all prices, e.g. tiles per 1000, are given in this form rather than converting to metric.

One pound (£1) contains 20 shillings (20s); one shilling consists of 12 pennies (12d.), each penny (1d.) dividing into two half-pennies (½d.) or four farthings (¼d.).

Weights

As with currency, imperial weights, ton, cwt, lb, and oz, are used throughout.

Measures

Imperial measures, yards and feet are used. In some cases it can be difficult to determine if a 'customary' or a 'statute' measure is being used. There is also the problem with the term 'rood', which can relate to both square and lineal measurements.

Square measure:-

Acre

The English statute or imperial acre of 4840 square yards, 40 rods x 4 rods.

Rood

A fourth part of an acre, a strip measuring 40 rods (1 furlong) x 1 rod.

Lineal measure:-

Rood or Rod

As a statute lineal measure this was 5 ½ yards or 16 ½ feet (a perch or pole) as used in southern, western and midland districts of England.

As a measurement of length in relation to wall building and drainage in Cumberland, Westmorland, Lancashire, Durham and Northumberland this was 7 yards. In Scotland the rod was usually 6 yards.

Appendix 2

Acts relating to duty on bricks and tiles

1784 24 Geo III s.2 c.24
An Act for granting to His Majesty certain Rates and Duties upon Bricks and Tiles made in Great Britain, and for laying additional Duties on Bricks and Tiles imported into the same

1794 34 Geo III c.15
An Act for granting to His Majesty certain additional Duties on Bricks and Tiles made in, or imported into, Great Britain [28th March 1794]

Tiles for draining lands may be made free of any duty – 'to make for the sole purpose of draining wet or marshy lands, Tiles Nineteen inches and three-tenth part of an inch in Length, and Thirteen inches and three-tenth part of an inch in breadth, bent into a semi-elliptical form – without being charged or chargeable with any duty'

1802 42 Geo III c.93
An Act for - - - ; and for allowing certain Draining Tiles to be made free of Duty [26th June 1802]

'For the sole purpose of Draining wet or marshy lands free of the Duties of Excise, Tiles not less than Nine inches long, such Tiles being in every other respect of the Description and Dimensions prescribed' in 34 Geo III c.15

1806 46 Geo III c.138
An Act for - - - ; and to exempt Tiles made for the Purpose of draining Lands from the Duties of Excise [22nd July 1806]

For the sole purpose of draining wet or marshy lands, free of the duties of excise, 'Tiles bent into a semi-elliptical Form, the Width of which, measured on the inside thereof, shall not in any part exceed six inches, and the height of which when so bent as aforesaid, taken from the outside of the Crown of the Arch thereof in a perpendicular line to the extreme Edge thereof, shall in all cases exceed the Width measured as aforesaid'

1815 55 Geo III c.176
An Act for allowing certain Tiles to be made Duty free to serve for Draining [11th July 1815]

To make 'for the sole purpose of serving for the Foundations or Support of Tiles bent into the semi-elliptical Form prescribed - - - flat tiles not exceeding one inch in thickness -- - having at one end a semicircular Projection, and at the other a Semicircular Arch or Indent, - - - such Tile being also not less than Nine Inches in Length and not exceeding Seven Inches in Breadth -- - being also perforated with circular Holes - - - '

Appendix 2 continued

Acts relating to duty on bricks and tiles

1821 1 & 2 Geo IV c.102
An Act for - - - ; and for exempting Tiles made for draining Lands from Duty [10th July 1821]

'Flat Tiles for the sole Purpose of serving for the Foundations or Support of such semi elliptical Tiles as shall be made and applicable and fit for the sole Purpose of draining'

1824 5 Geo IV c.75
An Act - - - to exempt - - - ; and to the Duty on Draining Tiles [17th June 1824]

'To make Tiles or Bricks for the sole Purpose of draining wet or marshy Land, without being charged or chargeable with any Duty for or in respect of such Tiles or Bricks: Provided always, that all such Tiles and Bricks shall be made upon the Land for the draining of which such Tiles or Bricks shall be used and employed, or within a Quarter of a Mile of such Land'

1826 7 Geo IV c.49
An Act to amend several Laws of Excise relating to - - - , Tiles and Bricks for draining - - - [26th May 1826]

'That from and after the passing of this Act it shall and may be lawful to and for any Person to make Tiles or Bricks for the sole Purpose of draining wet or marshy Land without being charged or chargeable with any Duty for or in respect of such Tiles and Bricks: Provided always, that all such Tiles or Bricks shall be stamped or moulded by the Person making the same with the Word "Drain" in or near the Centre of one of the Surfaces of such Tile or Brick'

1850 13 & 14 Vic. c.9
An Act to repeal the Duties and Drawbacks of Excise on Bricks [17th May 1850]

'That from and after the passing of this Act all the Duties and Drawbacks of Excise on Bricks --- are hereby repealed'

Appendix 3

Land drainage acts

1840 3 & 4 Vict. c.55 Mr Phillip Pusey's Act

1846 9 & 10 Vict. c.101 'The Drainage Act'
The first public money drainage act, 'The Drainage Act', administered by the Inclosure Commissioners for England and Wales

Altering and amending
1847 10 Vict. c.11
1848 11 & 12 Vict. c.119

1848 11 & 12 Vict. c.142
Companies Act – *The West of England & South Wales Land Drainage & Inclosure Company*

1849 12 & 13 Vict. c.91
Companies Act – *The General Land Drainage & Improvement Company*

1849 12 & 13 Vict. c.100
Private Money Drainage Act

1850 13 & 14 Vict. c.31 'The Second Drainage Act'
The second public money drainage act, administered by the Inclosure Commissioners for England and Wales

Altering and amending
1856 19 Vict. c.9

1853 16 & 17 Vict. c.154, 18 & 19 Vict. c.84, 22 & 23 Vict. c.82, 26 & 27 Vict. 140
Companies Act – *The Lands Improvement Company*

1860 23 & 24 Vict. c.169 & c.194
Companies Act – *The Land Loan & Enfranchisement Company*
Subject to the approval of the Inclosure Commissioners

1864 27 & 28 Vict. c.114
The Improvement of Land Act

Appendix 4

Some major tile-making families

Family member	Years	Tile -works	Occupation
DEMAIN			
Emanuel Demain [1]	1827-34	Earl of Carlisle's Tile-kiln	brick & tile-maker
	1836	Middle Farm Tile-works	brick & tile-maker
	1836-40	Becks [Toppin Castle]	brick & tile-maker
	1840	*Allan Grove Brick & Tile Works*	brick & tile-maker
James Demain son of Emanuel	1861-74	*Allen Grove Brick & Tile Works*	brick & tile-maker
Emanuel Demain [2] grandson of Emanuel	1876-95	*Allan Grove Brick & Tile Works*	brick & tile-maker
EDMONDSON			
Thomas Edmondson	1841	*Bassenthwaite Tile Kiln*	tile-maker
	1841-51	*Westward Park Tilery*	tile-maker
	1861-	*Bleatarn Tilery*	tile-maker
William Edmondson son of Thomas	1841	*Bassenthwaite Tile Kiln*	tile-maker
	1841-51	*Westward Park Tilery*	tile-burner
	1861-71	*Gaythorne Tilery*	tile & brick-maker
George Edmondson grandson of Thomas born Bromfield	1861	*Bleatarn Tilery*	tile-maker
George Edmondson Born Penruddock	1871	Cliburn – brick-works	labourer
	1877-91	*Julian Bower Brick & T W*	tile-mkr, manager
Ridley Edmondson Son of George	1911	Penrith Brick-works	brick-maker

Appendix 4 continued

Family member	Years	Tile-works	Occupation
LUCOCK			
Robert Lucock	1820-24	Netherby Estate	tile-burner
	1824-54	*Langrigg Tilery*	manufacturer
	1830-54	*Broughton Moor Brick & Tile Works*	manufacturer
	1831-54	*Curthwaite Brick & Tile Works*	manufacturer
[died 1854]	1836-	Plumbland	manufacturer
Joseph Lucock [1] brother of Robert	1820-24	Netherby Estate	tile-burner
	1824-31	*Langrigg Tilery*	tile-moulder
[died 1871]	1831-71	*Curthwaite Brick & Tile Works*	manager
Joseph Lucock [2] son of Robert	1854	R Lucock & Son [all Lucock tileries]	manufacturer
[died 1871]	1854-71	Joseph Lucock [all Lucock tileries]	manufacturer
Mary Lucock wife of Joseph [2]	1871-73	Broughton Moor & Langrigg	manufacturer
James Lucock son of Joseph [1]	-1851	*Curthwaite Brick & Tile Works*	tile-maker
	1871-76	" "	proprietor
	1881	Carlisle	brick & tile-mkr

Appendix 4 continued

Family member	Years	Tile-works	Occupation
PICKERING			
Joseph Pickering [died 1846]	1843	*Howgill Tile Works*	proprietor
James Pickering	1851	*Howgill Tile Works*	manufacturer
John Pickering Son of James?	1851	*Howgill Tile Works*	tile-burner
		Whitrigg Tile Works	manufacturer
	1859	*Johnby Brick & Tile Works*	tile-maker
Jane (Janet) Pickering Widow of Joseph [died 1894]	1846	*Howgill Tile Works*	
	1861-71	*Johnby Brick & Tile Works*	manufacturer
James Pickering Son of Joseph & Jane	1861	*Johnby Brick & Tile Works*	tile-maker
	1871-99	*Johnby Brick & Tile Works*	manufacturer
	1900-06	*Johnby Wythes Tilery Co Ltd*	manager
John Pickering Son of James	1891	*Johnby Brick & Tile Works*	manufacturer
Joseph Pickering Son of James	1891	*Johnby Brick & Tile Works*	tile-maker

Family member	Years	Tile-works	Occupation
TAYLOR			
Samuel Taylor	1861-65	*Hackthorpe Tilery*	tile-maker
	1866-67	*Troutbeck Brick & Tile Works*	tile-maker
	1871-74	*Threlkeld Brick & Tile Works*	tile & brick mkr
	1875-1906	*Culgaith Brick & Tile Works*	manager
[died 1906]	1897-1906	*Troutbeck Brick & Tile Works*	proprietor

Appendix 4 continued

Family member	Years	Tile-works	Occupation
TAYLOR continued			
John Thomas Taylor son of Samuel	1881-	*Culgaith B & Tile Works*	brick & tile-maker
	1910-14	*Sandysike B & Tile Works*	brick & tile-maker
John Fallowfield Taylor Son of Samuel	1891	*Culgaith B & Tile Works*	drain tile-maker
	1901	*Troutbeck B & Tile Wks.*	manager
	1908-25	*Culgaith B & Tile Works*	brick & tile-maker
George William Taylor Son of Samuel	1891	*Culgaith B & Tile Works*	drain tile-maker
	1901	*Troutbeck B & Tile Wks.*	tile-maker
Clement Taylor Son of Samuel	1891-25	*Culgaith B & Tile Works*	brick & tile-maker
Frederick Septimus Taylor son of Samuel	1901	*Troutbeck B & Tile Works*	tile-maker
George Taylor Brother of Samuel	1861-	*Hackthorpe Tilery*	drain tile-maker
	1871-81	*Troutbeck B & Tile Wks.*	tile-maker
Harold Taylor Son of John Thomas	1911	*Sandysike B & Tile Works*	brick & tile-maker

Family member	Years	Tile-works	Occupation
TWEDDLE			
Joseph Tweddle [1] died 1884	1847-84	*Sandysike Brick & Tile Works*	tile-maker
Joseph Tweddle [2] son of Joseph	1881-1901	*Sandysike Brick & Tile Wks*	brick & tile-maker

Appendix 4 continued

Family member	Years	Tile-works	Occupation
TWEDDLE continued			
David Tweddle son of Joseph [1] [died 1884]	1871	*Sandysike B & Tile Wks*	tile-maker
Archibald Tweddle ? brother of James	1851	*Brackenhill Tile Works*	tile-maker
	1854-63	*Wetheriggs B & Tile Wks*	tile-burner
James Tweddle ? brother of Archibald	1852	*Abbey Tile Works*	tile-maker
	1853-61	*Tarrasfoot B & Tile Wks*	tile-maker
	1862-71	*Troutbeck B & Tile Wks*	tile-maker
David Tweddle son of James	1871	*Troutbeck B & Tile Wks*	tile-labourer
John Tweddle [2] son of James	1871	*Troutbeck B & Tile Wks*	tile-labourer
John Tweddle [1] died 1888	1849-88	*Leeshill Tile Works*	proprietor
Alexander Tweddle died 1922	1876-01	*Sandysike B & Tile Wks*	manufacturer
William Tweddle [1] son of Alexander	1891	*Sandysike B & Tile Wks*	brick & tile-maker
Alexander Tweddle son of Alexander	1891	*Sandysike B & Tile Wks*	brick & tile-maker
Robert Tweddle son of Alexander	1891	*Sandysike B & Tile Works*	brick & tile-maker
William Tweddle [2] Son of Joseph [1]	1878-81	*Tarrasfoot B & Tile Wks*	brick & tile-maker
John Tweddle [3]	1901-14	*Kirkcambeck B & Tile Wks*	tile-maker

Appendix 5

Cubic yards of clay required to manufacture tiles

Tile size in inches	Cubic yards of clay	Quantity of tiles
2	1 ½	1000
2 ½	2	1000
3	2 ½	1000
4	3	1000
5	4	1000
6	5	1000
7	6	1000
8	1	42
9	1	35
Bricks	3	1000

Source:
CAS (Carlisle) DB74/2/41/21 Account of clay used at *Culgaith Tilery* 1885-1896
The clay royalty was six pence per cubic yard.

Weight of pipes per 1000 by bore, thickness and length

Bore.	Thick.	Weight of Pipes per 1000.			
		12 inches long.	14 inches long.	16 inches long.	18 inches long.
Inches.	Inch.	Cwts.	Cwts.	Cwts.	Cwts.
1	$\frac{1}{4}$	$11\frac{1}{2}$	$13\frac{1}{2}$	$15\frac{1}{4}$	17
2	$\frac{3}{8}$	17	20	23	$25\frac{3}{4}$
3	$\frac{1}{2}$	$34\frac{1}{4}$	40	46	$51\frac{1}{2}$
4	$\frac{1}{2}$	$45\frac{3}{4}$	$53\frac{1}{2}$	61	$68\frac{1}{2}$
5	$\frac{5}{8}$	$71\frac{1}{2}$	$83\frac{1}{2}$	$95\frac{1}{4}$	107
6	$\frac{3}{4}$	103	120	137	$154\frac{1}{2}$
7	$\frac{3}{4}$	120	140	160	180
8	$\frac{7}{8}$	160	$186\frac{1}{2}$	$213\frac{1}{2}$	240
9	$\frac{7}{8}$	180	210	240	270
10	1	228	$266\frac{1}{2}$	$304\frac{3}{4}$	343
11	1	$251\frac{1}{2}$	$293\frac{1}{2}$	$335\frac{1}{4}$	$378\frac{1}{2}$
12	1	$274\frac{1}{4}$	320	$365\frac{3}{4}$	$411\frac{1}{2}$

Source:
Hozier, W.W. (1870) *Practical Remarks on Agricultural Drainage* p 69

Glossary

ARCH-TILES see **TILES:-arch-tiles**

BENDER or BENDING BLOCK see **TILE:- tile-bender**

BOTTOM TILES see **SOLES**

BRICK
brick-covers
Wooden covers to protect rows of bricks drying in the open [*CJ* 8/6/1869].
brick-drain
A drain formed in the bottom of a trench, by setting bricks on edge to create the sides, and then laying bricks across them, giving an opening approximately four inches square. Bricks could also be used as a sole if conditions warranted.
An article of 1843 suggests that such drains were constructed in Wigtownshire, Scotland in the mid-1750s, at a depth of about 30 inches [*Transactions of the HASS* Vol. XIV].
brick-field
Described in 1801 as 'a field where bricks are made' [*SOED*], and in 1885 as 'a field or yard where bricks are made' [Ogilvie (1885)].The term was apparently English with no known examples in Scotland [Douglas & Oglethorpe (1993)].
There are numerous examples of its use in Cumberland, including Botcherby, Upperby, Kingmoor, Moresby, Cleator, Whitehaven and West Linton, together with one at Soulby in Westmorland.
fire-brick
Fire-clay, which has high silica content, is in Cumberland mainly found in the western coastal strip and was used to manufacture fire-bricks. Among other purposes these were employed to line the fire-holes of tile-kilns, with extra long bricks being manufactured for this purpose, and sold as 'Tile Kiln Bricks' [CAS (Carlisle) DMH/5/2/2, *CJ* 22/2/1856].
hollow-brick
Manufactured at a number of Works, hollow-bricks usually contained two circular apertures which ran lengthwise [See Figure 8.19 b].
perforated-brick
This was a brick which normally contained ten cylindrical opening through the depth of the body [See Figure 8.19a].

BURNER see **TILE:-tile-burner**

CAST & CASTING
The digging and turning, usually in the autumn, of clay that was to be left outside over the winter months. 'To be let the casting of clay' (Northumberland) [*CJ* 5/1/1839].

CLAMP

Clamp-kiln, field-clamp and brick-clamp are terms used to describe burning in the open covered with earth as opposed to within a kiln, no evidence has been found to suggest tiles were fired in this way.

CLAY

'The essential properties of clay are two: that when mixed with a certain proportion of water it makes a plastic material that can be moulded. Then when baked under certain conditions it becomes hard and durable' [Raistrick (1943)].

clay-crusher

A clay-crusher or crushing-mill was used for crushing the small stones and gravel found in some clay. As to whether clay was crushed or sent directly to a pug-mill, would depend on the number and size of stones it contained.

'Clay-Crushers' were advertised for sale among the contents of *Millrigg Tilery* in 1865 [*CJ* 3/2/1865]. In 1860 the sale of plant at *Whitrigg Tile Works* included 'Crushing-Rollers' [*CJ* 2/12/1860]. A 'Clay-Mill' was shown at *Sebergham Tile Works* in 1864 on the 1st edition O S map [Sheet XXXVIII].

'clay drainage pipe works'

'A site where clay pipes used for drainage are manufactured' RCHME (2000) *Thesaurus.*

clay-mill see **clay-crusher**

clay-pit

The bed from which clay was extracted determined the location of the tile-works. The description of the clay-pit often appeared in directories and newspapers. At Sandysike 'a bed of excellent clay exists in the township' [Bulmer (1884)] and at Millrigg 'an abundance of clay' [*CJ* 3/2/1865]. The description of Silecroft gave more detail 'a bed of clay 40 feet deep, from which bricks, tiles, drainpipes etc are made' [Bulmer (1901)].

In the 1890s when the surveys for the 2nd edition O S maps were carried out, the only indication that a site had existed was often the caption 'old clay pit'.

clay-washer

A 'clay washer' was a machine for washing stones out of clay, more usually in Cumberland a clay-crusher or grinding-mill was used. The only located reference to a washer in the County is at Calthwaite in 1860 [OS Sheet XXXIX].

fat-clay

Clay of a type which shrank on baking and was unsuitable for brick and tile-making without the addition of sand or other aggregate.

fire-clay

Clay with a high silica content used to manufacture fire-bricks was also recommended by Robert Lucock to be used in a fine-ground form to make the best mortar for laying fire-bricks in a kiln [CAS (Carlisle) D HUD 3/66/2].

keen-clay

Keen-clay was the term used by workmen on the Netherby estate for clay of a type suitable for coarse pottery, bricks and draining-tiles, with the added advantage of being free of small stones [Yule (1929) 391].

lean-clay

This was friable clay which was deficient in binding power, and therefore difficult to mould and making it unsuitable for tile-making.

CLOGS
Special types of clogs were produced for specific occupations, including a ditcher's clog, a pair of which is on display in the *Museum of Scottish Country Life.*

COLLARS
A 'collar' usually used with 1 ½, 2 and 2 ½ inch-diameter-pipes, was approximately three inches wide, into which were inserted the ends of two pipes, thus preventing earth entering at the join and silting up the pipes. The first located advertisements for these in Cumberland were in 1849, when they were on sale at *Holme Cultram Tilery* [*CJ* 21/9/1849]. In Westmorland they were manufactured in 1847 at *Hackthorpe Tilery* for use on the Lowther estate.

CONTRACT
The system of manufacture in the early years of the industry appears to have been by contract, for a term of years or for a stipulated quantity of tiles.

A landowner with a suitable bed of clay on his property, having erected a kiln and drying sheds, would put out the making of tiles to contract. 'One or more experienced persons to contract for manufacturing of draining tiles for a term to be agreed on' [*CJ* 31/10/1835].

'Clay ground will be found, and a proper Kiln & Drying Sheds erected. The contractor to find all labour, barrows, tools and coals' [*CJ* 23/1/1836].

Terms varied but generally included the preparation of the clay and the moulding and burning of the tiles. The contractor would find the labour, also provide equipment such as barrows and tools and purchase the coal for firing the kiln. The finished tiles would have to be loaded onto carts. In return the landowner purchased a given quantity of tiles, at an agreed price per thousand, over a fixed period usually one, two or three years. If the contractor could manufacture more tiles than was required to fulfil the contract, these could be sold on the open market at a higher price.

DRAIN-SLATES see SOLES

DRAINER
The term was normally applied to the labourer who dug and refilled the trenches, the description of such a labourer could be more specific e.g. field-drainer, land-drainer, tile-drainer, estate-drainer. A master-drainer employing labourers, or an estate-drainer or agent would be responsible for setting the tiles and supervising schemes.

DRYING SHADE see SHADE

DRYING SHEDS
Drying sheds in use in the early years were constructed of strong wooden posts, supporting a roof, usually thatched [Yule (1829) Hodges (1844)]. The structures which replaced these had slate roofs, usually Welsh slate which was thinner and therefore lighter in weight than local slate. The sides were constructed with a system of louvre-boards to allow the entry of air. Internally the walls were lined with shelves, and centrally there were one or more double sided sections running the length of the shed [See Figure 4.4].

EYE
An orifice or opening for the introduction or withdrawal of material, 'Kiln-ee, the orifice in a lime kiln from which the lime is drawn' Atkinson, J. C. (1868) *A Glossary of the Cleveland Dialect* quoted in Wright, J. (1898) *The English Dialect Dictionary.*
One instance found of its use for the fire-hole of a tile-kiln was at Petersyke, Rockliff '560 Fire Bricks for the 10 Eyes' [CAS (Carlisle) DMH/5/2/2 16th February 1825].

FIRE-BRICK see BRICK:-fire-brick

FIRE-CLAY see CLAY:-fire-clay

FOOTINGS see SOLES

FREQUENT DRAINING see THOROUGH DRAINING

FURROW DRAINING see THOROUGH DRAINING

GIN
 A machine powered by a horse, or other animal, which was harnessed to the free end of a horizontal beam, and by constantly walking in a circle provided the power to turn the cogs which were attached to the opposite end of the beam. Used extensively in agriculture, in tile-making it was the central spindle with knives attached, in the barrel of a pug-mill which was rotated [See Figure 4.2].
gin-house
The circular shed which housed the gin.
gin-ring
Open to the elements, apart from possibly a roof, these were shown on 1st edition OS maps at a number of tile-works. In 1878 the gin-ring at *Threlkeld Tile Works* was 31 feet in diameter [*CJ* 3/5/1878].

HOLLOW-BRICK see BRICK:-hollow-brick

HORSESHOE-TILE see TILES:-horseshoe

KILN
The structure used to 'burn' or bake, bricks and tiles. The type of kiln normally used in a small tile-works was an intermittent updraught kiln. This consisted of a single chamber, with fire-holes, 'eyes', on each side, and was worked on a cycle of fill, fire, cool and then empty, 'draw', 'A Kiln is now burned and will be drawn tomorrow' [CAS (Carlisle) D Lons L15/1/1/29].
In local dialect occasionally written as 'Cill', 'Kil' [CAS (Carlisle) D Lons L15/1/3/4], Tile Kill Inn' [1851 & 1861 Census, Great Clifton].
Scotch kiln
'A type of updraught intermittent kiln of rectangular plan and battered sides, but with an open top' [RCHME (2000) *Thesaurus*]. These often had storm shelters to protect the row of fire-holes down each side. The early kiln at Netherby was of this type [Yule (1829)].

Newcastle kiln
Named as such as they were widely used on Tyneside, this was a horizontal-draught kiln, also intermittent. The walls were heavily buttressed on each side, with a chimney at one end, and an entrance and two fire-holes at the other. Inside, the roof was barrel-shaped, and there were flues at the base of the chimney wall.
One brick built example was standing at Kirkcambeck in 2008 [See Figures 13.10-16], as was a two chambered kiln with a central chimney at Tarrasfoot [*Gazetteer* Figure 5.12].

MOULDER see **tile-moulder**

MOULDING FRAME see **TILE:-tile-mould**

MUG or MUGG-TILE see **TILES:-mug**

NEWCASTLE KILN see **KILN:-Newcastle kiln**

OFFAL WOOD
Offal wood and faggots such as tops and loppings of firs were also used as fuel in tile-kilns by estates which had a surplus of these materials. [CAS (Carlisle) DLonsL15 Box 1232].

PARALLEL DRAINS see **THOROUGH DRAINING**

PERFORATED-BRICK see **BRICK:-perforated-brick**

PIPES see **TILES**

PUG-MILL
A machine frequently horse powered, for cutting and mixing raw clay with water to produce the desired consistency [RCHM (2000) *Thesaurus*] [Douglas & Oglethorpe (1993)].

RUNNER see **TILE:-tile-makers-runner**

SCOTCH DRAIN-TILES see **TILES:-Scotch drain-tiles**

SCOTCH KILN see **KILN:-Scotch kiln**

SHADE
This term for a shed, or lightly constructed wooden building, largely obsolete by the mid nineteenth century, was still in occasional use in the early 1800s. Examples of this were at Petersyke Close, in which a 'Tile Kiln, Shade and other conveniences for making tiles are erected' [CAS (Carlisle) DMH5/2/2 16th February 1825], and in describing the situation at Langrigg in 1832, where 'The tempering mill is under cover in the centre of the extensive Drying Shade', [*CJ* 5/4/1828]. It was not restricted to tile drying sheds but applied to all sheds 'to be let the slating of some Cattle Shades' [*CJ* 15/6/1839].

SLATE-BOTTOM see **SOLES**

SOLE-PIPE and SOLE-TILE see **TILES**:-**tile-pipe**

SOLES

In some areas horseshoe-tiles were supplied with a separate flat sheet of clay to support the tiles in the trench when the ground was soft, this was a sole. In Cumberland, where as yet only one advertisement for soles, described as footings, has been located. Slate, particularly offal roofing slates, or broken tiles appear to have been used for this purpose. Wooden soles were also used; they were usually offcuts of larch, alder or other low priced woods [Dickinson (1850) 34].

Soles were called 'bottom tiles' in some areas. [Wiggins (1840) 352, Beart (1841) 93].

STAFFORDSHIRE PRINCIPLE

'He (Robert Lucock) has commenced the manufacture of draining tiles at Langrigg --- he intends to prepare them upon the Staffordshire principle' [*CJ* 21/8/1824].

Robert Lucock learned tile-making from Thomas Guy Patrick, a Staffordshire tile-maker brought to the Netherby Estate to set up a tile-works. [Lonsdale (1868) pp.37-39].

TEMPERING

'In the spring as soon as the frosts are gone, the process of tempering commences, which is done with the greatest care, either by a simple grinding machine, 'tempering mill', driven by a pony, or by manual labour'. [Yule (1829) p.39].

THOROUGH DRAINING

The system advocated by James Smith of Deanston and adapted by others, in particular Josiah Parkes, in relation to the depth of the drains, and the size of the tiles and pipes.

The principle of thorough draining was to provide every field that needed draining with a complete system of parallel underground channels, running in the line of the greatest slope of the ground. The channels sufficiently close to each other, that all of the rain in excess of that absorbed by the soil was carried off by the drains.

Also known as **furrow draining** (particularly in Scotland) from the custom of forming the drains in the lines of furrows.

From the number and arrangement of the drains the terms **frequent drains** and **parallel drains** were also used.

TILE

tile-bender or bending-block see **tile-horse**

tile-burner

The person responsible for burning bricks and tiles in a kiln, including ensuring that the kiln was correctly filled, and that the fires burned at the right temperature for the necessary period of time.

tile-hook

'The tile hook is an implement by means of which the pipes may be lowered from the edge of the trench and laid at the bottom' ['Drainage of Land' (1911)].

tile-horse
A form usually made of wood over which a sheet of clay, of the correct size, is pressed to create the desired shaped drain-tile [Yule (1829) p.391/2, Bell (1843) pp743/7].
In other areas the same object was described as a tile-bender or a bending-block. [Wiggins (1840) Plan iv, Beart (1841) 99].
tile-kiln-bricks see **BRICK:-fire-bricks**
tile-maker
The terms 'tile-burner' and 'tile-maker' seem, particularly in early advertisements, to describe the same person, who would contract with an owner of a works to supply tiles at an agreed price.
'Wanted an experienced maker of draining tiles' [*CJ* (1823)].
Wanted 'tile burner' 'He prepares the clay, provides the coal and everything necessary at his own expense and furnishes the kiln owner with tiles at an agreed price' [Yule (1829)]
As the industry expanded the hand-moulder was replaced by tile-making machines and the operatives of these and other equipment were the tile-makers.
tile-maker's runner
A boy, or possibly a girl, who worked with a **tile-moulder** bringing the tempered clay in lumps to the moulding table and removing the moulded tile, carrying it to the **drying shed**.
tile-manufacturer
A term used to describe the owner or lessee of a tile-works, who was also involved in the manufacturing process. In 1841, only Robert Lucock used this description, ten years later there were ten individuals who gave tile-manufacturer as their occupation.
tile-mould or **moulding frame**
The frame in which the thin sheet of clay was formed prior to moulding it on the **tile-horse** to create the shape of the drain tile [Bell (1843) pp.743/4/7].
tile-moulder
He worked at a moulding table, with sand, water, and a mould the shape of the tile. He was assisted by a boy who brought the clay and removed the moulded tiles [Yule (1829)].

TILE-BOTTOM see **SOLES**

TILE-PIPE see **TILES:-tile-pipe**

TILE WORKS
A 'Tile Works' or 'Tilery' in nineteenth-century sources, including Ordnance Survey maps and trade directories, would in Cumberland almost certainly relate to drainage-tiles. These terms are now used however to describe sites used for the manufacture of roof, floor and decorative tiles [RCHME (2000) *Thesaurus*].

TILE-YARD
Used occasionally in Cumberland as an alternative to tile-works, 'apply to Robert Lucock at the Tile Yard, Wragmire' [*CJ* 27/6/1835].

TILERY see **TILE WORKS**

TILES

According to the *Oxford English Dictionary* 'a thin slab of burnt clay, shaped according to the purpose for which it is required --- semi-cylindrical or tunnel shaped when used for purpose of drainage'. The term was in use at least as early as 1823 in Cumberland in advertisements in the *Carlisle Journal* and continued to be so throughout the nineteenth-century.

arch-tiles

Large diameter horseshoe-tiles [*CJ* 19/9/1862].

horseshoe-tile

A tile produced by moulding a flat sheet of clay over a horseshoe shaped wooden form approximately 12 inches long. This was the earliest form of drainage-tile produced in Cumberland.

mug or mugg-tile

A term used for horseshoe-tiles in Scotland [Douglas & Oglethorpe (1993) p.67, Fenton (1976) p.22] Also called 'common drain tiles' or 'saddle-back' tiles.

pipe

A pipe could be defined as the final stage in the evolution of the tile, round without a flat base and extruded from a machine rather than hand moulded.

Scotch drain-tile

The term used in Cumberland for tiles manufactured in Scotland, which were usually around 14 ¾ to 15 inches in length, longer than the standard Cumberland tiles.

tile-pipe or pipe-tile

These were the next stage after horseshoe-tiles, they could be described as either a pipe with a flattened base or a horseshoe-tile with a sole attached. The shapes of the apertures varied from almost round to oval, while in size they were produced from as small as one inch up to nine inches. Some early ones may have been hand-moulded, but from the 1850s the majority would have been machine made.

In the United States where the design of early tiles was based on samples imported from Scotland these types were called 'sole-tiles' [Weaver (1964) p.127].

tunnel-tiles

Similar to a horseshoe-tile but semi-circular [Wiggins (1840) Plan iv].

TUNNEL-TILE see **TILES:-tunnel-tiles**

WASHER see **CLAY:-clay-washer**

Bibliography

Primary sources

Beamish Museum Archive
Photographs

Cumbria Libraries (Carlisle, Local Studies Section)
Census Enumerations – Cumberland & Westmorland 1841-1901 (microfiche)
Ordnance Survey maps 1:10560, Initial survey, 1859-1865 Cumberland
Ordnance Survey maps 1:10560, First revision, 1897-1900 Cumberland
Ordnance Survey maps 1:2500, First revision, 1897-1900 Cumberland
Carlisle Examiner & North Western Advertiser [microfilm]
Cumberland News [microfilm]
English Lakes Visitor & Keswick Guardian [microfilm]
Wigton Advertiser [microfilm]

Cumbria Libraries (Penrith)
Cumberland & Westmorland Advertiser [microfilm]

Cumbria Archive Centre (Carlisle)
Carlisle Journal 1819 – 1885 all issues, 1886 onwards selected years
Carlisle Patriot
Cumberland Pacquet
Penrith Observer
Census Enumerations – Cumberland [microfilm]
Ordnance Survey maps 1:2500, Initial survey, 1859-1865 Cumberland
Ordnance Survey *Books of Reference* [dates as initial survey]
Ordnance Survey maps 1:2500, First revision, 1897-1900 Cumberland
Parish Registers – Baptism, Marriage & Burial [microfilm]
CAS (Carlisle) DB3/244 Rolled Plan 1841 Leapsrigg
CAS (Carlisle) D/BW/13/4/8/2 Book of maps re Brackenhill estate 1847
CAS (Carlisle) Finance Act (1909-10) TIR/4/ Valuation Books & Plans
CAS (Carlisle) D/CL/P/8/41 Thomas Hetherington
CAS (Carlisle) DRC/8/ Tithe Maps
CAS (Carlisle) DB74/2/41/21 Account of clay used at Culgaith Tilery 1885-96
CAS (Carlisle) DBS4/3/38 Aglionby Estate improvements 1854
CAS (Carlisle) DBS529 *Johnby Wythes Tilery Co Ltd*
Administrative Records
CAS (Carlisle) DBS529/1/1 Register of Directors 1901-1905
CAS (Carlisle) DBS529/1/2 Counterfoil Book of Share Certificates 1900-1907
CAS (Carlisle) DBS529/1/3 Register of Shares
CAS (Carlisle) DBS529/1/4 Minute Book of the Board of Directors 1900-1909
CAS (Carlisle) DBS529/1/5 Draft & Printed Reports and Balance Sheets 1901-1909
CAS (Carlisle) DBS529/1/6 Letters Companies Registration Office 1909

CAS (Carlisle) DBS529/1/7 Papers re the winding up of the Company 1910
CAS (Carlisle) DBS529/2/1 Valuation of Stock 1900-1907
CAS (Carlisle) DBS529/2/2 Ledger 1900-1908
CAS (Carlisle) DBS529/2/3 Sales Journal 1900-1908
CAS (Carlisle) DBS529/2/4 Petty Cash Book 1900-1908
CAS (Carlisle) DBS529/2/5 Cash Book
CAS (Carlisle) DCartC1 Copy of Will of Mr Robert Lucock
CAS (Carlisle) D/Hud17/158/1 Estate correspondence 1844-6
CAS (Carlisle) D/HG/214 Summary of income and outgoings for each named farm on Greystoke Estate 1893-1903
CAS (Carlisle) D ING 23 Building & Draining Accounts 1847-1864
CAS (Carlisle) D ING 46 Account of Costs for Draining etc 1843-1846
CAS (Carlisle) D Lons L 15/1/1/1-31, 15/1/2/1-6, 15/1/3/1-6 Hackthorpe Tilery
CAS (Carlisle) D Lons/W3/61 General Estate Cash Books – Greenbank Tilery 1859-62
CAS (Carlisle) D/Mil/Mounsey/153 Sale Particulars
2 Sebergham – Round Hill Estate 1864, 12 Cumwhinton 1924, 70 Kirklinton-Moorhouse & Newbiggin 1881, 187 Walton-Leapsrigg Estate 1910, 309 Lanercost-1920
CAS (Carlisle) D/Ric/154 Hayton Estates
CAS (Carlisle) DW9/51 Ewart Archive – Agreement – for clay for tiles 4th April 1864
CAS (Carlisle) Ewart Collection, ms note 1863, 'Crossings Tile Works'
CAS (Carlisle) DX50/1 DX50/2 Lonsdale Brick & Tile Works
CAS (Carlisle) DX558/77 Allen Grove Brick & Tile Works
CAS (Carlisle) DX1648/1/1 Copy licence to Thomas Nelson to allow the use of inventions in the manufacture of bricks and tiles
CAS (Carlisle) DX1648/2/1 Papers re the death of a boy using a pug mill erected on Thomas Nelson's land 1856
CAS (Carlisle) QRE/1/76 Brampton Enclosure 1778

Cumbria Libraries (Kendal Local Studies Library)
Ordnance Survey maps 1:10560 Initial Survey, 1856-60 Westmorland

Cumbria Archive Centre (Kendal)
Ordnance Survey maps 1:2500, 1:10560, Initial survey, 1856-60 Westmorland
Ordnance Survey maps 1:10560, First revision, 1896-8, Westmorland
CAS (Kendal) Finance Act (1909-10) WD/DV/2 Plan
CAS (Kendal) WD DF/Box 24/1 Papers re Gaythorne Tilery 1863-4
CAS (Kendal) WD DF Box 17/15 Culgaith Tilery 1859-60, Bleatarn Tilery 1859, Gaythorne Tilery 1861
CAS (Kendal) WPR7/1/5 Crosby Ravensworth, Tithe & endowment, Papers re Glebe lands in Lazonby. Letters about drainage, cost of tiles etc 1851-52, 1862-63
CAS (Kendal) WDSO 108/A3135 Bowtell 09,13,14 Cumbrian Railways Association – *Cockermouth, Penrith & Keswick Railway* notes and correspondence about personalities

Cumbria Archive & Local Studies Centre (Barrow)
Ordnance Survey maps 1:10560 Survey, 1842-48 Lancashire
Ordnance Survey maps 1:2500, Initial survey, 1888-1893 Lancashire

BIBLIOGRAPHY

Cumbria Archive & Local Studies Centre (Whitehaven)
CAS (Whitehaven) D Cu/5/82 1836/7 Kiln at Winscales
CAS (Whitehaven) D/Di/49 Dickinson Family
CAS (Whitehaven) D/Di/53/1 Troutbeck Tilery
CAS (Whitehaven) D/Lec/116 Clay Royalty, Dean
CAS (Whitehaven) D/Lec/119 West Park Tilery Documents
CAS (Whitehaven) D/Lec/144 Westward Tilery Sales Book 1852/3
CAS (Whitehaven) D/Lec/219 Clay Royalty, Caldbeck
CAS (Whitehaven) D/Lec/240 Bigrigg Tilery Clay
CAS (Whitehaven) D/Lec Box 21 Mineral Report 1878 Wigton

Dumfries Museum, The Observatory, Dumfries
Drain Tile Collection

Durham University Library Archives & Special Collections
Howard of Naworth Papers C612, C631/58

Ewart Library, Catherine Street, Dumfries
Annan Observer [microfiche]
Dumfries Times [microfiche]
Dumfries & Galloway Standard [microfiche]
Dumfries & Galloway Standard & Advertiser [microfiche]
Ordnance Survey maps, 1:10560, initial survey, 1854-8, Dumfriesshire
Ordnance Survey maps, 1:2500, initial survey, 1854-8, Dumfriesshire

House of Lords Record Office (The Parliamentary Archive) London SW1A 0PW
Acts relating to Duty on Bricks & Tiles

Lancashire Record Office (Preston)
LRO DDCa 1/116 - 1/121 Cavendish family of Holker Hall – Account Books
LRO DDCa 13/299 22nd May 1838 – 20th September 1843 Estate Accounts
LRO DDCa 13/300 29th September 1843 – 25th March 1844 Estate Accounts
LRO DDCa 13/301 28th March 1844 – 29th October 1845 Estate Accounts
LRO DDCL 1186/30 20th August 1839 John Whitehead
LRO DDCL 1195/32 Begbie – tilemaking 1843
LRO DDCL 1195/34 Scott - tilemaking 20th December 1843
LRO DDCL 1195/38 Scott – tilemaking 27th December 1843
LRO DDCL 2232/8 Clifton of Lytham - Josiah Parkes – erection of Tileries 1847
LRO DDCL 2232/12 Josiah Parkes recommending Scragg's Tile Machine 1847
LRO DDCL 2232/34 W. Garnett – Quernmore – decision to drain with tiles 1847

Lancaster University Library

Mitchell Library, North Street, Glasgow
Prize Essays & Transactions of the Highland Society of Scotland
Transactions of the Highland & Agricultural Society of Scotland

Mitchell Library, Patents Section, Information & Business Services, Glasgow
Tile making machine Patents

Museum of English Rural Life, Reading
www.rhc.rdg.ac.uk

Museum of Scottish Country Life, Wester Kittochside
Land Gallery – Completely Drained – Exhibition – Exhibits 1-20

Newcastle University, The Robinson Library: Special Collections
History of Agriculture Collection

Northumberland Record Office, Gosforth
[Now - Northumberland Collections Service, Ashington]
Ordnance Survey maps 1:2500, Initial survey, 1855-64, Northumberland

Personal collection
Billheads – drain tiles – tools – bricks – photographs

Private collections
Alston Moormaster, J. M. Paull, Letter Book, Transcripts 1866-68

Salt Library, Stafford
Misc.238 The Inge Family, Records of the Inge Family, compiled by Canon Charles
Cuthbert Inge, Typescript

Tullie House Museum, Castle Street, Carlisle
Drain Tile Collection

University of Cumbria, Ambleside & Newton Rigg
Journal of the Royal Agricultural Society of England

York Central Library
The Transactions of the Yorkshire Agricultural Society 1842 – 1853

Electronic Sources
http://stat-acc-scot.edina.ac.uk
www.historicaldirectories.org/
www.bodley.ox.ac.uk *The Builder* Vol.1 (1843), Vol.2 (1844)
www.oxforddnb.com
www.sine.ncl.ac.uk University of Newcastle upon Tyne
http://ads.ahds.ac.uk Northumberland \Sites and Monuments Record
www.archive.org
www.woodborough-heritage.org.uk
www.brocross.com/poynton
Archive CD Books (2004) *Soulby's Ulverston Advertiser*

BIBLIOGRAPHY

Theses
A.B. Humphries, *Agrarian Change in East Cumberland 1750-1900*
Thesis, University of Lancaster 1981
C.E. Searle, '*The Odd Corner of England*' *A Study of a Rural Social Formation in Transition, Cumbria c1700-1914*
PhD University of Essex, July 1983

Published printed sources & references
Adams, L.P (1932) *Agricultural Depression and Farm Relief in England 1813-1852*, King, London
ADAS (1973)
Old Underdrainage Systems, Field Drainage leaflet, Getting Down to Drainage No.12, MAFF
Allardyce, W. (1851) 'On the Application of Steam or other Power to the Working of Drain-Tile or Pipe-making Machines' *THASS*, July 1849-March 1851, New Series
Allbury, H.E. (1853) 'On the Farming of Surrey' *JRASE* Vol.14, 395-424
Anderson, V. R. & Fox, G. K. (1986) *Stations & Structures of the Settle & Carlisle Railway*, Oxford Publishing Company, Poole
Arbuthnot, C (1845) 'Letter on Deep Draining' *JRASE* Vol.6, 129-131
Arbuthnot, C. (1845) 'On Deep Draining' *JRASE* Vol.6, 573-4
Arbuthnot, C. (1849) 'On the Advantage of Deep Draining', *JRASE*, Vol.10, 496-506
Arkell, T. (1843) 'On the Drainage of Land', *JRASE*, Vol.4, 318-340
Armstrong, A. (1988) *Farmworkers,* Batsford, London
Bailey, J. & Culley, G. (1805) *General View of the Agriculture of Northumberland, Cumberland& Westmorland*, facsimile 1972, Graham, Newcastle
Bainbridge, G.H. (1943) 'Land Utilisation in Cumbria in the Mid-Nineteenth Century as revealed by a Study of the Tithe Returns' *CWAAS*, NS Vol. XLIII, 87-95
Bainbridge, T.H. (1944) 'Some factors in the Development of Cumbrian Agriculture, especially during the Nineteenth Century' *CWAAS*, NS Vol. XLIV, 81-92
Baker, R. (1844) 'On the Farming of Essex', *JRASE*, Vol.5, 1-43
Barnett, C. (1859) 'Report on the Exhibition & Trial of Implements at the Warwick Meeting' *JRASE* Vol.20, 313-326
Barrett, P & Co (1917) *General & Commercial Directory of Preston*, 12th edition, Barrett, Preston
Barrow-in-Furness (1870/1) *Commercial Directory of the Borough of Barrow-in-Furness* [CRO & Local Studies Library Barrow]
Beart, R. (1841) 'On the Economical Manufacture of Draining-Tiles and Soles' *JRASE* Vol. 2, 93-104
Beart, R. (1843) 'On the proper Materials for filling up Drains, and the Mode in which Water enters them' *JRASE* Vol.4, 411-430
Beastall, P.W. (1981) 'Landlords and Tenants' in Mingay, G.E. *Victorian Countryside* Vol.1, 428-38, Routledge, London
Becket, J. V. (2004) 'John Christian Curwen 1756 -1828' in *ODNB,* Oxford University Press, article 37334
Beesley, G. (1849) *A Report of the State of Agriculture in Lancashire*, Dobson, Preston

Bell, G. (1843) 'On the construction of an economical Tile-Work adapted to farms of ordinary size' *Prize Essays & Transactions of the Highland & Agricultural Society of Scotland*, Vol. XIV, 738-750

Bell, T. G. (1856) 'A report upon the agriculture of County Durham' *JRASE*, Vol.17, 86-123

Binns, J. (1851) *Notes on the Agriculture of Lancashire with Suggestions for its Improvement*, Dobson, Preston

Blenkinship, B. (1998) *Wetheriggs Pottery: A History and Collectors Guide*, Spencer

Bond, J. et al (1980) *Clay Industries of Oxfordshire: Oxfordshire Brickmakers*, Oxfordshire Museums

Boyle, R. (1851) 'On the Burning of Drain Tiles and Pipes' *THASS*, New Series

Bracker, P. (2002) 'Henry Turner: brick maker master 1804-1872' *Sussex Industrial History*, Issue 32, 2-7

Brassley, P. (2000) 'Land Drainage' 514-521 in E. J. T. Collins (ed.), *A H E W*, Vol. VII, 1850-1914, (2000)

Brassley, P. (2006) 'Wartime Productivity and Innovation 1939-45' in B. Short *et al*, (eds.) *The Front Line of Freedom: British Farming in the Second World War*, BAHS

Bravender, J. (1850) 'Farming of Gloucestershire', *JRASE*, Vol.11, 116-177

Brigden, R. (1983) *Agricultural Hand Tools*, Shire, Aylesbury

Brigden, R. (1986) *Victorian Farms*, Crowood, Marlborough

Bremner, D. (1869) *The Industries of Scotland*, reprint 1969, Kelley, NY

Broderick, G.C. (1881) *English Land and English Landlords*, Cassell, London

Brooks, G. (2000) 'Cumbrian brick and tile works: North Cumbria' *The Cumbrian Industrialist,* Vol.3, 49-59

Brown, J. (1989) *Farm Machinery 1750-1945*, Batsford, London

Brown, J. (1993) *Farm Tools and Techniques: A Pictorial History,* Batsford, London

Brunskill, R.W. (1990) *Brick Building in Britain*, Gollancz, London

Bulmer, T. & Co. (1883) *History, Topography & Directory of West Cumberland*

Bulmer, T. F. (1884) History, *Topography & Directory of East Cumberland*, Bulmer, Manchester

Bulmer, T. F. (1885) *History, Topography & Directory of Westmorland*, Manchester

Bulmer, T. F. (1886) *History, Topography & Directory of Northumberland*, Newcastle

Bulmer, T. & Co. (1901) *History Topography and Directory of Cumberland*, Preston

Bulmer, T (1908) *History, Topography & Directory of Westmorland*, Preston

Bunting, B. T. (2004) 'John Chalmers Morton 1821-1888' in *ODNB,* Oxford University Press, article 19366

Burke, J. F (1834) *British Husbandry; exhibiting the farming practice of various parts of the United Kingdom*, Vol.1, Baldwin & Cradock, London

Burke, J. F. (1840) *Husbandry*, Volume the third of *British Husbandry*, Baldwin & Craddock, London

Burke, J.F. (1841) 'On the Drainage of Land' *JRASE* Vol.2, 273-296

Butt, J., Donnachie, I. L. Hume, J. R. (1968) *Scotland: Industrial History in Pictures*, David & Charles

Caird, J. (1852) *English Agriculture in 1850-51*, 2nd edition, introduction G.E. Mingay, Cass, London, 1967

Caird, J. (1878) *The Landed Interest and the Supply of Food*, 5th edition, 1967, Cass

BIBLIOGRAPHY

Campbell, J. W. P. (2002) 'More on Pug Mills' *BBS Information* 89, 17

Cavendish, W. G. (1856) 'Report on the Exhibition and Trial of Implements at the Chelmsford Meeting, 1856' *JRASE* Vol.17, 564-581

Celoria, F. (1971) 'Edward Dobson's "A Rudimentary Treatise on the Manufacture of Bricks and Tiles" (1850) edited with an introduction, biography, notes, bibliography and index, *Journal of Ceramic History*, Vol.5

Challoner, Colonel (1850) 'On the Accurate Levelling of Drains' *JRASE* Vol.11, 114-115

Challoner, Colonel (1850) 'Report on the Exhibition and Trial of Implements at the Exeter meeting 1850' *JRASE*, Vol.11, 452-494

Chambers, J. D. & Mingay, G. E. (1966) *The Agricultural Revolution 1750-1880*, Batsford, London

Channing, F A (1897) *The Truth About Agricultural Depression: An Economic Study of the Evidence of the Royal Commission* Longmans, Green, & Co, London

Charnock, J.H. (1849) 'On Suiting the Depth f Drainage to the Circumstances of the Soil', *JRASE*, Vol.10, 507-519

Cheape, H. (2004) 'James Smith of Deanston 1789-1850' in *ODNB,* Oxford University Press, article 25822

Clapham, J. H. (1967) *An Economic History of Modern Britain* Vol.1 *The Early Railway Age 1820-1850* 2nd edition, Vol.2 *Free Trade and Steel 1850-1886,* Cambridge University Press

Clapham, A.R. (ed.) (1978) *Upper Teesdale*, Collins, London

Clarke, J.A. (1851) 'Farming of Lincolnshire' *JRASE*, Vol.12

Cockerill, J. & J. (1995) *Commondale Clay – Bricks, Pipes & Pottery*, Yorkshire

Colbeck, T. L. (1847) 'On the Agriculture of Northumberland' *JRASE* Vol.8, 422-437

Collingwood, R.G. (1913) 'Report of the Excavations at Papcastle, 1912' *CW2,* Vol. XIII, 138

Collins, E. J. T. Ed. (2000) *The Agrarian History of England and Wales,* Vol. VII 1850-1914, 2 parts, Cambridge

Collins, E. J. T. & Jones, E. L. (1967) 'Sectoral Advance in English Agriculture' *Agricultural History Review*, Vol.15, 65-81

Connolly, A. (2003) *Life in the Victorian Brickyards of Flintshire & Denbighshire*, Carreg Gwalch

Cook, H. & Williamson, T. (1999) *Water Management in the English Landscape: Field, Marsh and Meadow*, Edinburgh University Press

Cooke, T. (1849) 'Description and use of an Improved Agricultural Drainage Level, with the Process of Levelling, as required for Agricultural Purposes' *JRASE* Vol.10, 165-172

Cowie, J. (1845) 'On the improvement of waste land' *Transactions of the Highland & Agricultural Society of Scotland*, July 1843-March 1845, New Series, 452-455

Cox, A. (1979) *Survey of Bedfordshire: Brickmaking, A History & Gazetteer*, Bedfordshire C.C. / RCHM

Cox, A. (2002) 'The Pug Mill Reconsidered' *British Brick Society, Brick Information* 89, 9-14

Cox, A (2010) 'Brick and Tilemaking in the Nuneaton Area' *British Brick Society Information* 114, 11-23

Creasey, J. S. (2004) 'John Joseph Mechi 1802-1880' in *ODNB,* Oxford University Press, article 18491

Creasey, J. S. (2004) 'Henry Stephens 1795-1874' in *ODNB*, Oxford University Press, article 26384

Curwen, J.C. (1809) *Hints on Agricultural Subjects and on the best means of improving the condition of the laboring classes* 2nd edition, Johnson, London [Carlisle Library, Jackson Library M87]

Curwen, J.C. (1815) *The Rules and Proceedings of the Agricultural Society of Workington and the Reports to that Society by the President 1813 to 1814* Foster, Workington [Carlisle Library, Jackson Library M83]

Dalton, R. (2006) 'Aspects of farming and land management in southern Derbyshire in the early nineteenth century' *The Local Historian* Vol.36 No.2 106-120

Darby, H.C. (ed.) (1973) *New Historical Geography of England*, Cambridge Univ. Press

Davies, D.B. et al (1972) *Soil Management*, 4th edition, 1982, Farming Press

Davis, E. (2002) 'Clay Drainage Tile and Pipe Manufacture at Johnby Wythes, Greystoke, c1851 -1909' *CW* 3, Vol II, 261-275

Davis, E. (2004) 'Tilemakers of Threlkeld and Troutbeck' *MHAS Yearbook 2003 & Transactions* Vol 10, 9-13

Davison, P. I. (1986) *Brickworks of the North East*, Gateshead

Day, J. & Charlton, D. B. (1981) 'Excavation & Field Survey in Upper Redesdale Part III' *Archaeologia Aeliana* 5th Series, Vol. IX

Dempsey, G D (1852) *The Machinery of the nineteenth century; illustrated from original drawings, and including the best examples shewn at the Exhibition of the Works of Industry of all Nations*, Part 1, London

Denton, J.B. (1868) 'On Land Drainage and Improvement by Loans from Government or Public Companies' *JRASE*, Second Series, Vol 4, 123-143

Denton, J. B. (1883) *Agricultural Drainage: A Retrospect of Forty Years' Experiences*, Spon, London

Devine, T.M. (ed.) (1984) *Farm Servants and Labour in Lowland Scotland,* Donald, Edinburgh

Dickinson, W. (1850) *Essay on the Agriculture of West Cumberland*, Whittaker, London, Gibson, Whitehaven

Dickinson, W. (1853) *Essay on the Agriculture of East Cumberland,* Thurnam, Carlisle

Dickinson, W. (1853) *On the Farming of Cumberland*, Clowes, London, Callander & Dixon, Whitehaven

Dickson, R. W. (1805) *Practical Agriculture or a Complete System of Modern Husbandry*, 2 vols. Phillips, London

Dickson, R. W. (1815) *General View of the Agriculture of Lancashire with Observations on the means of its improvement*, revised & prepared for the Press by W. Stevenson, Shepwood, Neely & Jones, London

Directory of Clayworkers (1901) *The British Clayworker*, London

Dixon, E.E.L. et al (1926) *The Geology of the Carlisle, Longtown & Silloth District*, Geological Survey Memoir, HMSO, London

Dixon, H. (1845) 'On Socket Drain-Pipes' *JRASE*, Vol.5, 603-4

Dobson, E. (1850) *A Rudimentary Treatise on the Manufacture of Bricks & Tiles* 2 parts, Weale, London

Dobson, E. (1882) 7th edition of above, Crosby Lockwood, London

Donnachie, I. (1971) *Industrial Archaeology of Galloway*, David & Charles

BIBLIOGRAPHY

Douglas, G. & Oglethorpe, M. (1993) *Brick, Tile and Fireclay Industries in Scotland,* RCAHMS, Edinburgh

Dowell, S. (1888) *A History of Taxation and Taxes in England from the earliest times to the year 1885* 2nd edition revised, Longmans, London
Vol II *Taxation from the Civil War to the present day*
Vol IV *Taxes on articles of consumption*

Dudgeon, J. (1840) 'Account of the Improvements which have taken place in the Agriculture of Scotland since the formation of the Highland Society' *JRASE*, Vol.1, 59-112

Dumfries & Galloway Family History Society (1993) Census 1851transcriptions

Elliott, R. (1845) 'Report of converting into profitable tillage upwards of 100 acres of waste land' *THASS*, July 1843-March 1845, New Series, 217-223

Elliott, R. (1849) 'On Draining' *THASS*, July 1847-March 1849, New Series, 301-317

Erickson, A. B. (1950) 'Sir James Graham, Agricultural Reformer' *Agricultural History*, Vol.24, 170-4

Etheredge, F. W. (1845) 'On the cheapest and best method of establishing a Tile Yard' *JRASE*, Vol.6, 463-476

Evans, E. J. (2004) 'William Blamire 1790-1862' in *ODNB*, Oxford University Press, article 4339

Evans, G. E. (1969) *The Farm and the Village* Faber, London

Evershed, H. (1853) 'Farming of Surrey', *JRASE*, Vol.14

Evershed, H. (1856) 'Farming of Warwickshire' *JRASE* Vol.17, 475-493

Fahey, D. (2004) 'Rosalind Francis Howard 1845-1921' in *ODNB*, Oxford University Press, article 34022

Farey, J (1811-17) *General View of the Agriculture of Derbyshire* Vol.1 (1811) 446-457, Vol.2 (1813) 360-401 Sherwood, Neely & Jones, London

Farrall, T. (1868) 'A Report on the Agriculture of Cumberland, chiefly with regard to the production of meat' *JRASE*, Second Series, Vol.10, 402-429

Fenton, A. (1976) *Scottish Country Life,* Donald, Edinburgh

Ferguson, R. S. (1890) *A History of Cumberland*, Elliot Stock, London

Fitzrandolph, H.E. & Hay, M.D. (1927) *Rural Industries of England & Wales,* Vol. 3, *Decorative Crafts & Rural Potteries*, Clarendon, Oxford

Fletcher, T.W. (1961) 'The Great Depression of English Agriculture 1873-96' *EHR*, 2nd Series XIII, 417-32

Fletcher, T W (1962) 'The Agrarian Revolution in Arable Lancashire' *TLCAS* Vol.72, 93-122

Ford, W. (1842) 'Account of Mr. Irving's new Machine for constructing Tiles' *JRASE*, Vol.3, 398-400

Fox, H.S.A. (1979) 'Local Farmers' Associations and the Circulation of Agricultural Information in Nineteenth-Century England' pp. 43-63 in Fox, H.S.A. & Butlin, R.A.

French, H. F. (1859) *Farm Drainage: The Principles, Processes and Effects of Draining land with Stones, Wood, Plows and Open Ditches, and especially with Tiles*, A.O. Moore & Co, New York

Fulton, H. (1851) 'Drainage of Hethel Wood Farm' *JRASE* Vol.12, 149-151

Fussell, G. E. (1848) 'The dawn of High Farming in England: Land reclamation in early Victorian days' *Agricultural History*, Vol.22, 83-95

Fussell, G.E. (1952) *The Farmer's Tools*, reprint, Orbis, London, 1981

Fussell, G E (1966) *The English Dairy Farmer 1500-1900* Kelley, New York

Garnett, F. W. (1912) *Westmorland Agriculture 1800-1900,* Titus Wilson, Kendal

Garnett, W. J. (1849) 'Farming of Lancashire' *JRASE*, Vol.10, 1-51

Gillbanks, B. H. & Co (1857) *Directory & Gazetteer of Preston*, Bailey, Preston

Gillbanks, B. H. & Co (1858) *Directory & Gazetteer of Preston*, Bailey, Preston

Gillespie, J. (1868-9) 'Report on the Agriculture of Dumfriesshire' *THASS,* 4th Series, Vol.2, 270-325

Gillett, G (1869) *Commercial & General Directory of Preston*, Greenall, Preston

Gisborne, T. (1852) *Agricultural Drainage*, Second edition, Murray, London

Goddard, N. (1983) 'The Development and Influence of Agricultural Periodicals and Newspapers 1780-1880' *Agricultural History Review* Vol. 31.2, 116-131

Goddard, N. (1988) *Harvest of Change: The Royal Agricultural Society of England 1838-1988*, London, Quiller Press

Goddard, N (2000) 'Agricultural Institutions: Societies, Associations and the Press' 650-690 in Collins, E J T, *AHEW* Vol. VII 1850-1914, Cambridge University Press

Goddard, N. (2004) 'Chandos Wren Hoskyns 1812-1876' in *ODNB,* Oxford University Press, article 13842

Graham, J. R. G. (1840) 'On the Deanston frequent Drain System, as distinguished from and compared with the Furrow-Draining and Deep Ploughing of the Midland Counties of England' *JRSAE*, Vol.1, 29-33.

Green, F. H. W. (1980) 'Field Under-Drainage Before and After 1940' *AHR,* Vol. 28, 120-123

Grey, J. (1841) 'A View of the past and present State of Agriculture in Northumberland' *JRASE*, Vol.2, 151-192

Guthrie, G. (1843) 'On Old Brick Drains' *Prize Essays & THASS*, Vol. XIV, 45-46

Haggard, H. R. (1899) *A Farmers Year being his Commonplace Book for 1898*, Cresset Library edition 1987, Hutchinson, London

Hallas C (2000) 'The Northern Region' 402-410 in Collins, E J T *AHEW* Vol. VII

Halliwell, J. O. (1904) *Dictionary of Archaic & Provincial Words* 6th edition, Routledge

Hammond, M. D. P. (1977) 'Brick Kilns: An Illustrated Survey' *IAR*, Vol.1, No.2, 171-192

Hammond, M. (1981) *Bricks and Brickmaking*, Shire, Princes Risborough

Hamond, A. (1854) 'Report on the Exhibition and Trial of Implements at the Lincoln Meeting, 1854' *JRASE* Vol.15, 363-378

Handley, H. (1842) 'On the Drainage of Land' *JRASE*, Vol.3, 165-168

Harley, J.B. (1973) 'England *circa* 1850' 527-94 in Darby, H. C. (ed.) (1973) *A New Historical Geography of England*, Cambridge University Press

Harpur, F. (1911) *Land Drainage*, Estates Gazette, London

Hartley, M. & Ingilby, J. (1968) *Life and Tradition in the Yorkshire Dales*, Dent

Harvey, N. (1956) *Ditches Dykes and Deep-Drainage*, Young Farmers' Club Booklet No.29, Evans, London

Harvey, N. (1980) *The Industrial Archaeology of Farming in England and Wales*, Batsford, London

Hawes, S. (1858) 'Notes on the Wealden Clay of Sussex and on its Cultivation', *JRASE*, Vol.19, 182-198

BIBLIOGRAPHY

Hawksworth, C. (2006) 'Fergushill Tileworks – a short lived industrial concern on the Eglinton Estate' *Ayrshire Notes* No.32, 21-25

Hay, G. D. & G. P. Stell (1986) *Monuments of Industry: an illustrated Historical Record,* RCAHMS

Highland & Agricultural Society of Scotland (1851) 'Account of the Show of The Highland and Agricultural Society held at Glasgow in 1850' 'Implements' *THASS* July 1849-March 1851, New Series, 409-438

Highland & Agricultural Society (1878) *Report on the Present State of the Agriculture of Scotland* Neill & Co, Edinburgh

Hobbs, W. S. (1855) 'Report on the Exhibition & Trial of Implements at Carlisle Meeting' *JRASE,* Vol.16, 505-521

Hodges, T. L. (1844) 'On the cheapest method of making and burning Draining Tiles' *JRASE,* Vol.5, 551-9

Hodges, T. L. (1848) 'On Temporary Tile-Kilns' *JRASE,* Vol.9, 198-9

Hodgson, W. editor (1888) *Uncollected Literary Remains of William Dickinson,* Coward

Holderness, B.A. (1981) *'Agriculture & Industrialization in the Victorian Economy'* in Mingay, G. E. (1981) *Victorian Countryside,* Vol.1, 179-99, Routledge

Holderness, B. A. (2000) 'Investment, accumulation and agricultural credit', 863-929 in E. J. T. Collins (editor), *A H E W,* Vol. VII 1850-1914

Holderness, B.A. & Turner, M. editors (1991) *Land Labour and Agriculture 1700-1920: Essays for Gordon Mingay* Hambledon Press, London

Holland, C, Langley, A, Moore, A (2006) *Joseph Elkington, Warwickshire's Land Drainage Pioneer* Stretton on Dunmore

Holt, J. (1795) *General View of the Agriculture of Lancaster,* reprint 1969, Kelley, NY

Horn, P. (1980) *The Rural World 1780-1850,* Hutchinson, London

Hoskyns, C. W. (1852) *Talpa: or the Chronicles of a Clay Farm,* 3rd edition 1854, Lovell Reece, London

Hoskyns, C.W. (1856) 'On "Ridge-and-Furrow" Pasture Land, and a method of levelling it' *JRASE,* Vol.17, 327-331 [abridgement of this article reprinted in the *Carlisle Journal* 23rd January 1857 p.3 'Agriculture']

Hounsell, P. (2004) 'Robert Beart 1801-1873' in *ODNB,* Oxford University Press, article 48801

Howe, C. (2001) 'The Canney Hill Pottery' *The Local Historian* No.31.4, 230-246

Howitt, W. (1844) *The Rural Life of England,* Longman, London

Hozier, W. W. (1870) *Practical Remarks on Agricultural Drainage: Especially adapted to the Drainage of heavy land with some observations on subsequent management,* Blackwood, Edinburgh

Hudson, P. (2000) 'Quarrying and Extractive Industries' 41-62 in Winstanley, M. (editor) *Rural Industries of the Lune Valley,* CNWRS, Lancaster

Hughes, E. (1965) *North Country Life in the Eighteenth Century,* Vol.2 *Cumberland & Westmorland 1700-1830,* Oxford University Press

Humphries, A, (1996) *Seeds of Change* Newton Rigg

Hunt, J. (1841) 'On the Marquis of Tweeddale's Tile-making Machine' *JRASE,* Vol.2, 148-150

Hutchinson, H. (1844) *A Treatise on the Practical Drainage of Land* Houlston & Stoneman, London

Jackson, P.J. & Co (1880) *Postal Address Directory of the City of Carlisle*, Jackson, Newcastle

Jenkins, J.G. (1978) *Traditional Country Craftsmen*, Routledge, London

Johnson, C. W. (1847) *Modern Agricultural Improvements: being a Supplement to the British Husbandry of the Society for Diffusion of Useful Knowledge*, Baldwin, London

Johnstone, J. (1801) *An Account of the Mode of Draining of Land, According to the system practised by Mr Elkington*, Second edition, Corrected & enlarged, Phillips, London

Jollie's (1811) *Cumberland Guide & Directory*, reprint 1995, Moon, Whitehaven

Jonas, S. (1846) 'Farming of Cambridgeshire', *JRASE, Vol.7*

Jones, B. C. (1983) 'Carlisle Brickmakers and Bricklayers 1652 1752' *C&W* 2, 125-129

Jones, E.L. (1962) 'The Changing Basis of English Agricultural Prosperity 1853-73' *AHR*, Vol X, 102-19

Jones, E.L. (1968) *Development of English Agriculture 1815-1873* [Studies in Economic History] Macmillan, London

Joy, D. (1983) *The Lake Counties: A Regional History of the Railways of GB*, Vol. XIV, David & Charles, Newton Abbot

Keates, T. (1998) 'Reake Wood Tile Kiln' *The Cumbrian Industrialist*, Vol.1, 29-43

Keates, T. (2002) 'Field drainage techniques and their development in Cumbria' *The Cumbrian Industrialist* Vol.4, 35-51

Kelly, (1858) *Post Office Directory of Cumberland & Westmorland*, Kelly, London

Kelly, (1858) *Post Office Directory of Northumberland & Durham*, London

Kelly (1864) *Post Office Directory of Lancashire*, Kelly, London

Kelly (1873) *Post Office Directory of the Principal Towns and Adjacent Places of Cumberland & Westmorland*, Kelly, London

Kelly (1894) *Directory of Durham, Northumberland, Cumberland & Westmorland*, Kelly, London

Kelly (1897) *Directory of Cumberland*, Kelly, London

Kelly (1906) (1910) (1914) (1921) (1925) (1929) (1934) (1938) *Directory of Cumberland & Westmorland*, Kelly, London

Klippart, J. H. (1862) *The Principles and Practice of Land Drainage; embracing a brief history of underdraining; a detailed examination of the operation and advantages; a description of various kinds of drains; with practical directions for their construction; the manufacture of drain-tile etc* R. Clarke & Co, Cincinnati

Knapp, B.J. (1979) *Soil Processes*, Allen & Unwin, London

Lane, J. H. (1916) *Newton-in-Makerfield, with some account of its people-compiled from authentic sources*, with notes and reminiscences of Peter Mayor Campbell, The compiler, Newton-le-Willows

Laws, P. (1850) *The Prize Essay of the Newcastle-upon-Tyne Farmers' Club on Draining Strong Clays*, Dodsworth, Newcastle

Lawson, W. & Hunter, C. D. (1875) *Ten Years of Gentleman Farming at Blennerhasset*, 2nd edition, Longmans

Legard, G (1848) 'Report on the Farming of the East Riding of Yorkshire', *JRASE*, Vol.9, 85-136

Leslie, K.C. (1970/1) 'The Ashburnham Estate Brickworks 1840-1968' *Sussex Industrial History*, No.1, 2-21

BIBLIOGRAPHY

Linsley, S.M. (1982) 'The Eighteenth to the Twentieth Century: Agrarian Transformation
& Industrial Revolution' in Pevsner, *Northumberland*, Buildings of England, 84-104,
Penguin

Livesley, M. C. (1960) *Field Drainage*, Spon, London

Lonsdale, H. (1867) *John Christian Curwen – William Blamire: The Worthies of
Cumberland*, Routledge, London

Lonsdale, H. (1868) *Sir J.R.G. Graham, Bart of Netherby: The Worthies of Cumberland*,
Routledge, London

Lonsdale, H. (1872) *The Howards, Rev R. Matthews, John Rooke, Captain Joseph
Huddart: The Worthies of Cumberland*, Routledge, London

Los, A. (2008) 'From Brickyard to Builders Yard: An East Riding Study' *BBS
Information* 106, 13-32

Loudon, J. C. (1825) *An Encyclopaedia of Agriculture*, Longman, London

Lovat, E. (1831) *A Sketch of the Rural Economy of Lancaster*, Rickard, Burnley

MacDonald, J. (1908/9) *Stephen's Book of the Farm*, 5th edition, revised & rewritten, 3
vols. Blackwood, Edinburgh

MacDonell, O. S. (n.d.) *Thorston Hall a tale of Cumberland Farms in the Old Days*
Selwyn Blunt, London

MacKenzie, E. (1825) *An Historical, Topographical, and Descriptive View of the County
Of Northumberland* 2 vols, MacKenzie & Dent, Newcastle

Mangon, H. (1856) 'On certain Obstructions which form in Draining-Tiles' *JRASE*
Vol.17, 625-629

Mannex, P.J. (1849) *History, Topography & Directory of Westmorland & Lonsdale
North of the Sands in Lancashire*, Simpkin Marshall, London

Mannex & Co (1851) *History, Topography & Directory of Westmorland; & of the
Hundreds of Lonsdale & Amounderness in Lancashire*, Johnson, Beverley

Mannex & Co (1854) *History, Topography and Directory of Mid-Lancashire, with an
Essay on Geology* Bailey & Thompson, Preston

Mannex, P. & Co (1866) *Topography & Directory of North & South Lonsdale,
Amounderness, Leyland,* Preston

Mannex, P. & Co (1873) *Directory of Preston*, Preston

Mannex & Co (1877) *Directory of Preston*, Snape, Preston

Mannex, P. & Co (1881) *Topography & Directory of Preston, Lancaster & Districts*

Mannix & Whellan (1847) *History, Gazetteer and Directory of Cumberland,* Johnson,
Beverley, Reprint, Moon, Beckermet, 1974

Marshall, J.D. (1958) *Furness and the Industrial Revolution*, Barrow

Marshall, J. D. (1961) 'The Lancashire Rural Labourer in the early nineteenth century'
TLCAS, 90-128

Marshall, J. D. & Davies-Shiel, M. (1971) *The Lake District at Work: Past and Present,*
David & Charles, Newton Abbot

Marshall, J. D. & Walton, J. K. (1981) *The Lake Counties from1830 to the mid-twentieth
century*, Manchester University Press

Marshall, W. (1818) *The Review and Abstract of the County Reports to the Board of
Agriculture*, 5 vols., Longman, London, reprint 1968, Kelley, NY

Martin, J. (2004) 'William Lewis Rham 1778-1843' in *ODNB,* Oxford University Press,
article 23446

Martins, S.W. (2004) *Farmers, Landlords and Landscapes: Rural Britain 1720-1870*, Windgather Press

McKeever, R. & Layfield, J. (2004) *The Industrial Archaeology of South Ulverston*, The Authors

Millward, R. & Robinson, A. (1972) *Cumbria: Landscapes of Britain*, Macmillan, London

Milward, R. (1853) 'Experiment on Drainage at Different Depths', *JRASE*, Vol.14, 210-211

Mingay, G. E. Editor (1977) *The Agricultural Revolution: changes in agriculture 1650-1880* [Documents in Economic History] Black, London

Mingay, G. E. Editor (1981) *The Victorian Countryside*, 2vols, Routledge, London

Mingay, G. E. Editor (1989 *The Agrarian History of England and Wales* Vol. VI, 1750-1850, Cambridge University Press

Mingay, G. E. (2004) 'Sir James Caird 1816-1892' in *ODNB,* Oxford University Press, article 4339

Minutes of Proceedings (1872) 'Mr Josiah Parkes', *Institution of Civil Engineers*, Vol XXXIII, 231-236

Mitchell, G. S. (1894) *A Handbook of Land Drainage,* Land Agents Record, London

Mitchell, G. S. (1898) *A Handbook of Land Drainage*, Second Edition, Land Agents Record, London

Moore, R.W. (1905) 'Industries: Coal Mining' 348-384 in Wilson, J. (ed.) *VCH Cumberland*

Morris, Harrison & Co. (1861) *Commercial Directory and Gazetteer of the County of Cumberland*, Nottingham, Reprint, Moon, Whitehaven, 2000

Moss, A. B. (1880) *Arthur's Directory of Carlisle*, A. Barnes Moss, Carlisle

Moss, A. B. (1884) *Post Office Directory of Carlisle*, Barns-Moss, Carlisle

Mounsey, H. (1997) 'Rambling Reminiscences of 55 years ago on the Netherby Estate-Part two' *Bewcastle Journal*, Vol.7

Mutch, A. (1988) *Rural Life in South-West Lancashire 1840-1914*, Occasional Paper No.16, CNWRS, Lancaster

Neville, H. M. (1909) *A Corner in the North: Yesterday and Today with Border Folk*, Newcastle, Reid

Nicholson, H. H. (1942) *The Principles of Field Drainage*, reprint 1944, Cambridge University Press

Oakey's (1851) *Commercial Directory of Preston*, Oakey, Preston

Oakey's (1853) *Commercial & Trade Directory of Preston*, Oakey, Preston

Orwin, C. S. & Whetham, E. H. (1964) *History of British Agriculture 1846-1914*, Longmans, London

Oxford Archaeology North (2003) *Poplar Grove Farm, Nateby* Archaeological Evaluation Report

Palin, W. (1844) 'The Farming of Cheshire' *JRASE* Vol.5, 57-111

Parker, C. S. (1907) *Life & Letters of Sir James Graham, second Baronet of Netherby P.C. G.C.B. 1792-1861*, Vol.1, Murray, London

Parkes, J. (1843) 'Report on Drain Tiles and Drainage' *JRASE* Vol.4, 369-379

Parkes, J. et al (1843) 'Report on the Exhibition of Implements at the Derby Meeting 1843' *JRASE* Vol.4, 453-497

Parkes, J. (1844) 'Report on the Exhibition of Implements at the Southampton Meeting 1844' *JRASE* Vol.5, 361-390

Parkes, J. (1845) 'On reducing the cost of permanent Drainage' *JRASE* Vol.6, 125-129

Parkes, J. (1845) 'Report on the Exhibition of Implements at the Shrewsbury Meeting in 1845' *JRASE* Vol.6, 303-323

Parkes, J. (1846) 'On Draining' *JRASE* Vol.7, 249-272

Parkes, J. (1846) 'Report on the Exhibition of Implements at the Newcastle-upon-Tyne Meeting, 1846' *JRASE*, 681-96

Parkinson, J. (1861) 'On Improvements in Agriculture in the County of Nottingham since the year 1800' *JRASE*, Vol.22, 159-66

Parry, J. (2004) 'Sir James Robert George Graham 1792-1861' in *ODNB,* Oxford University Press, article 11204

Parson, W. & Bradshaw, T. (1818) *Staffordshire General & Commercial Directory,* Manchester

Parson, W. & White, W. (1829) *History, Directory and Gazetteer of Cumberland and Westmorland,* White & Co., Leeds, Reprint, Moon, Beckermet, 1976

Payne, S. H. C. (1845) 'Drain Level' *JRASE,* Vol.6, 247-248

Perren, R (1995) *Agriculture in Depression 1870-1940* Cambridge University Press

Perriam, D. R. (1982) *Denton Holme; A Brief History,* Carlisle Library 1BC9

Perriam, D. R. (1992) *Carlisle an illustrated history,* Bookcase, Carlisle

Perriam, D. R. (2000) 'Past & Present' *Cumberland News,* Carlisle

Perry, P. J. (1974) *British Farming in the Great Depression 1870-1914 an historical geography,* David & Charles, Newton Abbot

Pevsner, N. et al (1992) *Northumberland,* Buildings of England, Penguin

Phillips, A.D.M. (1969) 'Underdraining and the English Claylands, 1850-80: A Review' *AHR,* Vol.17, 44-55

Phillips, A. D. M. (1972) 'The Development of Underdraining on a Yorkshire Estate during the Nineteenth-Century' *Yorkshire Archaeological Journal,* Vol.44, 195-206

Phillips, A.D.M. (1981) 'Agricultural Improvements on a Durham Estate in the Nineteenth Century: the Lumley Estate of the Earls of Scarborough' *Durham University Journal* Vol.73 No.2, 161-168

Phillips, A.D.M. (1989) *The Underdraining of Farmland in England during the nineteenth century,* Cambridge University Press

Phillips, A.D.M., Editor (1996) 'The Staffordshire Reports of Andrew Thompson to the Inclosure Commissioners, 1858-68: Landlord Investment in Staffordshire Agriculture in the Mid-Nineteenth Century' *Collections for a History of Staffordshire,* Fourth Series, Volume Seventeen, Staffordshire Record Society

Phillips, A. D. M. (2004) 'Josiah Parkes 1793- 1871' in *ODNB,* Oxford University Press, article 21357

Phillips, A. D. M. (2004) 'John Bailey Denton 1814-1893' in *ODNB,* Oxford University Press, article 50168

Phillips, A. D. M. (2004) 'Thomas Scragg 1804-1886' in *ODNB,* Oxford University Press, article 50686

Phillips, A. D. M. (2004) 'Andrew Thomson 1824?-1870' in *ODNB,* Oxford University Press, article 52538

Pidgeon, D. (1892) 'The Evolution of Agricultural Implements', *JRASE*, 3rd Series, Vol.3, 238-258

Pigot & Co (1828/9) *National Commercial Directory; for 1828-29, Cumberland, Lancashire, Westmorland*, Pigot, London

Pigot & Co. (1834) *Directory of Cumberland,* Pigot, Manchester

Pitt, W. (1813) *General View of the Agriculture of the County of Worcester,* reprint 1969, Newton Abbot, David & Charles

Porter, F. (1882) *Postal Directory for 1882 of Cumberland*, Porter, London

Portman, Lord (1849) 'On the Stoppage of Drains by a Stony Deposit' *JRASE* Vol.10, 119-121 *JRASE*, Vol.3 169-216

Practical Agriculturist (1838) 'Agriculture of Cumberland' *The Farmers Magazine*, 332-335

Price, J.W.A. (1983) *The Industrial Archaeology of the Lune Valley,* CNWRS, Lancaster

Prothero, R. E. [Lord Ernle] (1912) *English Farming: Past and Present*, 5th edition, edited A. D. Hall (1936) Longman, London

Pusey, P. (1842) 'On the Progress of Agricultural Knowledge during the last four years' *JRASE* Vol.3, 169-216

Pusey, P. (1843) 'Evidence on the Antiquity, Cheapness and Efficacy of Thorough-Draining, or Land-Ditching as practised throughout the Counties of Suffolk, Hertford, Essex and Norfolk' *JRASE*, Vol.4, 23-49

Pusey, P. (1846) 'On Cheapness of Draining' *JRASE*, Vol.7, 520-24

Pusey, P. (1850) 'On the Progress of Agricultural Knowledge during the last eight years', *JRASE*, Vol.11, 381-438

Pusey, P. (1851) 'Report on Agricultural Improvements-VII Draining' *JRASE* Vol.12, 638-41

Quayle, B. (1794) *General View of the Agriculture of the Isle of Man*, reprinted 1992, Douglas

Raistrick, A. (1943) *Geology,* English Universities Press, London

Randall, J. (1877) 'The Clay Industries of Shropshire' *Industrial Archaeology*, Vol.12, No.3, 1977, 221-25

RASE (1846) *Meeting at Newcastle-upon-Tyne, The Hand-Book of Newcastle and Visitors Guide to the Show*, Gilbert, London

Rawstorne, L. (1848) *The New Husbandry or a complete code of Modern Agriculture*, Oakey, Preston

RCAHMS (1997) *Eastern Dumfriesshire an archaeological landscape*, HMSO, Edinburgh

Read, C. S. (1854) 'On the Farming of Oxfordshire' *JRASE* Vol.15, 189-275

Read, J. (1843) 'On Pipe Tiles' *JRASE*, Vol.4, 273-4

Report by the Committee (1847) 'Report of the Act 9 and 10 Victoria, Cap. 101 called The Drainage Act *THASS*, New Series, 610-617

Report by the Committee (1847) 'Supplementary Report to the Directors by the Committee on the Drainage Act' *THASS*, New Series, 627-628

Rham, W. L. (1840) 'Experiments on the Improvement of Poor Land by Subsoil Ploughing both with and without Underdraining' *JRASE* Vol.1, 257-262

Richmond, Duke of (1847) 'On the use of Peat-Tiles for Draining' *JRASE*, Vol.8, 570

Ridgway, C. (2004) 'George James Howard 1843-1911' in *ODNB*, Oxford University Press, article 34019

Ridley, M. W. (1853) 'Report on the Exhibition and Trial of Implements at the Gloucester Meeting, 1853' *JRASE* Vol.14, 343-373

Roberts, B.K. (1978) 'Man and Land in Upper Teesdale', 141-59 in Clapham, A.R (1978) *Upper Teesdale*, Collins

Roberts, C (1962) *The Radical Countess: The History of the Life of Rosalind Countess of Carlisle* Steel, Carlisle

Robinson, M. (1986) 'The Extent of Farm Underdrainage in England and Wales, prior to 1939' *AHR*, Vol. 34, 79-85

Rogers, G. (1986) 'Lancashire land owners and the Great Agricultural Depression' *Northern History*, Vol.XXII, 250-268

Rowley, J. J. (1853) 'The Farming of Derbyshire' *JRASE* Vol.14, 17-66

Royal Agricultural Society of England (1846) *Meeting at Newcastle upon Tyne, the Hand-book of Newcastle and Visitors Guide to the Show*, Gilbert, London

Royal Agricultural Society of England (1855) *A Catalogue of the various Agricultural Implements, Machines and other articles for farm purposes Exhibited at the Society's Show at Carlisle*, July 25th –27th, [Carlisle Library, Jackson Collection N4/14]

Royal Commission on Agriculture of England (1895) *Report by Mr. Wilson Fox on the County of Cumberland*, HMSO, London

Ruegg, L. H. (1854) 'Farming of Dorsetshire' *JRASE* Vol.15, 389-454

Samuel, R. (1977) 'Mineral Workers' 1-97 in Samuel, R. (ed.) *Miners, Quarrymen and Saltworkers*, Routledge, London

Scot, W. (1843) 'On the Substitution of Tubes made of Larch Wood for Drain Tiles' *THASS*, Vol. XIV, 99-113

Scot, W. (1847) 'Supplementary notice on the substitution of tubes made of larch wood for drain-tiles used in draining' *THASS*, July 1845-March 1847, New Series, 155-159

Scott, Hudson, (1855) *A Directory & Local Guide or Handbook to Carlisle and Immediate Vicinity*, Hudson Scott, Carlisle [Carlisle Library A62]

Searle, A. B. (1912) *The Natural History of Clay*, Cambridge University Press

Searle, A. B. (1936) *A Rudimentary Treatise on the Manufacture of Bricks and Tiles: Based on the Work of Edward Dobson*, Fourteenth edition, Technical Press, London

Selby, J. A. (2001) 'The Brick Kiln for the Oxford Canal Company at Fenny Compton, Warwickshire' *BBS* Information, No.85

Shepherd, M.E. (2003) *From Hellgill to Bridge End: Aspects of economic and social change in the Upper Eden Valley 1840-95*, University of Herefordshire Press

Short, B. et al (eds.) (2006) *The Front Line of Freedom: British Farming in the Second World War*, BAHS

Simpson, J. C. (1979) 'Agriculture and Land Drainage' in Kilgour, I. N. L. *Soils in Cumbria*, Soil Survey Record No.59, Harpenden

Slater (1848) *Cumberland Directory* [Carlisle Library 1B9]

Slater (1852) *Royal National Commercial Directory and Topography of Scotland with Carlisle*, Slater, Manchester

Slater (1855) *Royal National Commercial Directory of Northern Counties* Vol.2, *Directory of Cumberland*, Slater, Manchester

Slater (1869) *Royal National Commercial Directory of Cumberland and Westmorland*,

Manchester

Slater (1876/7) *Royal National Commercial Directory of the Counties of Cumberland and Westmorland and Cleveland District*, Slater, Manchester

Slater (1979) *Royal National Commercial Directory of Cumberland* [Carlisle Library 1B9]

Slater (1884) *Royal National Commercial Directory of the Counties of Cumberland, Durham, Northumberland & Westmorland*, Slater, Manchester

Slee-Smith, J. (n. d.) *Ancient Rocks in South Cumbria*, Cumbria RIGS

Smedley, N. (1976) *Life and Tradition in Suffolk, Norfolk and East Essex*, Dent, London

Smith, J. (1844) *Remarks on Thorough Draining and Deep Ploughing* 7th edition, Drummond, Stirling

Smith, R. (1856) 'Bringing Moorland into Cultivation' *JRASE* Vol.17, 349-393

Snell, J. (n. d.) *Wetheriggs Country Pottery*, Penrith

Spearing, J. B. (1860) 'On the Agriculture of Berkshire' *JRASE*, Vol.21, 1-46

Spring, D. (1955) 'A great agricultural estate: Netherby under Sir James Graham 1820-45' *Agricultural History*, Vol.29, 73-81

Spring, D. (1963) *The English Landed Estate in the Nineteenth Century: Its Administration,* Maryland, John Hopkins

Stevenson, C. (1853) 'On the Farming of East Lothian' *JRASE* Vol.14, 275-324

Stephens, H. (1846) *A Manual of Practical Draining*, Blackwood, London

Stephens, H. (1852) *The Book of the Farm*, Vol.2, 2nd edition, Blackwood, Edinburgh & London

Stratton, J. N. (1978) *Agricultural Records AD220-1977*, 2nd edition, Baker, London

Sturgess, R. W. (1966) 'The Agricultural Revolution on the English Clays' *AHR*, Vol. 14, 104-121

Sturgess, R. W. (1967) 'The Agricultural Revolution on the English Clays: a Rejoinder' *AHR*, Vol.15, 82-87

Tanner, H. (1858) 'Agriculture of Shropshire' *JRASE*, Vol.19, 1-64

Taylor, B.J. et al. (1971) *British Regional Geology: Northern England,* Fourth edition, HMSO, London

Thompson, F. M. L. (1963) *English Landed Society in the Nineteenth Century,* Routledge, London

Thompson, F. M. L. (2004) 'John Grey 1785-1868' in *ODNB*, Oxford University Press, article11550

Thompson, F. M. L. (2004) 'Philip Pusey 1799-1855' in *ODNB* Oxford University Press, article 22911

Thompson, H. S (1848) 'Report on the Exhibition & Trial of Implements at the York Meeting 1848' *JRASE*, Vol.9, 377-421

Thompson, H. S. (1849) 'Report on the Exhibition and Trial of Implements at the Norwich Meeting' *JRASE* Vol.10, 526-570

Thompson, H. S. (1852) 'Report on the Exhibition & Trial of Implements at the Lewes Meeting 1852' *JRASE* Vol.13, 302-346

Thring, D.T. (1913) 'Mole-Draining and the Renovation of Old Pipe Drains' *JRASE* Vol.74, 76-89

Torrens, H. S. (2004) 'Joseph Elkington bap.1740-d.1806' in *ODNB* Oxford University Press, article 61000

BIBLIOGRAPHY

Town & Country Directories (1898) *Dumfries, Kirkudbright & Wigtown Trade Directory*, Edinburgh

Trevor, A. P. (1983) 'Anglesey and Clay - Part 1 – Drain Tiles and Pipes' *BBS Information*, No.30, 10-11

Trimmer, J. (1853) 'Notes on the Geology of the Keythorpe Estate, and its relations to the Keythorpe System of Draining', *JRASE*, Vol.14, 96-105

Trotter, F.M. & Hollingworth, F.E. (1932) *Geology of the Brampton District*, Geological Survey Memoir, HMSO, London

Turner, M. E., Becket, J. V., Afton, B. (2001) *Farm Production in England 1700-1914*, Oxford University Press

Vince, J. (1992) *The Farmer's Tools*, Sorbus, Aylesbury

Ward, (1851) *North of England Directory*, Ward, Newcastle

Ward, J.T. (1967) *Sir James Graham*, Macmillan, London

Waring, G.E. (1879) *Draining for Profit and Draining for Health* 2nd edition revised & enlarged, Orange Judd, New York

Watkin, S & Whyte, I. (2009) *Floods in North West England: a history c.1600-2008*, CNWRS, Lancaster

Watt, K. (2002) 'Making drain tiles "home manufacture": Agricultural Consumers and the Social Construction of Clayworking Technology in the 1840s' *Rural History* 13

Way, J. T. (1856) 'On the Composition of the Waters of Land-Drainage and of Rain' *JRASE* Vol.17, 123-61

Weaver, M. M. (1964) *History of Tile Drainage (In America prior to 1900)*, The Author, New York

Webster, C. (1868) 'On the Farming of Westmorland' *JRASE*, Second Series, Vol.4, 1-37

Webster, W.B. (1848) 'On the failure of Deep Draining on certain strong Clay subsoils with a few remarks on the injurious effect of sinking the water too far below the roots of plants in very porous alluvial and peaty soils', *JRASE*, Vol.9, 237-248

Webster, W.B. (1850) 'On the mischief arising from Draining certain Clay Soils too deeply' *JRASE*, Vol.11, 311-313

Westminster, Marquis of (1849) 'On a Dress for Drainers' *JRASE*, Vol.10, 51-3

Wharncliffe, Lord (1851) 'On Draining, under certain Conditions of Soil and Climate' *JRASE* Vol.12, 41-62

Wheeler, W. H. (1883) 'On River Conservancy and the Cause and Prevention of Floods' *JRASE* 2ns Series Vol.19, 388-

Whellan, W. (1855) *History, Topography, and Directory of Northumberland*, Whittaker, London

Whellan, W. (1860) *The History and Topography of the Counties of Cumberland and Westmorland*, Whellan, Pontefract

Whetham, E. H. (1978) *The Agrarian History of England & Wales*, Vol VIII, 1914-1939, Cambridge University Press

Whetham, E. H. (1968) 'Sectoral Advance in English Agriculture 1850-80: a Summary' *AHR*, Vol.16, 46-48

White, R. (1840) 'Report of Several Operations in Thorough-Draining and Subsoil-Ploughing at Oakley Park' *JRASE*, Vol.1, 33-37

White, R. (1840) 'Second Report' *JRASE*, Vol.1, 248-252

White, R, (1841) 'Report of Results obtained in Thorough-Draining and Subsoil-Ploughing in the years 1840 and 1841' *JRASE*, Vol.2, 346-353

White, R. (1843) 'Report to the Honourable Robert Clive MP, on his Improvements by Draining and Subsoil-Ploughing', *JRASE*, Vol.4, 172-176

White, R.E. (1979) *Introduction to the Principles and Practice of Soil Science*, Blackwell

White, W. (1834) *History, Gazetteer & Directory of Staffordshire*, Sheffield

White, W. (1851) *History, Gazetteer & Directory of Staffordshire*, Sheffield

Whitehead, John & Co (n d) *Some Remarks on the Drainage of Land*, John Whitehead & Co, Preston [Hull City Archives DBHT/5/147]

Whyte, I. (2003) *Transforming Fell and Valley: Landscape and Parliamentary Enclosure in North West England*, CNWRS, Lancaster

Wiggins, J. (1840) 'On the Mode of Making and Using Tiles for Underdraining practiced on the Stow Hall Estate in Norfolk' *JRASE*, Vol.1, 350-356

Wiggins, J. (1847) *A Practical Essay on the most economical and effectual modes of Underdraining* Newman, London

Wilkinson, J. (1861) 'Farming of Hampshire' *JRASE*, Vol.22, 266-7

Wilson, J. (ed.) (1905) *The Victoria History of the County of Cumberland*, Vol.2, reprint 1968, Dawson, London

Wilson, J. M. Editor (n.d.) *The Farmers Dictionary or a Cyclopedia of Agriculture*, 2 vols. Fullarton, Edinburgh

Winchester, A.J.L. & Crosby, A.G. (2006) *England's Landscape The North West*, Collins & English Heritage

Winstanley, M. (ed.) (2000) *Rural Industries of the Lune Valley*, CNWRS, Lancaster

Wood, O. (1988) *West Cumberland Coal 1600-1892/3*, Extra Series XXIV, *CWAAS*

Woodcroft, B. (1854) *Subject Matter Index of Patents of Inventions*, Eyre & Spottiswood, London

Wright, P.A. (1961) *Old Farm Implements*, Black

Wright, T. (2003) *Brickworks: a Gazetteer of Brick and Tile Manufacturing Sites in North East Hampshire*, 2nd edition, The Author

Wright, W. (1861) 'On the improvements in the Farming of Yorkshire since the dates of the last Reports in the Journal' *JRASE*, Vol.22, 87-131

Young, A. (1813) *General View of the Agriculture of Lincolnshire*, London, Reprint 1970, David & Charles, Newton Abbot

Yule, J. (1829) 'An Account of the Mode of Draining, by means of tiles as practised on the Estate of Netherby, in Cumberland, the property of Sir James Graham, Bart MP' *Transactions of the Highland Society of Scotland*, New Series Vol.1, 388-400

Yule, J. (1830) 'Reports of Select Farms: III. Netherby-Appendix: An Account of Under Draining, by means of Tiles' 49-68 in Burke, J.F. (1834-40) *Husbandry*, Volume the Third, Baldwin, London

Index

Draining the Cumbrian Landscape

[See pages 205-219 for a separate Index to the *Gazetteer of Sites and Manufacturers* CD]

Abbey Holme agricultural society 44
Abbey Tile Works (Abbey Tilery) 75, 77, 114
Abbey Town 97
agents (representing tileries) 102-3
Aglionby estate 46
agricultural depression 107-9, 123
agricultural labourers 114
Aikbank Tilery 101
Ainslie Brick & Tile Machine Co., The 59, 64
Ainslie, John 56, 59, 66
Ainstable (CUL) 46
Akehead, Wigton 52
Allan Grove see *Allen Grove*
Allen Grove Brick & Tile Works 31, 112, 120
Allenheads Tile Works 93
Alnwick (NBL) 16, 24
Alston (CUL) 93, 103, 142
Alston Moor 142
Annan (DFS) 24, 37, 67, 85, 102, 120
Appleby (WES) 36, 97
Applegarth (DFS) 132
Armstrong & Hodgson 77
Askrigg Hall, Skelton 132
Aspatria (CUL) 65, 66, 111, 115
Atkin, Thomas 31
Ayrshire (SCT) 16, 37, 56, 82, 103

Barker, John 46, 104
Barnard, Lord 137
Barrow (LAN [F&C]) 93
Barrow in Furness agricultural society 44
barrow (tile & brick): 22-3
  -planks 22-3
Barton, Preston (LAN) 92
Bassenthwaite Tile Kiln 103
Baty, James & Son 116, 128
Beart, Robert 20, 24, 25, 55-58, 64
Beart's Patent Brick Company Ltd, The 55
Beaty Brothers 116, 123
Beaty, James 110, 124
Beaty, John (Rockliff) 29
Beaumont (CUL) 96
Beaumont Tile Yard 23
Becks, Hayton 30
Bedford, Duke of 55, 57

Bedfordshire, 6, 55
Beith (AYR) 37, 82
Bell, Thomas 117
Bell, William 65, 66
Belsay (NBL) 145
Bender (tile) 23
Benn, Joseph 97, 104
Beverley (YKS) 59
Bewcastle (CUL) 77, 123, 149
Bigrigg Tile Works 73
Birneyknowe Tile Works 62
Blackburn, Quintin 13
Blackwell Road Steam Brick Works 116
Blamire, William 44, 52
Bleatarn Tilery 80, 97, 117
Blenkinsopp Tilery 81, 83, 93, 144
boiler: 120, 129
  Cornish 118
  Lancashire 128
  tubular 118
  vertical 118
Bolton Fell End agricultural society 44
Bolton Tile Works 64, 97
Bonshaw Tile Works 120
Boon Tile Leading 50
Border Union Railway 101
Botcherby Brick & Tile Works 20, 116, 128
Bothel (NBL) 37
Boustead, Roland 102
Bowness (CUL) 16
Boyle, Robert 56
boys (employed) 33, 56-9, 63, 95-6
bracken 5
Brackenhill estate 67
Brackenhill Tile Works 67, 97
Bradley, William 12
Braidwood Tile Works 125
Brampton (CUL) 150
Brayton (CUL) 43
Brayton, Thomas 64, 65
brick: 26, 104, 118,
  -arch 9
  -barrows (see barrow)
  -covers 163
  -drains 9, 163

INDEX

INDEX

INDEX

Tile-works described in the

Gazetteer of Sites and Manufacturers

In the interests of economy the *Gazetteer* has been produced as a CD (contained in a sleeve at the back of the book). Details of the standard layout and content of entries are given at the beginning of the *Gazetteer*. The major sites and manufacturers arranged according to traditional counties and parishes are listed below. In addition to these, possible sites and brick and tile-makers not linked to specific works, are included in the *Gazetteer* under relevant parishes. The *Gazetteer* is paginated independently, and has its own index which is printed after this list.

[1] Cumberland

ALSTON
Skelgill Tilery
How Hill Tile Works
ARLECDON
Dickinson & Dalzell
ARTHURET
Brackenhill Tile Works
Sandysike Brick & Tile Works
Netherby Tile & Brick Works
ASPATRIA
Hayton Tile Works
Brayton Demesne Tile Works
Old Domain Brick & Tile Works
BASSENTHWAITE
Bassenthwaite Tile Kiln
BEAUMONT
Beaumont Brick & Tile Works
BEWCASTLE
Kinkry Hill Drain Tile Works
BOLTON
Bolton Tile Works
BOOTLE
Bootle Tile Works
BOWNESS
Joshua Ward Brick & Tile Maker
Glasson Tile Kilns
Millrigg Tile Works
BRAMPTON
Middle Farm Tile Works
BRIDEKIRK
Broughton Moor Brick & Tile Works
BRIGHAM
Hundith Hill Tile Works
Jonah Dixon

BROMFIELD
Langrigg Tilery
CALDBECK
Eller Beck Brick & Tile Works
Caldbeck Tile Works
CAMERTON
Seaton Tile Works
Moorhouseguards Brick Works
Camerton Brick & Tile Company
Seaton Fire Brick Works
CARLISLE
Blackwell Road Steam Brick Works
Botcherby Brick & Tile Works
Murrell Hill Brick Works
Carlisle Pottery, Thomas Nanson & Co
Wragmire Tile Works
Upperby Brick & Tile Works
CASTLE SOWERBY
Lambfield Tile Works
CLEATOR
Aldby Brick Field
COCKERMOUTH
Kirkgate Brick & Tile Works
William Mackreath
Rt Smithson Brick & Tile Manufacturer
CROSSCANONBY
Birkby Brick & Tile Works
CROSTHWAITE
Lair Beck Brick & Tile Works
DALSTON
Broadfield Brick & Tile Works

DEAN
High & Low Edge Tile Works
Edge Tile Works
DEARHAM
Dearham Tile Works
DRIGG
Dickinson, Dalzell & Thompson
EGREMONT
Bigrigg Tile Works
FARLAM
Kirkhouse Brick & Tile Works Ltd
FLIMBY
Eagle Gill Brick & Tile Works
Gillhead Brick Works
GREYSTOKE
Troutbeck Tilery – P. Miller & Co
Troutbeck Brick & Tile Works
Johnby Brick & Tile Works
Threlkeld Tile Works
Greenah Craggs Brick & Tile Works
HARRINGTON
Harrington Brick Works
HAYTON
Toppin Castle Brick & Tile Works
Allen Grove Brick & Tile Works
HESKET-IN-THE-FOREST
New Inn Tile Works
Calthwaite Tile Works
HOLME CULTRAM
Abbey Tile Works
Brownrigg Tilery
Abbey Town Brick Field
HUTTON-IN-THE-FOREST
Whitrigg Tile Works
IREBY
Robert Cowx Brick & Tile Maker
IRTHINGTON
Glebe Farm Tile Yard
Laversdale Lane End Tile Works
IRTON
Irton Tile Kiln
ISEL
Sunderland Tile Works
KINGMOOR
Kingmoor Brick & Tile Co Ltd
Kingstown Brick Works
Richard Wright
KIRKANDREWS-UPON-ESK
Barns Tilery

KIRKBRIDE
Pow Hill Brick & Tile Works
KIRKLAND
Culgaith Brick & Tile Works
KIRKLINTON
Newbiggin Tile Works
Young's Close Tile Works
Moorhouse Tilery
Close House Brick Works
LAMPLUGH
John Dalzell
LANERCOST
Kirkcambeck Tile Works
Lees Hill Tile Works
MARYPORT
Nicholson & Pearson
Maryport Brick & Tile Works
MILLOM
Dickinson, Dalzell & Co
William Bradley Brick & Tile Maker
MORESBY
Scilly Bank Brick Kiln
NEWTON ARLOSH
Longlands Head Brick & Tile Works
PLUMBLAND
Robert Lucock
ROCKLIFF
Petersyke Tile Works
SCALEBY
Longpark Brick & Tile Works
SEBERGHAM
Sebergham Tilery
Goose Green Tile Works
STANWIX
Eden Place Tile Works
Linstock Tile Works
Houghton Tile Works
STAPLETON
Cracrop Tile Works
Crossings Tile Works
Middlefoot Brick & Tile Works
TORPENHOW
Bewaldeth Brick & Tile Works
WALTON
Leaps Rigg Brick & Tile Works
WESTWARD
Joseph Hodgson
Westward Park Tilery
Curthwaite Brick & Tile Works

202

WETHERAL
Cumwhinton Tile Works
Cocklakes Tilery
Cumwhinton Brick & Tile Works
Carlisle Brick & Tile Works
Crown Brick & Tile Works
WHICHAM
Silecroft Brick & Tile Works
WHITEHAVEN
Richard Sanderson Tile Maker
Thomas Jackson & Co
Greenbank Tilery
Whitehaven Fire Brick Company
Whitehaven Brick & Tile Co Ltd
WIGTON
Parkgate Tilery
Sheffield's Brick & Tile Works
WORKINGTON
Thomas Greggins
Winscales Tile Works
WREAY
Potterpits Tile Works (Chapel Hill Tilery)

[2] Westmorland

APPLEBY
Burrells Tilery
BROUGHAM
Julian Bower Brick & Tile Works
CLIFTON
Wetheriggs Brick & Tile Works
CROSBY RAVENSWORTH
Gaythorn Tilery
DUFTON
Coatsike Tile Works
KIRKBY LONSDALE
Lupton Tile Works
KIRKBY STEPHEN
Sandriggs Brick & Tile Works
KIRKBY THORE
Acorn Bank Brick & Tile Works
LOWTHER
Hackthorpe Tilery
MORLAND
Morland Tilery & Brickfield
WARCOP
Bleatarn Tilery

[3] Lancashire (Furness & Cartmel)

BARROW
Furness Brick & Tile Co
CARTMEL
Holker Tilery
DALTON
Hindpool Tile & Brick Works
Armstrong & Hodgson Drain Tile Manufacturers
Sandscale Brick & Tile Works
Roose Tile Kiln
ULVERSTON
Priory Brick Works
Isaac Ireland Brick & Tile Manufacturer
Sandhall Brick Works

[4] Northumberland

ALLENDALE
Allenheads Tile Works
HALTWHISTLE
Blenkinsopp Tilery
Featherstone Tile Works
South-Tyne Brick Works, Nelson & Co
Hartleyburn Tile Works
Errington Reay & Co
Melkridge Brick & Tile Works

[5] Scotland

ANNAN
Howgill Tile Works
Whinnyrigg Tile Works
CANONBIE
Tarrasfoot Tile Works
Woodhouselees Tile Works
SANQUHAR
Sanquhar Brick & Tile Works
CAMBUSNETHAN
Wishaw & Coltness Brick, Tile &
Pottery Works
CARNWATH
Lampits Tile Works

Index

Gazetteer of Sites and Manufacturers

[See pages 191-199 for a separate Index to *Draining the Cumbrian Landscape*]

INDEX

INDEX

INDEX

INDEX

Potts, Thomas (Bowness) 27
Potts, Thomas (Lanercost) 126-7
Pow Hill, Kirkbride 26, 115-7
Pow Hill Brick & Tile Works 115-7
Preston Quarter, Whitehaven 178
price of tiles (see tile: prices)
Priory Brick Works 222
Pristol Cottage, Walton 161
publican (see innkeeper)
pug-mill 3, 21

quantity see clay-quantity
quarry 17

Rae, John 233-4
railways (see also sidings) 119
Ramshay, John 32
Reake Wood Tile Kiln 216-7
Reay, Roger 228
Reay, William (Bolton) 23
Reay: (Haltwhistle)
  William 231
  George T (son) 231
  Isaac (son) 231
  Robert William (son) 231
Red Brick Works 75
Red Hill Brick Works 135
Redhill, Irthington 107
Red How, Lamplugh 125
Renwick, William 46
Reynolds, John 84
Rice Head 4, 5
Richardson, Jos & Son 171-2
Richardson, Robert 122-3, 167-8
Richardson, William 81, 147-8
Riddle, Robert 226
Ridley, John 22
Ridley, Messrs 79-81
Ridley, Robert 231-2
Ritson, George 16
Ritson, James 38
Ritson, John 16
Ritson, William 140-1
Robin Hood 18-19
Robinson, George 60
Robinson, James 157-8
Robinson, John (Carlisle) 234-5
Robinson, John (Hayton) 88
Robinson, Thomas 59
Robinson, Thomas W 80
Robinson, William (Cartmel) 217
Robinson: (Bowness)
  William 27
  Joseph (brother) 27
  Richard (brother) 27
  Amelia (cousin) 27

  William (cousin) 27
Robson, Henry 225
Robson, Thomas & Co 50-1
Rockliff (Rockliffe) (CUL) 141-2
Rome, Joseph 178-80
roof-tile 39, 42, 172
Rooke, John 40
Roose Brick Field 221
Roose Brick Kiln 221
Roosecote, Dalton 221
Roose Tile Kiln 221
Rosley, Westward 162-3
Round Hill Farm, Sebergham 147
Rowrah, Winder, Lamplugh 5
Rowntree, John 231
Rowntree, William 232
Royal Oak Inn, Winscales, Workington 188
royalty (see clay-royalty)
Ruddick:
  John 126
  George (grandson) 126
Ruleholme, Irthington 107
runner (see tile: -runner)
Rush, Joseph 141-2, 237-8
Rush, Peter 151
Russell:
  Thomas 148-9
  Thomas (son) 148-9

St Helen's Colliery & Brick Works Co Ltd 190
St Helen's Street, Cockermouth 65
Salt Cotes, Holme Cultram 101
Salthouse, Brick Works 216
Sanderson, Henry 198-9
Sanderson, John 46
Sanderson, Richard 46, 62, 177-8
Sanderson, Thomas 213
Sanderson:
  William 46
  William (son) 46
Sandford, Drigg 74
Sandhall Brick Works 228-9
Sandhall Cottages 228-9
Sandriggs Brick & Tile Works 206-7
Sandscale Brick & Tile Works 220
Sandysike (CUL) 9
Sandysike Brick & Pipe Works 9
Sandysike Brick & Tile Co Ltd 9
Sandysike Brick & Tile Works 9-13
Sandysike Brick Works 9
Sandysike Tile Kiln 9
Sanquhar (DFS) 240-1
Sanquhar Brick & Tile Works 111-2, 240-1
saw mill 54, 78, 82, 103, 145
Scaleby (CUL) 143-4
Scilly Bank, Moresby 136-7

INDEX